My Yoke Was Coke

Sandra Whitt Horsley

Although based on a true life story, names have been changed where necessary to protect the innocent. Any resemblance to real persons, living or dead, is purely coincidental.

SECOND EDITION

Manufactured in the United States of America

ISBN: 0-533-15386-7 Library of Congress Catalog Card No.: 2005909714
098765432

To Walter Lee Freeman

My first love, my now love, and my forever love.

I love you, I live you, and I am you.

ACKNOWLEDGMENTS

First of all, I would like to give honor to Jesus Christ, who is the head of my life. I would like to thank God for Prophetess Mae who told me in the '70s about my book. Of course, I didn't believe her because I was a dope dealer. To my sister, Mary Brandon (Sugar Bear), who has gone home to be with the lord, I will always love her. To Mischelle Standifer, who without her fingers helped me type, and renamed my book. Thank you Mischelle, I love you. To Uncle George (Bubba) Whitt, an old and very wise man who always kept me laughing. Special thanks to Patrick Price the deacon of my church; he can sell the white off rice. Special thanks to my nephew Artis (Noonie) Johnson. He finished typing it. Love ya! Mr. Walter Lee Freeman, thank you for being here for me, I love you.

1

It started October 1977, in Eastwyck Apartments in Decatur, Georgia. A young lady 28 years of age, and about five feet four inches. Her hair was medium brown and her skin was like honey. She had dark brown eyes with dimples high on her cheekbones. She was a fast moving girl with plenty of energy. Her name was Sandra Whitt, better known as San. She got up one morning getting ready for work. She worked at a printing company. That young lady was nobody but me. At work, there was this white boy who always fucked with me. His name was Joe. Joe said, "Hey San, do you know what this means?" showing me a burning cross-tattooed on his arm. (My mother told me if I ever saw one, what it meant—KKK.) I said, "Hell yeah, I know. But, do you know what this means?" and hit him over the head with a crate. He staggered over by the machine. All the bosses ran over and asked me to report to the office. Mr. Young said, "Sandra, we have got to let you go."

I said, "But Mr. Young, he started fucking with me first; he pulled his shirt up and showed me that KKK cross. So I hit him."

"You're fired," said Mr. Young.

I said, ' 'Okay, fuck it," and left the plant crying. Then I said as I was getting into my car, "Lord, have mercy! What am I gonna do now (with heavy tears falling down my face)? Jesus help me, I just don't know what to do." I have the apartment. I made it home. Looking at all four corners of the walls, my kids' pictures, the phone bill, rent, and in the refrigerator. By then the telephone rang. It was Sugar. "Hey, what's happening?" I said. "How did you know I was home?"

She said, "I called your job to tell you about the basketball game we have tonight and they told me that you were fired."

I told her what had happened. I said, "I won't be late picking you up; I'll be there about 6:45, okay?" I picked Sugar up on time. We had red, white, and blue uniforms. Sugar lived on the West Side of Atlanta in the Cascade area. We left her house and headed for the Martin Luther King Gym. The game had started and we were winning. Sugar and I made a fast break going down court. This big chick was already down there. Sugar had the ball, shot it and missed. We went up for the rebound; while coming down with the ball, that fat ass-chick fell on my leg. I was screaming very loud because my leg was in a lot of pain. The coaches all ran over to see about my leg. I hollered out, "Sugar, please don't let them mess with my leg, just let's go." My tendon was out of place. After the coach looked at it, he decided that I should see a doctor. Sugar and I got into the car—she was driving—and we went straight to Grady Hospital. They put a cast on my leg.

Sugar looked at me in a strange way, she said, "San, what are you going to do?"

I said, "Do about what?"

"You know that you don't have a job or insurance and you can't get unemployment with that cast all the way to your ass."

"Damn," I thought, "what in the fuck am I going to do?"

I said, "I know, I'll wait two weeks and go back to the doctor to see if he will cut the cast down to my knee, how about that?"

Sugar said, "Maybe that will work."

"Okay, let's go."

Sugar said, "Go where?" I told her to drive my car down to my mother's house so that I could pick up my children, and then take us home because the cast was on my driving foot, plus I was all drugged up.

When we got there, everybody wanted to know what happened. My mother lived in a government project. We finally headed for Decatur going home. After getting home and into the bed, I started worrying about my bills.

A week passed; Sugar went to pick up my last check from the printing company. It was only $250.00. That was enough to give Mama fifty dollars, pay my phone, light and gas bills; I still didn't pay the rent that month because they was going to turn everything off. The next week I was to go to the doctor then to the unemployment office. I went to the doctor's first. He took my cast off and put a half one on me.

The unemployment office lady said, "You would have to wait eight weeks for penalty."

I said, "Damn, what the fuck now?" I walked off.

When I got outside, I saw my uncle riding down Marietta Street. I yelled out, "Big H! What's going on, where are you going?" He pulled over and asked me did I have my car. I said yes.

"Would you come over to the house tonight? I got something I want to talk to you about."

Nodding my head, I said yeah.

He said, "Okay, I'm going home right now." He drove off and I hopped to the parking lot to get my car.

While riding down Peachtree Street listening to some music, I decided to go right on over to his house. He lived in East Atlanta off Moreland Avenue. When I got there, I parked my car on the left side of the one-way street. I hopped on up the steps and went into the den where he was. He had a bunch of kids and the house stayed dirty all the time. Big H said, "Come on in, San. Listen, I have something that will make you a lot of money if you know how to deal with it."

I said, "What, what is it? Please tell me, because you can see that I can't work."

He said, "It is illegal and I don't even know a damn thing about it."

"Tell me, Big H, what? Damn," I said.

"San, it's cocaine."

I said, "Cocaine!" My eyes widened. I said, "Where it's at? When do you want me to start?"

"Wait now, don't rush. We have got to get this thing together. I wish that Aunt Hazel was out of jail." (Aunt Hazel was my aunt.)

"Why do we have to wait? Hell, you don't know and I damn show don't know. I'll tell you what, I'll go down to the state penitentiary Sunday to see her and get the information we need, okay?"

Big H said, "Are you sure?"

"Hell yeah, I'm going." That following Sunday I went down to the prison to see her. I gave her the low down.

She looked at me and said, "Baby, I got eight years for that shit. Honey, please don't get involved, San."

"Aunt Hazel, I got to; I'm messed up and don't have any money. Just tell me what to do and how to watch for the police and the robbers."

"Look, who introduced you to that shit, San?"

"Big H told me that we can make lots of money if I knew how."

"Well, I'll tell you what, check it out and see how much money is in it for you and come back down here next week then we will discuss it, okay baby?"

"Dog, Aunt Hazel, I thought that I would have some money this week. Okay aunt-tee."

I left the prison headed back for Atlanta; I went straight back to Big H's house and told him what Aunt Hazel said. Big H said, "The man will be over here to meet with you Tuesday, which was November, the 16th."

"Ah shoot, why won't he come now or tomorrow?"

"Honey, you got to wait on him."

I could hardly wait until Tuesday got here. On Monday, I took my kids to the Hawks basketball game; the game didn't even interest me because I was thinking about the next day. After the game, we went home; I put my kids in bed. Then I got in there myself. It was Tuesday morning; the children were gone to school and I was waiting on the telephone to ring. I would not leave the house for anything. I wouldn't even go to the mailbox. It was 11:30 in the morning; I decided to fix me some cheese and eggs with bacon. By the time I finished the bacon and started to put the eggs in the frying pan, the phone rang. I threw the eggs in the pan and jumped to the phone, it was my sister.

"Hello! Hello, San, what are you doing?"

"Who is this?"

"What's wrong, girl, this is me, your sister."

"Oh, I thought it was somebody else because I was waiting on a very important phone call."

"Okay, I'll call you back later. I didn't want anything, just to say hello. How's your leg?"

"Well, my leg is fine. They are going to take the cast off Thursday, okay? Bye." Damn. I wish the fuck he will call. I headed back for my eggs; before I got there the phone rang again. I ran over to the phone again, falling over everything. "Hello, hey, what's happening? Are you ready?"

My eyes bucked and I had a big grin all over my face. "Yeah, when can I come?"

"He will be here at 3:30, so you be here at that time and no later 'cause those people are always on time."

"Okay Unc," I said, "I'll be there. Bye." I ate my breakfast, turned on the music, and cleaned up my house, waiting on the clock to strike. It was now the time. I went over there and a medium height Italian was standing in the den. Big H said, "This is San." He looked up and said, "Hey man, this is a female; you told me Sam."

Big H said, "No, I said San. She's my niece and she knows everybody in Atlanta."

Julio said, "I've been in this shit a long time; we have never dealt with a female, not even my wife."

"Please, mister," I said, "give me a chance. Just let me try. I'll be good."

He said, "No, no women."

I looked at him with kind of a sad face; I turned and walked through the hall going out of the door. When I got half way he said, "Sam." I stopped and turned around hoping that he would change his mind and he did. "Come here for a minute. Look, Sam."

I looked at him with glittering eyes, "It's San," I said.

He said, "Can I call you Sam?"

I said, "Yeah."

"What can you do? How much can you sell?"

I really didn't know what to say because this would my first time. So I said, "I can sell all you got."

He smiled at me and said, "No, Sam, not all I got because I have enough for thirty people giving them ten keys a piece."

I didn't ever know what a key was.

"Well, I can do lots."

He then pulled a Ziploc bag out filled with cocaine. It looked like diamonds and seashells. That stuff was very pretty. He gave me a six-hundred dollar bag, an eight-hundred-dollar bag, and two bags worth two hundred dollars each. I still didn't know how much that I would make yet, and I didn't even worry about it.

"Okay, Sam, let's get to work. I'll be seeing you."

I turned to walk off. He stopped me again. "Oh, I forgot to tell you that if you fuck up the money, we fucks up the lives."

Then I said, "If you fuck up the stuff I'll do my best to find you and fuck you back up."

"Sam! Guard the dope with your life, okay?" he said, with a smile.

So, I walked on out the door. I didn't do anything until I got the cast off my leg and back down to talk with my aunt. When I went back to the prison to talk to her, I gave her the low down. "Aunt Hazel, the stuff I saw and got is way, way bigger than you ever dreamed of. That man got pounds and pounds of that stuff."

"Well, San, if you are going to do it, good luck, baby. What you do is find Bippy, he'll show you the ropes."

"Where can I find him?" I asked.

"San, all you got to do is go to Auburn Avenue. You'll see him."

"Okay, Aunt Hazel," I said. "When I make my first one thousand dollars, I'll send you two hundred dollars, okay?" She looked at me with a frown. "Hey, I'm going to do it bigger and better," I said.

It was time for me to leave and I kissed her and left her some money. She waved at me and said, "Be careful, baby, just be careful." I just smiled and walked on to the car.

I went on down the highway listening to Patti Labelle's "It's a Joy to Have Your Love." The first place I went to was Auburn Avenue. I went up and down Auburn, Foote Street, Old Wheat Street and Edgewood Avenue. It was getting late and I hadn't found Bippy yet, so I decided to go into the Bell Street shop. I saw Head. "Hey, Head, have you seen Bippy?"

Head was a six-foot-seven-inch fat man and he worked there. Head said, "Naw, but go check the street in about an hour."

It was six-thirty then. I went to the hotdog stand to get some hot dogs so that I could kill some time. After getting the hot dogs from the curb service, I drove off eating them on the way back to Auburn Ave. By the time I got to Piedmont & Auburn, who did I see coming out of Kat's Liquor Store with a bottle of wine? It was Bippy. I quickly jumped in the other lane and pulled into the liquor store parking lot.

I jumped out of the car all excited and waving my hands saying, "Bippy, Bippy, come here!" Bippy was a pretty-haired six-foot man with a nice complexion, but he had very bad skin—plus he was a junkie.

"Yeah, baby. What's happening?"

"Guess what?" I said, not giving Bippy time to say a word. He looked down at me. "I got some pure cocaine to sell and a whole lot of it. Aunt Hazel told me to find you and that you will show me the way."

"Ah, shit, San, you ain't got no shit like that. Hell, you are a square-ass working girl and I know that you don't fuck around."

"Bullshit, nigga. I got the stuff. Wanna see?" He stood there nodding, rocking, and leaning, looking at me real crazy. "Look motherfucka: Just get in the fuckin' car." Bippy and I got in the car. I pulled one of the bags out and started to show it to Bippy.

He flashed and said, "San, what in the fuck? Hey," he said, saying it real quick. "Man, don't pull that shit out right here. What the fuck wrong with you? Are you crazy?"

"Hell, naw, I ain't crazy. You want to see it don't you?"

But Bippy was looking all around. "But not right here. Take this goddamn car around the block or something. Don't show me shit right here. Damn, g-i-r-l, you're crazy."

I said, "Un-huh." I put the bag between my legs and drove the car down Auburn Avenue and took a right turn off Auburn onto Butler Street.

While driving, Bippy asked, "San, where in the fuck did you get all that shit, man? Do you know what kind of time a nigga will get?"

"Un-huh," I answered, not having a clue. "I really hadn't thought about that kind of time and anyway they don't know that I got it. So what's the beef?"

"Listen, girl, you can't pull that dope out just anywhere."

I said, "Why not? Hell, they won't think a woman like me would have sense enough to sell dope."

"Baby, that's not the point. The point is you have me in the car with you and you know that I been down many times and got a case pending now."

O-o-h, I thought. I looked at him but really didn't understand what he was talking about because I had never been to jail. "Okay, Bip. I'll pull into the corner market." It was right down the street on Butler. I parked the car, reached between my legs, and showed Bippy the cocaine.

"Oyo-wee, goddamn and good God almighty. Baby, baby, baby! Let's get rich, San. This is all a mother fucker need. Girl, you are ever too straight. Goddamn, San! Uh-uh-uh, boy, boy, boy." I looked at him carrying on and didn't know a damn thing he was talking about.

"What Bippy? What? Tell me what?"

"Listen, baby. You got to get some cut."

"Cut! What is that? I don't know nothing 'bout no cut, and what do you do with it anyway?"

"Okay, San. People put cut on dope to stretch it."

"Uh-uh," I said. "I ain't fuckin' with that shit, no way. Don't you know that the man might kill my goddamn ass? Hell naw."

After a second or two, Bippy thought about it and it was like he saw his boat coming in. Like this was his time. He said, "Okay, baby. It's gonna take a little time and then you'll see. Now give me a little to test ...you know I got to see if this is the shit or are you just shittin?"

I said, "Test? For what? Goddamn! I ain't got time to be playing." I'm figuring this junky was trying to mess me around.

"Goddamn! You don't know a mother fuckin' thing, do you? Just let me see how the mother fuckin' shit is. Damn."

I said, "Okay, motherfucker. Just a little bit." I didn't even know what a little bit was. I gave him damn near a gram ...dumping it out with a card onto a dollar bill. This nigga flipped into the junky mode on me, right before my eyes. "Now, San. Take me to Auburn Avenue's shooting gallery." I told him I don't know where no shooting gallery is. He hurried up and told me, "Just crank up and drive the mother fucka back to Auburn Avenue and let me out."

"Oooh, now you ain't gonna show me how to sell this shit, huh?"

"Naw, baby," Bippy said. "I just want to check it to see what it is all about. You just wait. Better yet, drive around or something so that you won't be seen stopping and waiting 'round here."

"Okay," I replied, as I cranked the car and drove back to Auburn Avenue. Bippy got out up there by the Royal Peacock.

Bippy said, "Look, baby. Pick me up right back here in about twenty minutes." He got out and slammed the door and ran down the street. I watched him as he ran, then started talking and laughing to myself as I looked at the girl in my rearview window, saying, "You gonna get paid now!" I pushed in my favorite eight tracks and let Patti Labelle do her thing as I drove around downtown. The music was blasting. My car was shining rolling on my spotless whitewalls. We're talking spic-and-span. The music was very loud because I was feeling good about what I was going to do.

I went back to pick Bippy up. You know he was right where he said he'd be. That nigga was sweating and blowing. I pulled to the right side across from the Royal Peacock. He ran across the street and jumped in saying, "San, baby. Now is the time. Let's get the dollars. Girl, this mother fucka is a monster. I mean, a cold-blooded killer! You have got to get some cut, San, or you might kill a mother fucka. Hey, I ran half a quarter and that mother fucka made me snatch the work out and run. Take me out to your house so that I can make some phone calls. Believe me, sister. I know who you need to see just. Just hang tight, babe."

I drove off, moving toward I-20, Decatur bound. It was like I couldn't go fast enough, but I knew I had to keep my cool. We got off at Candler Road headed for my apartment. We turned right into Eastwyck Village down the driveway. I parked the car and got out. I unlocked the burglar bars in a hurry and we both rushed into the house.

"Look, San, I'm gonna get off one more time before calling."

"Hell naw, I ain't giving you no more shit until you help me sell some."

"Wait a minute. I still have some more of mine. Just let me get off, all right?" Bippy told me to give him a spoon and a piece of cotton.

"Hey, mother-fucker, where you think you gonna get some cotton? You know damn well niggas don't use cotton swabs," I said smiling.

Bippy said, "Get it out of one of you cigarettes, okay?" He poured the cocaine onto the spoon.

"Damn, Bip. Do you gotta go through all that? Why don't you use just the spoon and the cocaine?"

Bippy schooled me: "To keep from getting trash fever, dummy." I didn't like this nigga insulting me in my house using my shit, but I knew Bippy didn't mean nothing by it. He was just teaching me something, and believe me, if Aunt Hazel sent me to him, he knew his stuff.

"Who you calling a dummy, dummy?" I said, smiling.

Bip just smirked and said, "Just watch and learn, okay, because you are going to be seeing a lots of this."

"Naw, hell, I ain't gon put that cocaine in my arm, no-o-o, not me."

"Wait a minute, baby. Just be cool. I didn't mean it like dat. I'm merely saying that you will have a lot of people coming buying and checking real soon."

"I ain't gonna fuck with no lotta people." Bip still breaking it down to me, went on to say, "Listen, will ya? Damn. If a nigga buy some weight, he's gonna want to bring his tester, right?"

"Oh, no," I said.

"Shut the fuck up and let me get a hit, then I'll take you to sho 'nuff school. Just be quiet."

I was staring because I had never seen that before. Bippy said, "Don't look at me like that. Hold my arm."

I reached for his arm then he said, "Hold it above my elbow and squeeze real tight." As I grabbed his arm, I wanted to make sure I was doing it right so I asked, "Talking bout right here?"

Looking like I wasn't moving fast enough for him ...like I was holding up his groove, he said, "Yeah, yeah, yea, right there ...hold it, and hold it." Bippy hit his self in the pit of the arm. I saw the blood running into the work. "Woo-wee, you got it, you got it," Bippy said. "Just be cool, and turn my damn arm a loose." He went in and out; in and out, then all of sudden he went to the window with the thing in his arm. I watched him carefully. "Hey, Bippy. Why are you peeping?"

He turned around and said, "Be quiet. Don't you hear something out there?" Looking out the window with him, I said, "Where?"

"Just shut up so I can watch, 'cause somebody's out there." I asked, "What are they doing out there? Ain't nobody gon' come here."

"Be quiet, San. Damn. Let me go!"

"Let you go? Where you going?"

"I forgot you don't understand." He was talking and still peeping ...moving from one window to the other ...front to the back and I was behind him. "Damn, quit following me. Can I please peep by myself? Damn, San. You'll fuck up a wet dream." He finally took the work out of his arm and washed it out.

I said, "When you goin' call the people?"

"Wait a minute, baby. Let me come down a little bit. Don't you know nothing about coming down? I sho' be glad when you learn, 'cause you will blow a nigga's high real quick. Just don't ask me nothing right now." That nigga was still pacing the floor, looking out the door, in the window, and the closets. Woo-wee! He freaked me out. I didn't know what to do. It was real serious at first, but suddenly I started laughing. He looked at me and said; "Now I'm a cartoon, huh?" I laughed out real loud this time. He said, "Okay, mother fucka. You'll see what it's about real soon."

"Okay, Bip, okay. I'm gonna be real quiet."

"Naw, you can talk now. I'm out straight, now."

"Well tell me this, Bip. Why do that stuff have you doing all that?"

"Damn if I know. All I know is the shit fucks with me and I like it."

"Well Bip, what do it feel like?"

"I feel like skeeting and can't even get a hard dick."

"Why?"

"Girl, this shit is something else. If you do too much you can't get hard and if you do a little you will fuck a bitch to death. Look, baby. If there's a freak in a mother fucka, this cocaine will definitely bring it out."

"I know that I don't want no shit to make me skeet and ain't no dick in me, shit!"

Bip cracked up and said, "You crazy."

I could tell Bip was ready to do the do. "Okay, baby. Now let's get down to the real biz," Bip said as he picked up the phone and starting dialing the number. I watched him dial the number with my hand on my chin. "Hey, is Jeff there?" Bip looked like he was taking care of some important stuff, getting connected to whoever Jeff was. Whoever was on the phone must have said yes 'cause he winked his eye at me. No later than that, Bip spoke into the phone, "Jeff, what's going on? Look here, man. Don't you remember Aunt Hazel's niece? Yeah, that's her, that's right. Well anyway she has got some cold bad shirttail and you need to check it out." Jeff wanted the number where he could call Bippy back. "Hell naw, nigga. You got to deal with me. I know what you wanna do .... okay, okay." Jeff wanted to know when Bip could bring me over. Bippy said, "What time do you want us to come over?" (They were talking back and forth on the phone.) Jeff must have wanted to know what time was it now. I heard Bip answer, "It's about 10:30 P.M." Jeff jumped on that and wanted to know if Bip could bring me and "the stuff" right on over because Bip put his hand over the mouth of the receiver to see whether I could leave right then. "San, can you leave right now?"

Without hesitation, I answered, "Yeah, but how far do we have to go?" Not that it really mattered.

"Just right over there by Greenbrier in those apartments. It won't take too long."

I nodded my head, saying yes. Bib spoke back into the phone, "Okay, Jeff. See you in a minute." While he was hanging up the phone he said, "Let's ride, Big Money, let's ride." We started gathering keys, pouches, shoes, and hats together. Then we headed out of the door toward the car.

We both got into the car. I backed out of the driveway headed for Campbellton Road. While riding, Bippy started to hip me a little because he knew that I didn't know what was going on. "Look, baby. I want you to listen very closely." My ears were wide open. "You have got to handle it like you know what you are doing because this is a young nigga and he is very swift. Plus, he's been in the game for quite some times. I use to work for him. Okay, you show him the two ounces."

Not having a clue, I asked, "What ounces?"

Bippy answered, "Okay, okay. The two big ones." I lifted up what I thought he meant. "Yeah, that's right. Now, he's gonna ask you the price of one, then the price of two. So, what you gonna say?"

Grinning, I answered, "$2400."

I felt Bippy turn his head real quick and he said, "Hell naw, fool. That's your price!"

I said, "Oh. It is. Well, what is his?"

"Let me see ..." figuring Bippy. "Tell him $1500 for one and $1400 a piece for two ...which would be $2800. Yeah, and the money you have over—is yours."

My eyes got big ...very big. I started smiling ...all my dimples showed. "Bip, you mean if he buy the ounces I'll have $400 of my own?"

"Hell yeah, you could have more than that, but you want the best price plus the best stuff in town."

"Oooh, I see."

"Girl, we are going to bust Atlanta wide open. We are going to supply the whole damn city, Miss S-A-N ...the Lady with the Sack. You just don't know, girl. You are gonna to be the baddest bitch in town—that is, other than the white girl."

"What damn white girl?" I wanted to know who I needed to outdo.

Bippy laughed out very loud.

"I'm talking about the cocaine. They call it 'girl,' and heroin, they call it 'boy.' Now he will probably try to catch."

I asked, "Catch who?"

"You, stupid. Come on San. Use a little common sense, will you?"

We were now at the apartments: Appletree. Bippy said, "Turn, left—right here, San. Go straight to the back." Soon after we got to the back, Bippy asked while pointing, "You see that Fleetwood to your left? Park right next to it."

I needed to know, "Whose car is that? It sure is a pretty gold and white."

Bippy was focused on our mission. He said, "Don't worry about the car. You'll have one soon enough. Anyway, it belong to Jeff."

I said, "Ooh, that nigga must be tough."

Bip went on to say, "Yeah, the young nigger is bad, but you are going to be badder than he'll ever be."

I said, "For real?" Bippy nodded his head, saying yes.

We got out of the car and went to the door. Bip rang the doorbell. A guy answered. I could hear the voice from the outside. "Who is it?"

Bippy answered, "It's Bippy, baby. Open up, let us in." The man from the other side of the door opened it. I took a deep swallow because my nerves started jumping. This nigga didn't have on no shirt, but I saw a shoulder holster; the 9 mm was in his hand. That really scared me a little.

We walked on in. The guy told us to have a seat and that he'll (referring to Jeff) be with you all in a minute. This living room was lavender and white: The sofa was a huge pit group, white with lavender pillows. The drapes were pinned, striped lavender and white. The carpet was lavender dressed with a coffee table with all mirror. One side of the wall was mirrored with a white stereo. He had a whole lot of crystal, a built in bar, and it was white trimmed in lavender with all kinds of stuff to drink. The guy asked us would we like something to drink.

I said, "Yeah, a coke." Bippy hunched me and I looked at him and whispered, "What's wrong?"

Bippy said, "Get some cognac."

"But I don't drink."

Bippy went on, "San, it's time to grow up, baby."

I said, "Well, order for me."

"Hey, man. Fix us two yaks with some coke."

The guy said, "You got it." When the guy came from behind the bar he had some real pretty glasses: crystal, at that. He laid the coasters on the table and gave us the glasses with napkins.

I kinda whispered to Bip. "Bip, this man is straight, huh?" Bip was sipping his drink and nodding his head, yes. Bippy said, "One day, baby, you will be the same way or better."

I said, "I sure hope so."

By the time I tried to sip my liquor, another guy came out of the dining room. I looked at him with the glass up to my mouth. I be damned if he didn't have a gun also, but it was a sawed off shotgun. I said to Bippy, "Damn, why all the guns?"

"Hey kiddo, when you get where this nigger is, you will need all kinds of protection. You will be able to pay niggers to watch you while you sleep, eat, go to the store, and while you sell dope.

You see, he don't just sell cocaine, he sells heroin also and that bring on the bad guys."

"Ooh."

The guy said, "Bippy and young lady, Jeff is ready for you all now." We went through the dining room into the kitchen. The dining room was all white with a little lavender trim; the kitchen was the same. Here we go; the nigger at the table was Jeff. The nigger was fine as hell; he was about six feet or six feet one, slim and built. His hair was going to the back with some waves; he was brown complexioned weighing about 160 pounds and his teeth were like pearls. He had a big scale on the table in front of him, a tray, and a sifter ready to go to work.

When we walked in he said, "What's happening man? So this is big San, huh?"

Bippy said, "Yeah, you remember her don't you?"

"Yeah man, Aunt Hazel only showed me a picture of her, I never did get to meet her in person. Damn, you are just as pretty as your picture."

I started blushing because the nigger was fine.

Bippy said, "Jeff, do you want to check the stuff out or not?"

"Bip, tell me something, is this your lady?"

"Oh man, you know damn well that San ain't my woman so stop bullshitting."

"I'm just kicking the game a little."

"Okay, game kicking. Come on, San, let the nigger see what you've got." I opened my pouch doing exactly what Bippy had told me. I handed him one of the ounces. The expression on Jeff's face made me feel good because he had never seen anything that pure. He put the stuff Bippy told me to get out just a little, about a half of gram. He ran it through the sifter twice and called for one of them to come and shoot it. "Hey Bo," he said, "come and check this shit out for me." Bo came into the kitchen with a top, a needle, and the cotton. He didn't have to use the tie like Bippy.

Jeff put some cocaine in the top; Bo already had the water in the works. He squirted the water in to the top, took the inside of the work out and stirred up, and then he took his cotton out of his mouth and put it in the top. He then put the stem back into the work, laid the needle on the cotton, and drew it up. He just opened and closed his hand about three times. Wham, the blood ran in the needle real fast. He pushed it in half way and stopped. He looked at Jeff, nodding his head, yes, and told Jeff, "Man it's too strong." So he pulled the work out with the other half still in there; he sucked the blood from his arm and said, "damn" and went into the bathroom.

Jeff said, "San, San, what do you want for this?"

"$1,500," I said.

He said, "Do you have two?"

I said, "Yes."

"Okay, give me two." My eyes were glittering. He got up and looked in the cabinet and got a briefcase. He counted $3,000.00 cash dollars and said, "Thanks, baby. Look ah here, where can I get in touch with you tomorrow night or early Friday morning?"

"Just call Bippy, he'll find me."

"What's your number, Bip?"

"Man, you know damn well I ain't got no phone; I'll probably be over to San's house anyway so call us over there."

"Here", he said, handing me his phone pad, "Write your number in there for me pretty." Jeff said, "Listen baby, big San (smiling), if your people keep you straight, hey it unlimited what we can make; what's your man name?"

"I don't have one."

"Oh no," said Jeff.

Bippy said, "Hey man, lay off, this is going to be strictly business and no love affairs." Bippy was laughing 'cause he knew that he was going to get paid just as soon as we got back.

All three of us got up from the table. Jeff walked us to the door saying, "Please be where I can find you, okay, because I turn a lots of blow."

I said, "Just call, we'll be there." He opened the door himself and let us out. We walked to the car real fast. I unlocked the door, jumped in, and reached across to open the other one for Bippy. I cranked the car up and backed out, rocking and talking. "Bippy look, I made $600.00 clear for myself, how about dat? Here you take the two hundred dollars over, okay?" "Naw, San, just give me some cocaine and stop me on the way so that I can buy a new work. Hey hold up, let me go and check to see if Jeff got a little personal boy. Let me have $50.00."

"Here, Bip, take the one hundred bill 'cause he gave me all one hundred dollar bills. He'll give you change." Bippy jumped out of the car and ran back to the apartment. That money really excited me. I started talking to myself, "Now I can give my mama one hundred dollars and put Christmas in the layaway. This is easy, I like it." By the time Bippy came back to the car, "Let's go San. You can go straight home cause I got the work from Bo."

"Okay," I said.

We headed for Decatur, back home. "San, tell you what I'm going to do. I'll be with you until you learn the game, then I'll let you handle it, okay?"

"Naw Bip, you can help me. You know that I don't know and remember what you said about needing protection?"

"Yeah, but San, face the facts, I'm a junkie."

"So as long as you get what you need you won't get sick will you?"

Bip smiled and said, "Will you do that for me?"

"Sure," I said. We made it to the house. It was late, plus I was tired and I told Bip that he could sleep on the sofa. So I went upstairs to get some covers for him. "Here Bippy, here's your cover."

"Thank you San." I turned to go back upstairs, "Sandra, can I get off?"

I looked at him and said, "Help yourself, just clean up your mess. Good night, Bippy."

"Hey you know that I'm good at that."

After getting upstairs, I looked into the room at my children and they were sleeping very sound. I started to think, Damn, I've got to get someone here with them when I have to leave. Oh, I know, I'll get my brother, he's not working. Yeah, that's what I'll do in the morning. I pulled off my clothes and went to bed.

2

On the following morning, my kids were up and getting ready for school, they were old enough to fix their own breakfast. Harry said, "Come on, Cocoa, let's eat so we can go. It's getting late."

"Okay, boy, I'm coming." Cocoa went downstairs, saw Bippy lying on the sofa, and ran straight to my room.

"San," she said and came over to my bed, shook me, and woke me up. "Wake up."

I was lying on my stomach and I looked up at her.

"Uh, wake up, there's a man downstairs. Who is it?"

I sat up in the bed, "Oh baby, that's Bippy, a friend of Aunt Hazel's."

By then Harry came into the room and said, "What, what's wrong?"

I said, "Nothing, sweetheart, just a friend of our aunt is downstairs and your sister wanted to know who it is. Hey, babies, what time is it? You all are going to be late."

"San, I told Cocoa to get up."

"Well, I'll get on up and help you all out, okay?" I got up helped my daughter get dressed and fixed them a bacon sandwich and sent them on out of the door. It was 8:20. I ran up the stairs to count the money, because I didn't last night.

As I was counting, the phone rang and it was Big H. "Hello, hey, what's going on San? How did you do so far?"

"Well let me tell you this; I sold two of those big ones and I think that the rest will be gone before the day is over. I met this friend and he knows everybody."

"Damn, San, that's good 'cause I ain't doing nothing yet. Well, what's his name?"

"Look, Uncle, I'll tell you 'bout it later, okay? I gotta clean up and be on my way. I will bring the money over later on, okay?"

"Hey, if you want me to I'll come and get it."

"Naw, that's all right. I'll be coming that way real soon."

"Okay then." I said bye real quick.

As I was hanging up the phone, I said, "Damn. What the fuck he want to run at the money for?" By that time, Bippy was awake. As he stretched, he said, "Who was that and what was that all about?"

"Oh, it was Big H. He was just being nosey, wanted to know had I sold any cocaine; Bip do you want some bacon or something?"

"Yeah, just a little bit and some juice."

"I ain't got no juice, but I got Pepsi Cola. Do you want half of it?"

"Yeah, I'll take it."

The bacon was already done, so I scrambled some eggs and we were eating. We talked about what we were going to do today. "Sister San, I'm going to call a couple more people, okay, to see if they need some girl. You know Thursdays are the beginning of the weekend."

"Why starting on Thursday?"

"That's when all the thieves get paid."

"Ooh yeah?"

He nodded his head in a yes motion. "Yeah baby, let me take some of my medicine then we will go to work."

"Oh hell, hell no, nigger. You'll be peeping all day long."

"Naw, naw, now I'm going to speedball." Looking at him with my nose tooted up, I said, "What in the hell is that? Now you got to do something else."

"Look, speedball is when you mix the boy and girl together, and when you mix them together it mellows you out. It will have me so calm that I won't peep as hard."

"Ooh, okay, I hope so. Go on now so we can get started on the thing."

Bippy got all his stuff together for him to get off, but this time he put the heroin in the spoon the same way he did the cocaine, but only he took a cigarette lighter and burned the bottom.

I was looking all the time, watching and following him. When I saw that, I asked him, "Why do you have to burn that one?"

"Damn, San, this is boy; you have to cook this shit first. Look, let me get off. You ask too many questions and seems like you ask more questions when I try to get off."

"Okay, I ain't gon bother you no more, just tell me is it gonna be good?"

"If you wait, you'll see," he said, shaking, his head in a no, no manner. I must have been getting on his nerves.

After he cooked the boy, he poured the last little bit that I gave him into the spoon and stirred it up with the inside of the work. I said, "You need a little bit more?"

"Hell naw, what you wanna do, kill me? Just save it, I'll get around to doing it." He then asked me for a tie.

"A tie, what kind of tie?"

"Come on, just hold my arm like you did before."

I walked over to him. As I was getting ready to grab his arm, I asked him, looking at him, "Who held your arm last night?"

"Just hold my damn arm." He had the work between his teeth. "I used the telephone cord."

I squeezed his arm again; this time it didn't work as fast as the other time. "Come on San, squeeze."

"Bip, I'm trying. You want me to hit you?"

"Turn my arm a loose; I'll hit it, damn." He went over, sat in a chair, and crossed his leg with his left arm in between his legs. The needle was in his mouth, and he was trying to find or make a vein come up. He felt up and down, up and down; he even hit the arm but nothing happened. He uncrossed his legs that way and crossed them the other way so that he could try the other arm.

I said softly, "You think you gon get it?"

With the work in his mouth, he said, "Oh, oh." He pressed hard in the pit with his index finger, I saw the vein show up. He took the work out of his mouth and felt for the vein again and it was still there; he stuck it in and pulled the inside of the needle back and the blood ran in, he pushed it in a little more than half way, this time he uncrossed his leg and stood up saying, "N-o-w, woo wee." He was looking at me like he was on top of the world. "Girl, good God a mighty, my, my, my, heaven must be like this." He started to push the rest of it in; after all of it was in, he didn't even jack it, he came out and put his arm to his mouth to stop the blood. He got a cup of water to wash his work out. "Now San, this is the way a nigger likes to feel, not too high and not too down."

I still didn't know what he meant, so I just nodded my head. "Come on now, call the people."

"There you again, rushing. Will you give me just ten minutes?" He looked to the ceiling and blew.

"But you said that you were mellow."

"Hey by the time you get your clothes on I will be ready, okay?"

I nodded my head and ran out of the kitchen into the living room and on up the stairs. I put on blue jeans, tennis shoes, and a navy blue sweatshirt, put my shoulder-length hair into two ponytails, grabbed my pouch with the cocaine and money in it, and hollered downstairs at Bippy. "Hey there, I'm ready like Freddie."

Bippy said, "Come on baby, 'cause ain't nobody home, let's just ride and catch the early bird. Some of the eight ball and quarter people should be out looking by now."

"Eight ball and quarter, what's that?"

"Damn you need a triple beam to weigh that shit out."

"Naw, I can't do that, I got to sell the six hundred pack and the eight hundred pack."

"But you might not find nobody that want to buy it like that, so we will have to break it down a little until you re-up."

"But that ain't gon mess up, is it?"

"Naw, hell naw, you'll come out on top again."

"Wait a minute, let me see. Call Jeff 'cause I can't weigh it up because I don't know how."

I said, "Shit, me either."

"Damn, San, we can't let the nigger know that you don't know how to weigh it."

"Well, what can we do, Bip?"

He had his hand on his chin thinking. He took his hand down quickly and said, "Where's Fat?"

"Fat, talking about my kid's daddy?"

"Yeah."

"Honey, please, that nigger might tell my mama and I haven't even told her yet."

Bip said, "Hey baby, that's the chance we have got to take."

"I don't know about that," I said.

"Well how in the fuck you think we are going to do it?"

"On no," I said. I was looking and thinking, walking in and out of the kitchen. I stopped for a minute and looked at Bippy smiling, and saying, "I know, I got it, let's go over to his brother's house. He will teach me because he been doing drugs even before Aunt Hazel went to jail."

Bip said, "Okay, let's go." He didn't even wash his face or nothing. I forgot to offer him a towel and toothbrush; I guess he didn't want one 'cause if he did, he would have asked me. We went out of the kitchen door and got into the car. Bippy said, "Do you know where he lives?"

"You know I know where he lives," I said.

Bippy asked "Well, how far is it from here?"

I answered, "Not too far, we just got to go to the Glenwood exit, then we will be right at it." We got to his street and I said, "There's his car in the driveway." He had a green Electra 225, about a 1973, and it was very clean. He lived in a little green and white house, his name was Willie, but everybody called him Will. He was five feet, eleven inches tall, weighing about 155 pounds. His hair was very bad, just like his brother's. His wife was pregnant; she was five feet, one inches and dark complexioned. She weighed about 145 pounds, and she was big. She already had two little snot noses already around there. I got by the car by myself first to make sure that Will knew Bippy and hoped that he wouldn't be mad at me for bringing somebody over to his house. I rang the doorbell twice and no one answered. I could see someone peeping out of the curtains, so I then knocked hard on the door. He opened with a smile. "Hey lady, what's going on and what storm brought you over here?"

"Look, I got something I want to show you, but first I want to know if you don't mind if Bippy can come in?"

"Bippy! Yeah, talking about Bippy from Auburn Avenue?"

"Yeah, that's him."

"Naw, I don't mind, shit we go a long ways back," Will said.

"Okay, wait, let me tell him to come in." I went to the bottom of the steps and motioned him to come in. He got out of the car and ran in.

Bip said, "Yeah, what's happening man? Long time no see. What are you doing for it now, are you still tilt tapping?" he asked with a smile on his face.

"Well, you know how that goes, if I find a good lick, I'll damn well take it off, but other than that, I'm handling a little boy and girl."

I looked at him and was glad Bippy capped it off for me, because I didn't know what to say. "Will, this is what brought me over here. Ah, I got some cocaine for sale, do you want to buy some?" I asked him.

He looked at me and laughed then said, "Hot damn, not the little working lady. Hey man," looking at Bippy. "I know damn well," he said and paused for a minute. "Um ah, come in the kitchen." We followed behind him. Then he said, "Fat know you got this?"

I said, "Naw (real quick), and don't tell him."

Will said, "Why not? Shit, he can help you move it, too."

"Well, I just don't want him to know," I said.

"Okay, Ms. Lady, show me what you got."

I asked, "Do you have a triple bean?"

He said, "Naw, but I got some cheater spoons."

"Cheater spoons, what's that?" I asked him.

He went into the silverware drawer and got some spoons and all of them was different. I opened my pouch and pulled one of the bags out; it was the $600 one.

He looked and said, "Goddamn, San, open it up. Where in the hell did you get it from?"

I said, "Never mind that, do you want it?"

"Pass it over here, let me check it out." Will got the sifter and a plate with a playing card already on it. "Wait a minute, Will, before you mess it up, are you gonna buy some?"

"Look, Ms. Lady, whatever I fuck up, I'll pay for, okay?"

"Okay," I said. He put half of the cocaine in the little sifter at a time. He separated the rock from the shake; he snorted some in his nose. It stung his nose a little and he said, "What you will sell an eighth for?"

"Will, to tell the truth, I don't even know how much they cost. This is the reason I came over here."

Will said, "Most people sells them for $225.00 to $250.00 with a little cut on them, but since yours is pure, hell, I just don't know."

"Okay, Will, do me a favor, see how many eighth's is in there." He took the card, filled the eighth spoon with the shake, and put a few gravels of rock on it. He came up with four eights out of the $600.00 sack. So I counted them and said, "Damn, Bippy, I can sell them for $200.00 a piece and still make $200.00 over on this." Damn! I got happier and happier, my nerves got stronger and stronger, and my mind was thinking money, money. "Look Will, since you helped me, I'll let you have it for $200.00, okay?"

"Well look ah here, San, I think that I have about $500.00–$550.00. What will you give me for that?"

"Just give me the $500.00 and take three of the eights."

He got up, went into the bedroom for the money, and came back in counting. He had fives, tens, and twenties totaling up to $500.00. While he was counting, he asked, "Do you want me to seal that other eighth?"

"What do you mean? Put it in a smaller bag?"

"Yeah."

He left the money on the table for me to double count and walked over to the sink and looked up the sealer. While waiting on it to get hot, he asked, "Is that all you have?"

"No. I have another bag, but it's an $800."

"Do you want me to break it down for you?"

"Yeah, please, if you don't mind."

He sat down at the table and started to sift again. He separated the shake and the rocks again. This time he came up with six eighths and a little more.

"Let's put some cut on this extra to see what it will take."

He put one spoon of cut and one spoon of cocaine that totaled a whole eighth. He ran all of it in the sifter. Then he got a spoon and ground all of the rocks together; then he ran it through the sifter about three more times.

Bippy was sitting patiently then asked, "Let me try that."

"Yeah, let Bippy try," Will said, "you know he's an expert tester."

"Okay, Bippy. Where's your stuff?"

"I left it out in the car. Let me out, man."

"Go up there and tell Ann to let you out."

Bippy jumped up and yelled for Ann.

While Bippy was gone, Will sealed the eighths up. When it was all over, I had seven eighths and one with some cut on it.

Bip got back in and Will put about 1/5 in the cooker. Then Will said, "Bippy! How about going in the bathroom to handle your business?"

"Okay, but where is it?"

"Go out the door to the left."

Bippy went on to the bathroom then Will continued schooling me, "Now you listen, San. You can have this spoon because you will need it. You need a triple beam and when you get it, let me know. I will show you how to work it. But as long as you are doing eighths and quarters, you won't need it. Now I want you to watch carefully as I fix two of these for you, and then I want you to do the rest of them. This is the best way for you to learn."

"Oh, okay."

He sealed up two eighths and brushed all the cocaine that was on the plate back together. "Hold it," he said as he was reaching for the plates.

"What are you doing?"

"I'm just trying to see if you are measuring it right."

"Oh, I see."

Bippy came rushing back from the bathroom and said, "Let me out, man! Let me out. I've got to walk! Let me out the back door ...'shit's too strong."

"But how can that be?" I asked. "I gave him some at home and he didn't react like this."

"That's why it needs a cut," Will explained. "You see, cut give it the rush."

"Well, is he going to be all right?" I was scared.

Will smiled and nodded his head, "Goddamn, girl. You've got a monster. Look, you don't need to sell that shit like that. That stuff will burst a motherfucker's heart, girl!"

We watched Bippy walk back and forth, up and down. Then he decided to come inside. When he got in, he was blowing and breathing hard. The sound of his voice scared me; he sounded as though he was hoarse. He said, "Um-um, um, boy, boy, boy ...m-a-n! She's got a cold-blooded killer." He looked at Will and then continued, "Baby, baby, baby! If a nigger don't know how to handle that, he'll be in trouble. Say, San! Why don't you put one on it, it'll still be just as strong."

"Nah. We are going to leave it just like it is. I'll do the next package I get like that, all right?"

Sweating, Bippy said, "Let's just go, baby."

"Okay. Let me fix these eighths up."

"Are you all right, Bippy, man?" Will asked.

"Yeah, man. That shit had me for a minute, but you know that I can handle it."

I finished fixing the stuff up and we got in the car and left.

Time was flying and I still had to go to Big H's house to drop the money off and pick up some more cocaine, but I wanted to finish selling all that I had first.

While riding, Bippy said, "Let's go through the Avenue to see what's happening down there."

It was in the afternoon and I was hoping that the time was right, but nevertheless I went anyway. We were at the intersections of Auburn and Foote Street and while turning the corner some bearded man notice Bippy and yelled, "Hey Bippy! Where you going?"

"Ah, man, just riding. What's up?"

"Look-a-hear, get touch with Jeff for me. I need to get two eighths and I need them quick."

"Hey baby, you ain't got to go no further. What do you want?"

Bippy opened the car door and pulled the front seat up to invite the guy in. When he got in he said, "Oh, ah, how you doing, Ms. San?"

I looked back to check out who was calling me by name and sure enough I recognized him, "Goddamn, I didn't even recognize you with that beard, Pretty Boy."

He was a real slim goody with a beautiful low-cut black beard and slick hair with a real pretty black complexion and big brown eyes. He was tall, too. I was checking out his long legs and firm buttocks in his well-fitted black pants. Woo boy! They were tight as hell ...showing everything. I loved to watch pretty booties and this nigger had one ...um, um. I heard him ask, "So when will you Aunt Hazel get out?"

"She's due out next month. I don't know the exact date."

"Look man," Bippy said, "What do you want to do? You want some girl or not?"

"I know ain't no motherfucker trusted you with no weight, man."

"Fuck all that. Do you want it or not?"

"Yeah, let me check it out."

"San, pull the car over and let me drive so you can show that thang to Pretty Boy."

I pulled over and stopped. Bippy got out and I slid over to the passenger's side while he was walking over to the driver's seat. Bippy adjusted the seat, got in, and stepped on the gas. I said, "Hey man, you ain't got no license so quit fucking around."

"Show this nigger the shit."

I went into the pouch and pulled out one eighth and turned it around so that he could check it. He tore the bag open with his teeth and got his little spoon out then snorted some.

"Damn, San! You got this kind of thang?"

"Well, Pretty Boy, now you know. How about that?" I smiled and showed my dimples, "How about it?"

"What do you want for a quarter?"

"That's two eighths, right?"

He nodded, yes.

"Give me $400."

"Four hundred?" He looked shocked; "It's a bet. Let me have'em so that I can go to work." He went into his pocket and counted out $400 to me. I then reached for my pouch and pulled another eighth out and gave it to him.

"Listen baby, y'all need to give me a number so I can get in touch with you because I'll be through with these in no time."

I wrote the number down and gave it to him. He said, "Let me out man, right here ...naw ...go up to Boulevard. My car is down the street." We let him out on Boulevard and while closing the door he lean over and whispered, "You're badder than you look, Ms. San."

"Get on 'way from here, nigger," Bippy said. We switched seats again because I didn't want to take the chance with lawless Bippy driving without a license. I drove on off.

"Damn Bippy, we didn't need but $400 more and the rest is ours."

"You need $500 more."

"No, um—"

"Yes, you do. Remember your brother-in-law?"

"Oh, that's right. But get it right, he ain't my brother-inlaw."

"Whatever, you still need another $500. Listen, if you want, you can re-up now with the money you have already made."

"Nooo, I'm going to sell all of the first then go back. I don't want to mix my money with the man's money, okay. Now let's get something to eat, Bip."

"Okay."

"Where do you want to go?"

"What do you want to eat?"

"You know what I want: a T-bone steak, baked potato, and garlic bread from a white folks place. I've never been to Hungry Bull."

"Go 'head. Do get what you want."

We headed for the steakhouse and on the way, Bippy said, "Listen baby, why don't you give me a little hit and a couple of dollars then I'll get out close to the shooting gallery."

"Aw, Bippy, I thought that you wanted to eat with me."

"I don't want no food no way. This stuff have you where you don't want no food."

"Okay, then. But listen—I'll be back for you in about one hour from now. But before I drop you off, let me call my brother to see if he will go over to my house to see about my children."

"Look, there's a phone, San. Go ahead and call him now."

I pulled over in front of the phone booth and parked. I grabbed my pouch and gave Bippy some out of the shake pack, then I gave him $50 to buy some "boy" and whatever. As soon as he got his stuff, he was ready to fly high.

"Look here," he said, "pick me up from the Rib Shack when you're done eating."

"Dog, I really wanted you to go with me ...but I guess now I'll be alone."

He started to get out the car and then I said, "Hey! At least you can wait until I make the phone call." I got out the car while Bip was looking at his thang. I walked up to the phone booth and dialed the number.

"Hello?"

"Hey, Mamma. What are you doing?"

"Baby, you know that this sugar is still bothering me and we don't have any food down here."

"You ain't got no money?"

"Naw. My food stamps are gone. I used the last ones yesterday. I'm going to try and borrow some from my neighbor."

"Don't borrow, Mama. I got some money for you, okay?"

"O-o-h boy! But where did you get money?"

"Ah, girl, don't worry about it. I got it. I was headed out to eat."

"With who?"

"Myself. But I'm not going now. I'll be straight down your house. Is Poo-Poo there?"

"Yeah. He's outside somewhere."

"Well, you tell him not to leave because I want to talk to him about something. Okay?"

"Alright."

"Okay. Bye, Mama."

I hung up the phone real quick and I was grinning because I felt so good about being able to go to my mama with money. I had some money for my mama. It was a joy to take some money to my mother.

I was skipping and smiling calling out to Bippy, "Bippy! I got them, so I will meet you at the place, okay?"

He got out and I drove off.

I drive fast anyway so I got down to Mama's house in about 12 minutes going by the Federal Penitentiary. My mother lived in government projects. I was one of eight girls and we had four brothers. All but three of us lived at home with four bedrooms. I parked in the back of the apartment. After I got in the house, my little brother and sister saw me and started smiling. It was as though they knew I had something for them. Well, they were right. "Where's Mama?"

My baby sister who was only eight years old said, "She'sup there in the living room."

I went toward the living room with my sister and brother following behind me. I reached over and kissed my mother while she was watching the soap operas. I then opened the pouch and pulled out some money. I counted out $200 for Mama. Her eyes widened. They were big and bright as though she had seen a ghost. Laughing, she got up off the sofa and grabbed me and said, "Thank you, Jesus, thank you. He's always on time."

"That's right, Mama. Regardless to how you get it, you got it!"

"Sandra, where did you get it?"

"Ah, Mama. I didn't steal it, so don't worry. It's all good."

She looked at me so funny 'til I had to lie a little bit, "Okay, Mama. I met a rich boyfriend and he really likes me. He wants to take me out of town. That's what I need to talk to Poo-Poo about. By the way, where is he? Come here, Tony," I said to my 13-year-old, dark-skinned baby brother. "Go look for Poo-Poo for me."

Tony went out the front door to get Poo-Poo. They both burst back into the door huffing and puffing, then Poo-Poo said, "Hey, Big Sister! What's going on?"

I looked at him and said, "You better slow down, Big Brother. You are gaining weight. You are going to be fat in a minute." He was 23 years old and stood about five feet eleven inches and weighed about 185 lbs and had curly hair. He'smy oldest brother and was four years my junior.

"That's just what I've been doing... jogging all day."

"Look here. Come outside and let me holler at you."

We started to walk out the door then I turned around and said, "I'll be right back, Mama."

"Look here, brother." I was motioning my hands, trying to persuade him into moving in with me. "I've got a chance to make lots of money, but I need you to move with me so that you can be there with the children whenever I have to go out. Now, I ain't going to be stealing or robbing or nothing like that. This is different."

"How different?" Poo-Poo asked.

"I'll tell you about it when you come over to the house."

"I can't go tonight because I've got to take care of some business, okay?"

"Uh-uh. I didn't want to talk about it tonight, anyway. Just get your grip together and be ready tomorrow."

"What time will you need me?"

"Well, It'll be after school."

"Okay, then."

We went back into the house. I was just smiling.

Mama asked, "What's the matter?"

"Mama, you'll see. I just feel good, good. I got to go now because I've got to meet my friend and go home to feed Harry and Cocoa. I'll check you later, Poo-Poo. See ya, Ma."

"Okay, Bye."

I walked out the door and by the time I got to the car, Mama was at the door watching me. She was waving at me and I was smiling and blowing the horn. It was time to pick Bippy back up. I turned on the Patti LaBelle's tape; "It's a Joy to Have Your Love" was playing. I rocked on down to Auburn Avenue. When I got there, Bippy wasn't around so I got out and went into the Rib Shack to get a BBQ sandwich and Pepsi-Cola. I didn't have too much time because I had to get home. I went to the counter and ordered. The waitress asked, "What part do you want?"

"Give me the short end for here."

She laid a napkin and silverware and came back with water and my Pepsi. "That will be $3.22, please."

I opened my pouch and gave her a $5.00 bill and told her to keep the change. I felt good because I had never been able to tip a waitress much. I looked around and spotted Bippy. He came over to me and I said, "There you are."

"Look here. I talked to those people, plus I talked back to Jeff; this is what he needs."

"Okay."

"Big Rob wants to check out a half ounce."

"What's a half?"

"That would be four eighths and Jeff wants another ounces and Lil Duey wants a quarter."

"Wait a minute. Are you talking about Duey who owns the club on Simpson Street?"

"Yeah, you know him. You also know Bob. He use to be your step-daddy."

"Bob? Oh, Fat Daddy Bob ...okay. I do know him."

"Come on, they are waiting."

"Wait. Let me get my food. Shit, I've paid for this and anyway, I've got to check on my children before I do anything."

"Aw man, okay then, get the sandwich and eat it on the way. I'll be outside making a phone call to tell them to give us an hour."

He walked out of the door real fast just as the lady handed me my sandwich. I covered it with my napkin and went out the door eating a piece of rib. When I got to the car, I forgot that I had left my Pepsi so I ran back to get it. Bippy saw me and said, "Hey baby, you're already fast, but you gonna have to move a little faster because in this game when you slow, you blow."

"Come on. I'm ready," I said returning with my drink.

"Now, I talked to all three of them. They are waiting on us, so how much stuff you got?"

"About nine eighths left."

Bippy started doing the figures, "Let me see, Bob wants four eighths, Duey wants two eighths ...that makes six and you'll have three left. Okay, now what we will do is get them first. Then we'll go see about the kids, call your uncle so you can re-up, then we'll call Jeff back to let him know, okay?"

"Come on, Bippy. I've got to go home."

"Shit, fast as you drive, hell it won't take no time."

We got in the car and went to the club on Simpson Street. Fat Daddy Bob was out in the parking lot waiting. He spotted us and yelled, "Hey, baby girl! What you doing messing with this shit?"

"It's a long story."

"Look here, what's your phone number?"

"I'll write it down," Bippy said, "just take care of the business."

"What will it take?" Bob asked.

Before I could say anything, Bippy said, "It will take a two."

Bob looked at me and asked, "Will it, baby girl?"

I nodded my head, yes.

He said, "Okay, I'll take my daughter's word for it and if it don't, I'll call."

"Aw motherfucker, it's fire! I've checked it," Bippy said.

"How much is it, baby girl?"

"Eight hundred dollars."

"Damn! That's all? I'll be calling you later on tonight if it's all right."

Bippy said, "We'll be there."

"Okay, yes man," Bob said. He counted out six 100 dollar bills and the rest in 20's. I then pulled out four eighths and handed them to him. He said, "Hey baby, why do you have it separated like this?"

"Because I'm just learning."

He smiled and opened one of the packs. "Damn! I didn't have to open it, I could smell the shit in the bag."

He balled it up in his hand and hit the car and said, "Check y'all out later."

"Okay, Fat Man," said Bippy.

"Drive baby, drive your car."

"Damn, Bippy," I said, "You know everybody who sells drugs."

"You're gonna know them too after a while. Just keep hanging with me."

"Turn down Ashby Street and go the West End because Duey will be in the Sears parking lot; that's only five minutes away."

We turned into the lot and Bippy got out to go talk to him. I sat there and was amazed how people were walking all around but no one paid any attention to us. They had no clue as to what were transacting. Not long, Bippy came back with Duey. They got in the car and I showed him the stuff real quick like. He looked at it and then at me and asked, "How much?"

"Four hundred."

"Oh yeah, I've got $500. What can you do with that?"

"Nothing, motherfucker, god damn you're already getting a play, so take the quarter that you asked for."

He looked at Bippy and said, "Kiss my ass, nigger and get out of my business."

"Wait a minute," I said, "I've got to go. I can't do nothing with no $100. You've got to have $200."

All his money was in $10's and $20's. I counted out $400.

Before he got out the car he said, "Okay, San, I'll get with you tomorrow ..."

"That's right, bastard," Bippy said, "get the fuck out."

"Ah, nigger. You can't blame me for trying. Damn! Let me out this motherfucker, man!"

"Get out, nigger," Bippy said while pulling the seat up.

"Hey, Bippy, I'm serious. I'll check you later, okay ...just kicking it ..."

"Hey, I know what the deal is. Bye, nigger. Let's go and see about Harry and Cocoa."

"Listen," I said, "What now?"

"Listen," he said, "We've got to go toward your uncle's house to get to your house, right?"

"Right."

"Okay, then, let's stop by his house and pay and pick—then stop by Church's Chicken and get the kids some food. Take it on home and feed them. While we're there, call Jeff. Okay?"

"I thought you were going to say something else."

We went down Ashby Street to I-20 East heading to my uncle's. We got off at Moreland and went to Glenwood, turned on Browns Mill. I parked the car in front of the house. I told Bippy to wait until I came back. I got out and went in. You never have to knock because the door is always open. I was walking very fast, plus I talk fast, so this was going to be quick. I remembered what Bippy had told me ..."You already fast, but you need to get faster ..."

His daughters and all were there. I walked on in and said, "Hey y'all! Where's Big H?"

"He's in the den, San."

I walked in the den and when I saw him I said, "Hey, Big H. I got your money so get me ready." He was sitting down. He looked at me with a big smile and said, "Julio left you five ounces already ounced up."

I clapped my hands and said, "Thank you, thank you! Woo-wee! I am so happy." I counted the money out to him and gave him $3,800. He went behind the sofa, pulled out a brown paper bag, opened it, and counted five different packs. But there was six in there. I said, "Hey, there six in there."

"Yeah, I know. After you sell the five, the sixth one belongs to you." "Golly! I'm about to get stuff! They still the same price?"

"Yeah. We will see you tomorrow and give you something personal."

"But I don't do it."

"Hell, he knows that. He wants to satisfy you."

"Believe me, Uncle. He has satisfied me. Tell him that all right."

"I'll tell him tomorrow. Give me the bag and I'll put it back in there. I've got to go feed my children."

I was putting the stuff back in the bag as I was still talking: "Okay, Big H. I've got to run now. I'll check you out tomorrow. Okay, boy?"

I was really stepping. All I could do was think positive, watch, listen and learn more because I wanted to be good at whatever I was into. I went out of the door in a flash, kicking my heels. Everybody in the house said good-bye. I didn't even respond. I got in the car real quick because to me it was just like a job and it was time for my break. I got in the car and Bippy asked, "Well, did you get it?"

"What you think, la-la. Bippy, you know what? I'm going to be a bad bitch ...I'm talking real bad. I want to sell dope 'til I fall out. I want to get some burglar bars, I got to do it up right."

Bippy looked at me, rocking, smiling then said, "That's the kind of attitude you've got to have, baby! Hey! I damn sure like that! Handle things, baby, handle it. Put the music on."

We stopped at the chicken shack ordered a family pack with corn on the cob, bread, and sodas for Harry and Cocoa. Bippy suddenly remembered, "Look-a-here, you need to get a sifter because you know you got some eighths and quarter people. How many did you get?"

"Six, baby."

"We're going to roll, now."

We made it to the house and I said, "Come on, Bippy, so we can call Jeff. Take the chicken on in the house. I've got to ask my neighbor if she'll watch the kids for me." I went over next door to ask and she said yes. I gave her $20 and ran back home.

Harry and Cocoa were in the kitchen eating their chicken. "Hey, babies," I said.

"Hey," Harry said. "San, where you been?" Harry is the one always wanting to know where I've been; where I'm going and what time I'll be back. I just ignored him, grabbed a wing and ate it as I spoke to Bippy, "Bippy, did you make that call?"

He had a drumstick in his mouth but still talking and reaching, "Pass me the phone."

"Here," I said, as I passed him the phone. Bippy made the call to Jeff and I could hear him talking ...

"Jeff, what's happening?" Jeff wanted to talk with me because he had Bug at his house and that Bug wanted to get two ounces if it's the same way that he had gotten it. Bippy told him it was the same way. Jeff asked for me.

When I got the phone, I said, "Hello."

Jeff spoke, "Listen, Pretty. Did Bippy tell you that I wanted one ounce of those things?"

"Uh-uh."

Jeff went on, "Well, I got a friend over and he spends big money. If it's like the others, he'll be buying four or five ounces per week."

"Oh yeah?"

"Yeah. Now understand—instead of the one, bring three," Jeff said.

My eyes bucked and I turned to Bippy while putting my hand over the mouthpiece of the phone. "Bip! Guess what? He wants three; one for him and two for a friend."

Bip told me to hang up and let's ride. I spoke back into the phone, "Okay, I'll be there in a minute." I dialed the phone to call my neighbor. "Hello, Gwen. Come on. I'm ready." Gwen didn't hesitate. She told me she was on her way.

As soon as I hung up the phone, I went straight to the front door to open it for her. I walked toward the bathroom, unzipping my pants 'cause I really had an urge to go. I told Bip to let me use the bathroom 'cause he had beat me in there. When I got done, Gwen was right there ...ready to go. I kissed Harry and Cocoa and told them I'd be back in about two hours. "Come on, Bippy." He came on out the door with me like roadrunners. While going to the car, I said, "Bippy! I like this world. This is easy, huh?"

Bippy said, "It seems like it now, baby, but you've got a long ways to go. You know, San—you can get there quick, but the key is to stay there."

I said, "Um, I'm gonna stay. Just watch and see. I'm gonna stay."

We drove off, heading towards Jeff's house. We pulled up in the parking lot. Right next to his car was a triple black limo. I couldn't help myself: "Good-god-ah-mighty! Whose car is that?"

Bip answered, "That must be Bug's car. He's top-notched. He's one of bigger buyers. He goes cross the waters to get his shit. He buys keys."

By this time we had approached the front door. Bip knocked. He didn't think to ring the doorbell.

"Yeah!" Someone from the other side of the door yelled.

Bip said, "Bip and San." We were told to come on in.

After we got in, Jeff looked out from the kitchen and said, "Baby, I ain't gonna hold you up. Come on back here." When I got in the kitchen I saw a little short man—about five foot seven with nappy hair. He must have been about 45 years old and had a stocky build. He was wearing a three-piece suit with two diamonds glistening from the lighting. This man looked impressive and came across very conservative. He had a cigar in mouth and gold tooth at the bottom of his mouth.

Jeff introduced us. "San, this is Bug; Bug, this is San."

Bug nodded his head, saying, "Pleased to meet you, I guess."

I said, "How do you do?" I blushed, looking like a young girl going on her first date. I did not know what to say.

I don't think Bug noticed anything, but he asked, "So, this little girl is who got the blow, Jeff?"

"Yeah, man. You know I told you it was a female who had the pack."

Bug just looked and said to me, "Let me see one of those ounces, baby."

I felt that he got over the fact that he was dealing with a female, so I went on into my pouch and pulled one out for his inspection. With obvious experience, Bug put the pack up to his nose. When he did that, I noticed his shoulder holster. I knew then, without a doubt—Bug was packing, and it wasn't white stuff. "Damn," I thought to myself. "Everybody selling dope carries a gun."

While he was opening my pack, he asked, "How much, baby?"

Without hesitation, I answered, "1400 apiece."

"Okay," Bug said, "Just let me check this out." He reached into his briefcase and grabbed a little test tube. He put a little cocaine down in it, put a top on it and shook it up. The man was maneuvering like a pharmacist. Looking in the tube, I noticed that the contents of the tube were blue, and after adding the cocaine, it changed colors just a little. "Damn, this is about 93 percent cocaine. Give me three ounces." I realized that I had only brought three—one for Jeff and two for Bug.

Jeff spoke up, "Man, you asked for two and I was getting one so I told her to just bring three."

Bug knew that he had changed his "order." Then he said, "I know, I know, but man, let me get all three 'cause I'mon my way out of town." Jeff didn't get a chance to respond when Bug turned to me, "Hold it ...you got anymore of this handy?"

"Yeah. I can get some like now, real soon," I answered.

Bug insisted that he was leaving town and wanted to know just how soon. I convinced him that I could get it before he left—that is, if he could wait an hour.

But Jeff spoke up, again. "Hey, go on and let him get those now."

Bug asked me, "How much do I owe you, baby?" It didn't take me long to figure this: I answered, "$4200." Bug didn't blink an eye. He put his cigar back in his mouth and reached in his grip and pulled out a stash. Like a teller at the bank, Bug counted out thirty $100 bills and the rest in 50's and 20's. He picked up the ounces he tested from and asked, "Now, where are the other two?"

"Oooh, I'm sorry. Here you are." I handed him the other two ounces.

"Look San," Jeff said, "you ain't no more on you, right?"

"Yeah, I got about three eighths ..."

"Sell me them until I get the others. What you want for all three?"

"Give me $500."

"It's a deal, San. I see me and you are going to be sho-nuff, all right," Jeff said. He yelled from the kitchen, "Hey, Bo! Come here, man."

Bo came to the door. "Yeah, Jeff."

Jeff instructed, "Look in the bedroom on the dresser and bring me that little pouch."

"Will do," said Bo as he walked away. I was thinking and listening.

By now, Bug had put all his stuff away and asked, "Well, man. Get somebody to let me out (referring to the parking arrangements in the lot). I got a long ride. I'll be in touch with you sometime next week. I'll call first to make sure that the little lady is still in pocket."

"Okay, man," Jeff said. By this time, Bo was back with the pouch. "Bo, give me that pouch and ah, let him out."

Bug turned to me as he was leaving behind Bo. "Take it easy, baby girl. It was nice meeting you."

"You, too," I said with one of my pretty smiles. He just don't know, that smile was cause I came with three ounces and some eighths and I was leaving with his money plus another $500 I was not expecting and a shake. I had a shake eighth and Bippy was using it.

Bippy said, "Give me that, baby, so you can go on and take care of your business. Here's the three eighths that I had left." I thought he was going to try and make a pass with his lying ass, but he didn't. He said, "Hey, baby, go on and get the stuff so you can get on back."

"Jeff!" I called out to him, "will it be asking too much if you come out to my house to pick it up because my kids are home and I'm kind of tired, plus I got a babysitter and I promised her that I would be back in two hours. I've been gone almost that long."

Jeff said, "No problem. I can't leave right now, but I'll be there in about one and a half hours—just as I cut some of this dope up, all right."

Bippy jumped in, "Hey, man. Can I get a little bit before I go?"

Jeff said, "Naw, man. I got to take care some business right now."

Bippy said, "Okay, well let me get 50 from you, okay?"

Jeff called out, "Hey, Bo! Get a funk 50 for Bippy."

Bippy looked at me, "San, will you get that for me?"

I said, "Yeah." I handed Jeff $50 and he gave it back to me saying, "Naw, that's all right, Pretty. I owe him more than that 'cause he brought you to me."

Bippy was concentrating on what he wanted and said, "Ah man, it won't take me long. Let me get a little hit."

Jeff spoke to Bippy, "Go ahead. But don't take long."

I said, "Please don't."

Bippy walked out of the kitchen and left me alone with Jeff. I caught him staring at me then he asked, "San, what's your man's name?" I told him I didn't have a man right now. He jumped right on that as if he didn't believe it. I assured him that I didn't have a man and he wanted to know why not.

I said, "Because, I just don't. Anyway, why do you want to know all that?"

Jeff spoke in a different tone, "Any man in his right mind wouldn't pass you up ...if you know what I mean."

"No—I don't what you mean."

Just then, Bippy came running back saying, "Let's ride." He thanked Jeff and told me, "Come on, San. Let's go."

As we were walking out of the kitchen toward the den, I heard Jeff, "Hey, San. You forgot to give me your address."

I realized that he was right. He was coming by to pick up his package. I responded, " Oh, yeah. It's 2401 Eastwyck Road. You'll find it off Candler Road." When he asked for directions, I continued. "Take I-20 East; get off at Candler Road, turn left. At the second traffic light, take a right. I'm in the 2nd driveway on the right—#23. It's the first apartment on the right. It is fenced in. You can't miss it. My car will be parked out in front of the door."

Jeff said, "Okay, baby. I'll call you when I'm on my way." Jeff spoke to Bippy, "Okay, Mr. Bippy. I'll see you later."

Bippy was feeling real good. He had just had a speedball. He went out of the door moving real fast—and I was just moving ...Bip was already at the car when I got to the door saying, "Come on, San! What you waiting for?"

"All right, all right, here I come." I turned around and looked at Jeff and said, "I'll see you when you get there."

Jeff grinned and said, "Hey, don't fall asleep on me because I most definitely will be there."

I said, "All right," and walked to the car looking right at Bippy.

I unlocked the door and got in to reach over to unlock Bippy's side. "Bippy, listen. I know you are speeding for something, but guess how much money?"

Bippy said, "Tell me about it later ...just let me enjoy this high."

I said, "Oh, okay." Even though I really wanted to talk about it, right then! We rode the rest of the way in complete silence.

As soon as I got home, I wanted to go straight to bed. I don't know what Bippy was doing downstairs because I was too sleepy and tired to even think about it. I do know that the babysitter was knocked out and Bippy must have woke her up and let her out. I had already forgotten that Jeff was coming. It was later than he said when he eventually got there. I heard a knock on the door (I didn't have a doorbell). I could hear it real good, but I didn't want to get up out my bed to answer it. I dragged up as the knock got louder with persistence. I looked out the window with my raggedy, but real comfortable, nightgown on. My eyes were bucked and I put my hands over my mouth saying with anticipation—"He's here, he's here." I was hoping that Bippy heard him at the door, but Bippy was in the damn bathroom. He had to have heard him, but Bippy must have had that damn needle in his arm.

He yelled, "San! Check the door. Hey, San!" It felt like I was sleep-walking and all of Bippy's yelling wasn't helping anything.

I yelled back, "I heard you the first time."

He wouldn't give it up, "Well check it out. It might be Jeff."

I started down the steps and caught myself. I looked down at my gown and yelled as I was running back to my bedroom and looking out the window as I passed it I could see the top of Jeff's head. "Hold on a minute! I'll be right down." I looked in the chest of drawers and grabbed a pair of jogging shorts and sweatshirt. I put them on real fast and went downstairs without any shoes on. Nearly out of breath, I opened the patio door and looked up at this tall handsome man. I motioned him with a grin to come in.

As he walked in he said, "I thought it was too late, but something came up and we ran out of 'boy' and 'girl,' so I had to go find some 'boy,' hoping that I could count on you to be here waiting for me since I kind of 'reserved' some 'girl' with you."

I told him to come on in and have a seat. Jeff continued to talk, "Damn. I sure am tired," while rubbing his eyes. I noticed he had on a rust sweater, rust pants, and some rust and blue suede shoes; a blue leather jacket with rust buttons top-stitched in rust. I mean, this man was together! His bracelet was solid gold with "Jeff" laid in diamonds. Draped in his gold chain around his neck, he complemented the rest of his diamonds with two more on his manicured hands. Snapping back to the business at hand, he said, "San, San, San. What's going on baby? Listen, I know I told you I was coming over for one ounce but I need two. But look, if you don't have but the one, I can work with that. I need two because I got some people buying a little more than before. Baby, you are gonna supply the whole territory—as long as this shit stays straight."

I said, "Umm-hmm. I got two just for you. I figured you would ask for another. Hold on." I ran upstairs, looked under my mattress and got the two ounces. I made a mad dash back down. When I got there, Jeff was nodding with the money in his hand. "Hey!"

He sitting and looking up at me. "Yeah, baby. We gonna make a killing!" He got right back on the same subject—just that quick.

I followed suit, "Here you go, Jeff," handing him the 2 ounces.

"Here, baby, count your money. Damn, San, do you mind if I open one to get me a little hit out of here?"

"Nooo, go ahead," I said.

He opened up one of the ounces and pulled a little bottle with a little spoon on it from his pocket. He then took a little straw, stuck it in the ounce, and thumped it. He thumped the ounce about three more times. He then took a lighter to seal the ounce back up.

Amazed, I said, "Hey, I didn't know that you could seal it like that."

Jeff explained, "Naw, baby. This is just the lazy way. Hey, where's Bippy?"

I told him that Bippy was in the bathroom. Jeff laughed and said, "I should have known that."

"Yep! That's where he is," I confirmed. Jeff then snorted some cocaine, snorting a total of four times—alternating nostrils. I said, "Why you gotta do it so many times right behind the other?"

Jeff just grinned and answered, "I'm used to it, baby. I can handle it. For one thing, I've snorted too much 'boy.' That shit got me fucked up! Here," passing me the little bottles, "you want a hit?"

I scooted in my chair and answered, "Naw. I don't want none. I don't do it anyway."

He said, "That's good. But you keep fucking with it and you will be."

I didn't hesitate, "No, no. I ain't never done no drugs before."

He snorted again saying, "If you keep that thought in mind, you won't. But if you ever fuck up and let a nigga introduce you ...ah baby, you'll be doing the same thing I am. And anyway, it won't hurt you. But listen to this! Don't ever let no mothafucker talk you into that heroin thing, baby. I mean, if you do ...your whole clientele will be different. That shit brings on the robbers and police!" As I was looking and listening, I thought about the money he had given me. I slid it under the table and curiosity took over. "What will it do to you?"

"What will 'what' do to you?"

"The cocaine."

"Oh, it will keep you watching, keep you up ...have you where you can hear a mile. It keeps you alert. But the part I like, it makes me freaky. Oooh yea!"

I smiled and said, "What do you mean—'make you freakish?'"

"Okay, let me see how can I explain this to you." He snorted again. "Okay. You see the little I've snorted and I'm already high. This is just enough to—excuse my expression—fuck a lady to death. Now if I overdo it, I can't even get up a hard dick. Too much makes my dick heavy, not hard."

I laughed and said, "What do you mean by it makes it heavy not hard?"

He smiled back and answered, "A heavy dick has to be pushed in. It's all balled up and thangs. But when this mothafucker get's hard ...Lord have mercy on you."

I jumped back, "Me!"

"Naw, baby. Not you," he said. As he was getting out of the chair to leave, Jeff threw a cute little kiss at me. "Look, I gotta go, now, but I do want to talk to you when my head is real straight."

"Okay. How about Sunday?" I asked.

Jeff didn't hesitate: "Yeah. Sunday's good for me. Will you cook dinner?"

"Yeah, I gotta cook anyway. I told you I have two kids," I said, heading to a the living room to get a picture of Harry and Cocoa. When I got back, I said, "Look. Here's a picture of them."

"Hey, you got some fine looking kids. They both look just like you."

Blushing from his underlined compliment, I said, "Oh, you think so?"

Jeff handed the picture back, "Here, put them back for now. I gotta hit the road. I got a pretty good ride ahead of me."

Taking the picture, I said while walking Jeff to the door, "Okay."

We could hear Bippy talking from the closed bathroom, "We'll check you tomorrow, Jeff."

Jeff said, "Ah, you motherfucker ...that shit got you ears wide open, ain't it?"

Bip answered back, "Ah, nigga. Go head on."

Jeff grinned while looking at me and gently touched my cheek, "Let me ride, baby."

I hesitantly opened the door to let him out. When he finally left, I locked the door and turned my back leaning on it with the picture of my kids still in my hand, thinking: Damn! That nigga know he's a fine-assed nigga. I snapped back and went into the living room to return the picture to its place. As I started upstairs, I yelled through the bathroom door at Bippy, "See you in the morning."

"Okay, baby. Goodnight. I'll be out of here in a minute."

I ran on up the steps and looked in on Harry and left there to check in on Cocoa's room to make sure my babies were all right. I finally got to my room, which is in the middle of theirs. I pulled off my clothes and put my comfortable gown back on. I got on my knees and started right in:

Dear Lord Jesus,
Thank you for watching over me and my children. Lord, I'm not praying to you 'bout no dope. Nor am I thanking you for the drugs. Lord, I'm thanking you for protecting me and watching out for my children because I know that I'm new to this. So would you please keep on watching over us? [I looked up and continued on]. Thank you Jesus.

I got up and jumped in bed.

3

It was morning. I could tell because even though I was in a deep sleep, I could feel somebody shaking me, trying to wake me up. It was Harry.

"San, San, wake up. We are ready to leave for school and we need some money."

I woke up, rubbing my eyes, scratching my head, and yawning, "Look over there in the top dresser drawer and get ya'll a dollar apiece." Harry got the money out of the drawer and headed for the door with his books in his hand. I asked him, "Is your sister ready, yet?"

"Yeah. She's down in the kitchen eating some cereal."

"Okay, then, baby. Hey, how does she look?"

"She looks good. She got a dress on."

"Well, who combed her hair?" I jumped up as I was picturing what she looked like.

"Ms. Gwen braided it for her."

"Oh! That's a relief. Ya'll hurry up now so you won't be late for the bus. Look, Harry. Poo-Poo will be here when you all get back from school, okay?"

"Where will you be?

"Mama got to go and put some X-mas in layaway."

"Oh? So you gonna be able to get what we asked for?"

Proudly, I said, "Yeah, baby. Thank the Lord."

"Who gonna give you the money? Is it Pat?"

"Boy! Get on out the door and stop worrying me, okay? I'm sleepy."

"Okay ...see you later, San."

I smiled, "Okay, baby. Go get your sister before she eats too much."

Harry went down the stairs saying, "Let's go, Cocoa. The bus will be here in 5 minutes. Come on, girl."

"I'm coming, boy," Cocoa answered as she was coming out the kitchen. "San give us some money?"

"Yeah, now come on, girl, get your books, put your coat on. It's kinda cold." Harry was protective of Cocoa. Always looking out for his sister. Cocoa went along with Harry. She was crazy about her big brother. They both left out for school.

Even though I fell back to sleep I was shortly awakened by the telephone ring.

"Hello?"

"What you doing?"

"Who is this?" I asked kind of quickly.

"Poo-Poo."

"Oh, hey, bro. You on your way?"

"Yeah. I'm downtown now. I'll be there on the next bus."

"Okay."

"Hey, you get something to eat?"

"Yeah. If not you can go to the store to get you some."

"I'll be there."

"Okay, bye." I hung up the phone and went back to sleep 'til my brother got there.

There was a knock on the door. It was so loud that it woke Bippy up. Bippy got up to see who it was. When he opened I heard him say, "Damn, man! You knock so damn hard ..."

Poo-Poo was laughing. "Well, well, if it ain't the Bippy! What you doing sleeping over here?"

"Man, go 'head on ..."

"What's happening, Bippy?"

"Nothing, man. She got to be upstairs."

Bippy went back to the sofa to lay down as Poo-Poo came up the stairs. I turned over and said before I could see him yet, opening my eyes to recognize him at the same time, "Who is it? Oh, Poo-Poo." I smiled and sat straight up in bed. "Well bro. Let me talk to you. Let me tell ya' what I'm into. First let me brush my teeth and wash my face, okay?" I got up to go to the bathroom. As I got up, Poo-Poo looked down beside the bed. He saw some thousands of dollars. While

I had gone to the bathroom, Poo-Poo went back to the bedroom saying, "San, where you get all that? What is this? Just how much is this? Girl, Mama gon ask questions."

"Wait. I'll tell you. You're gonna like it ...just let me brush my teeth, man. Pick it up for me." (The money had fallen as I got out of bed).

While he was picking it up, he was shaking his head. Poo-Poo said, "San! Come here."

"Okay. Wait a minute," I said with the toothbrush still in my mouth. I came out of the bathroom with a towel over my face, drying off. I threw the towel on the bed, slipped by gown over my head, and began putting my clothes on. Bippy replied, "You still show your ass."

"Ah, bro. I got on my 'brother drawers' on. What? You're my brother so I want to look ..."

He cut me off, but before he could say anything, I said "Ah, just shut up!" Smiling, I asked him to pass me my shorts and sweater from off the chest of drawers. He threw them to me and I went on and got dressed. I sat on the bed and motioned him to sit with me.

"Gimme that money, Poo." He handed it to me.

"Now. Talk."

"Okay. Wait."

"Come on! Where you get it from? What you doing?"

I lifted up the mattress and got the pouch from underneath it. He looked shocked as I opened it and pulled more money out. then I pulled the cocaine out. His eyes stretched very wide.

"San! You done gone crazy. What you been doing, robbing or something?"

"Naw, man."

"Well—where did you get all that money from?" Not giving me a chance to explain, Poo-Poo kept with the questions. "San, that's a lots of money, girl. What are you doing? What's that stuff in the envelope?"

Knowing what he was referring to, I asked, "What envelope?"

"The clear one."

I laughed and said, "This is what I'm into, bro. Now I need you to be by my side. Stay here with me. I mean live with me for a while, okay? I need a man around the house because Bippy will be gone in a minute. You know he don't like being way out here. Plus, he can't drive too much 'cause he don't have no driver's license. He's usta being around people: his kind of people."

"Ah, that junkie motherfucker ain't going no where."

"Don't call him that."

"Why not? He's the one that got you in this shit. Let me go talk to him. I don't appreciate that nigga!"

"Hold it, Poo-Poo." I was pulling on him as he started out the room. "I found him 'cause an Italian gave it to me and I went and got Bip to help me sell it." I held on to his arm because he was furious. "Listen, Poo-Poo. Just listen for a damn minute. Close the door."

Poo looked at me, tapping his feet with his arms folded. "San, I don't like it. You can get killed or go to jail." I could see the worry in his eyes. "Girl, I love you. I don't want nothing to happen to you. You just don't hear of a woman doing this kind of shit. I'm talking about big shit. Tell me, something. Are you using it?"

"No, no. Look, Poo. We are going to make it big, bro. That's why I need my favorite brother 'cause I love and trust you the most."

"Hey! A motherfucker gonna take one if it comes to fuckin' with you. Damn that pissed me off."

"Please don't be, okay?" I kissed him on the jaw.

Poo smiled and said, "Let's get down, sis. God damn, I got to respect you 'cause you been a bad ...well! Do it! I got your back. We've got to get some guns, you know? You know me. If you gonna do it—you got to do it right!"

I jumped up and down, hugging and kissing him. He pulled my arms away and got my sho' nuff attention. "Now, we can't tell mama right now, okay?"

"Okay. I'll tell her that the children's father gave me some money. She knows he does illegal things."

"Yeah. That will hold her."

"Plus, I told her that I met a nice man. I thought this much money was a lot. I mean like ...almost rich! But anyway—let's eat and make some decisions."

My brother loved to clean house, plus he was a very good cook. That's the way our mother brought us up; doing these things for ourselves. After the food was cooked, all three of us sat at the table to eat.

Poo-Poo said, "Bippy?" Bippy looked up at Poo. "Man, go wash your face and brush you teeth. You need a bath, nigga."

Bippy said, "Fuck you, Poo-Poo. Let me go."

"Sho nuff, man. You need a one."

"Yea, yea, yea. Just let me eat first, will ya'?"

"But still, wash your fuckin' face and brush you teeth—first."

Bippy got up and headed to the bathroom. He wasn't at all embarrassed. He just said, "Gimme a toothbrush and a rag, nigga."

Poo-Poo pointed at the floor over by the door where there was a grip, "Look in that grip. There's a new toothbrush in it. It's blue. Now use it."

"Shit on you, jive-ass nigga." Bippy got the toothbrush and went upstairs. He got a face rag, brushed his teeth, washed his face, and came back downstairs to eat. We looked at him. As I was eating, Poo-Poo said, "Now don't you feel better?" Bip shot a "bird". "Now all you need to do is shave and bathe, you funk-ass nigga."

"Just eat, big ol' motherfucker."

After we ate, Bippy took a bath. I gave him a pair of warm-ups to put on. Poo-Poo said, "I'll wash your shit, man, and take it to the wash house to dry it."

"Yeah, thanks, Poo."

"Don't thank me. Thank the water, with you stankin' ass." Poo was laughing. He went on to the bathroom upstairs to wash Bippy's clothes. Bippy said, "San! You got a crazy-ass brother."

"Who you telling? He's been that way all his life."

"Listen, San, now. You can say that you are on your way."

"Oh! The thanks goes to you." I looked at Bippy. "Thank you, for helping me."

He blushed and said, "What I'm gonna do is get you a few more customers and book 'cause that's all you need."

"But Bip ..."

"Naw, Naw, nowl. Ain't no if, ands, or buts about it. I've gotta do my thang. And my thang ain't big time. Hey, baby! This shit fits you. You know what, San?"

"Uh-uh, what?"

"You are a bad, bad lady. You know it and I know it, too. Hey baby! You are faster than I expected. Girl, when you do roll—look out, nigga, cause San will be taking over."

I smiled. "Bippy! You really think I can do it?"

"Ah, girl, deep down you know it."

"Well Bip, I know I need to go to the store and buy a sifter, some seal bags, and a seal-a-meal, plus a triple beam. You know I ain't got no more eighths, just two ounces left."

"Damn, San." Bip looked at the stash. "Why don't you let me and Poo-Poo go to the store."

"Okay ...will you do that?"

"Let me get Poo-Poo."

"You can drop your clothes off at the wash house while ya'll go to the store. Look, Bippy, do I have to get seal bags? Isn't there something else I can put it in, 'cause I want mine to be different."

"Oh, hell yeah! You can get some sandwich bags and tie them up."

"Okay ...then get the sandwich bags for me here."

Bippy went to the steps to get Poo-Poo. "Big boy, come and go with me to the store for your sister."

Poo-Poo yelled back, "Okay. Wait a minute. Let me ring out your clothes."

"Bring them with you."

I gave Bippy $100 to get all the stuff I needed. As I was handing Bippy the money, he said, "Listen at me. Now, you don't pay nothing 'til I finish. Let's stop at the Third World to get some cut."

I took a deep breath, ready to open my mouth ...

"Don't say a word. Now listen—you got two ounces left, right?" I nodded my head, yes. "Okay, remember the eighth that's cut?"

"Yeah."

"Look, let's put a one on one of the ounce to see what it would be and if it straight as I think it is, you can put the other ounce in with the cut ones and you will have three ounces that will have the same strength."

"Well, do we have to try that much at once? Can't we try a quarter? Okay, Bippy. I know that I don't know much, but what

I'm saying is if you put a one on an ounce, we can check a one on a quarter ...can't we?"

"Damn, that the same thing! Why didn't I think of that ...'cause if it don't take it, we can put a half ...."

"Yeah. That's what I'm talking about."

"You are catching on very quickly."

"Well, look Bippy. Ya'll better hurry, 'cause you know I'm suppose to meet the big man today."

"Okay. Let's go, Poo-Poo."

Poo-Poo was coming down the steps with Bippy's clothes. I handed my brother $50 to have for his pocket. I said, "Here, Poo-Poo. This is for you."

"What's this for, San?"

"Just keep it and get you something. Bippy, I'll give you yours when you get back, 'cause you might stop."

"All right. Let's go."

I let them out of the door and said, "Hey, please bring me some Pepsi in the bottle."

When they got back, they had everything I needed. Bippy even brought some cards that spelled C-O-C-A-I-N-E. I said, "Get me a plate, Poo." He got a plate out of the cabinet. I reached for the plate and opened one ounce of cocaine to pour on the plate. I started to pour ...Bippy snatched the plate and said, "Hey! That plate's damp! You put it on there and you won't have any cocaine!"

I patted my chest saying, "Oh, my God."

Bippy dried the plate off and handed it back to me. I poured the cocaine on the plate. I did just like Will told me to. I sifted it and separated the rocks; then I sifted the cut. I looked in my pouch and got the spoon Will gave me.

Bippy said, "Ain't you gonna use the trip?"

"I don't know how, yet. Do you?"

"Naw."

"Well, let's go with what we know for now."

"Okay, Mama. You handling it."

I took two spoons of cocaine, two spoons of cut and sifted them up together. Bippy was watching me and I asked, "Bippy, you ready?"

"Hell yeah. I've been waiting."

Poo-Poo looked carefully and said, "Damn, San. You act like you been doing that." I just smiled and said to Bippy, "Where's your spoon?" "Right here, babe. Just put it in." I put about two in there. Bip went into the bathroom. I said to Poo-Poo, "Pass me that other block out of the bag, bro. That's all right ...I'll get it, 'cause I want to get some ice for my drink." I got up to get some ice and drink. I poured it into a glass and said, "Umm, this is good. You want some, big boy?" "Yeah. Gimme me little bit ...leave it in the bottle, San." I had the glass up to my mouth while looking at him. "Huh." "Hey, what's Bippy gon do?" "He uses the needle." Poo looked at me and asked, "He's a junkie?" "Yeah." "But suppose he dies?" "Ah, boy. He ain't gon die." "You ought not let nobody do that in here. Something might happen." I could see the fear in his face. He was frightened, but tried not to show it.

Bippy came back out the bathroom, sweating, peeping, walking, and talking. He went from window to wing. This time Poo-Poo followed him.

He looked back at Poo-Poo and said, "Damn, you following me, too." "What you looking for?" "None of your damn business. Now I got to put up with you. Can't you see I'm speeding and peeping?"

Poo-Poo laughed hard as hell. Bippy was still in the window. He put his ear to the front door. I laughed out 'cause Poo-Poo was laughing.

Bippy looked around the whole room saying, "This shit ain't funny. I hear somebody out there, don't you?" Poo-Poo said, "Yeah. I hear somebody ...it's a monster!" "Fuck you, Poo-Poo! San, listen." Bippy had his ears to the door telling Poo-Poo, "Be quiet, man. Don't you hear it?" "Ha-ha-ha-ha."

"Be cool, man. Shut the fuck up." Bippy was still looking at the windows, the ceilings, and all around. Then Bip asked me, "San, it's too strong ...can I shoot my boy?"

"Yeah, go ahead. You want some more girl?"

"Naw, not right now."

I went on back to work with the cocaine. I said while laughing with my hand over my mouth, "Now, I can put the rest of the cut in."

Poo-Poo was laughing so hard he had tears in his eyes. "So, now I need six more spoons of cut." I sifted six spoons and opened the other bag of cocaine and mixed them together.

The telephone rang. I answered to my mother on the other end: "Hello."

"What are you doing?"

"Oh, nothing—just finished eating."

"Who cooked?"

"Me and Poo-Poo."

"Tell Poo-Poo that Linda called and said she needs some money for the children's X-mas."

Linda was the mother of Poo-Poo's children. I figured this was a good time to tell Mama about my good fortune.

"Okay, Mama, I'll tell him. Look, Mama, Pat gave me some money." Pat was Cocoa and Harry's no-good daddy. "So I'll bring you some so you can get the children something for X-mas, okay?"

"Well, ain't you got to get Harry and Cocoa's stuff?"

"Yeah, but Pat went out of town and came back with lots of money."

"Oh, boy! Thank you, Jesus! God knows that I didn't know where or how we were going to make it. Baby, the Lord sure answers prayers."

"Believe me, Mama, I know. He answers mine, too. I have thanked him also."

"Okay, baby. Don't forget to tell Poo-Poo what I said."

"Okay, Mama. I'll talk to you later."

As soon as I hung up the phone, Poo-Poo lashed right in. "What Mama say?"

"Nothing, but Linda called and said she needs some money for the kids' X-mas."

"Damn. I ain't got no job and no money to buy them nothing."

"Don't worry, Poo-Poo. We will call her to see what they want, okay? I'm making money so I can use it wisely. Everybody in my family will have a good X-mas from now on."

The telephone rang, again. This time is was Fat Bob: "Hello, may I speak to San?"

"San's speaking."

"Hey, baby. This is you stepdaddy. I need to see you again. This time I want a half ounce."

"Listen, can you come this way?"

"Where are you, baby?"

"In Decatur."

"God damn. You know niggas don't fuck around too much in Decatur. Tell me how to get there."

"Okay, take I-20 East, get off at Candler Road, turn left, and take a right at the second red light. I'm in the second building on the right, #3."

"Gotcha."

When I hung up the phone, I said to Poo-Poo, "Guess what? That was Fat Bob. He wants some cocaine."

"Talking about our stepdaddy?"

"Um-huh. He mess around, too. But he sells it though."

Bippy walked in saying, "Now, I'm straight."

"Come on, Bippy, help me bag it up."

"How you want it?"

"Okay, let's bag the two ounces back up and break the other one down. But of the other one, I made one half ounce for Fat Bob and four eighths for whoever."

The phone rang, again. "Hello." It was Duey.

"San, what's happening?"

"Me, I hope."

"I need two eight balls, right now. How soon can you bring them?"

"Can you come my way?"

"Where you at?"

"On Candler Road."

"Good. I'm right on Flat Shoals ...tell me how to get to ya'."

I gave Duey the directions and right before I hung up he said, "I'm in a hurry, okay?"

"Okay. I'll see ya' when I see ya'."

When I hung up the phone, I just started bouncing in the chair. I said, to Bippy, "That was Duey, and Fat Boy called also. Duey wants a quarter and Fat Boy wants a half ounce."

Bippy just grinned, "Handle it, baby."

Duey came, then Bob came and left. That was very fast. The money was growing and growing. My nerves were getting stronger and stronger. I wanted to sell more and more so I got Bippy to call Jeff, but he looked like he was falling asleep.

Bippy said, "Take you time, baby. They will be coming so fast after a while that you will be tired of 'em and trying to find a place to hide."

"I'll be glad when it does. Make me tired. I want to get tired."

"We'll see ...Hey San? You might have to break that other ounce down by tonight."

"I hope not. Maybe Jeff will call. Maybe that man that was over there will come back."

"Ah, now you rushing things."

"Naw, I'm just teasing. But I do want to sell all this before I go back."

"Well, listen. Call Big H. Find out what time you need to meet the man over there."

I dialed the phone and asked the person on the other end, "Is Big H there?"

"Hold on."

I put my hand over the mouthpiece and told Bippy that they told me to hold on. Before Bippy could respond a man came to the phone he said, "Hey, now."

"Big H, this is San."

"What's going on?"

"Oh nothing. Look here. What time am I suppose to be there?"

"He'll be here 'bout 8:30 ...9:00. He just called. Well, how you doing on the other back?"

"I just got two left."

"What!! God damn, girl, you are rolling. I done sold a little bit, but not nothing close to what you have done. You are something else. Pretty soon you'll have a Cadillac."

"No, not for a while, 'cause I got to take care of my mama, sisters, and brothers."

"Well, okay, then. I'll see you later."

As I was hanging up the phone, I told Bippy that he'd be there 8:00, 9:00, and that was cool. I was figuring that maybe by then somebody will want some more.

Time was really flying. It was almost time for my kids to come home. What was I gonna cook?

Long by now, Poo-Poo was all in my head. He asked, "Hey, what you gonna cook ...those kids gon be here soon, won't they?"

"Some Italian spaghetti, salad, and garlic bread. Cocoa love that. Here, Bippy, here's $100. Go to the mall and buy you a shirt and a pair of pants."

"And don't forget some Jockey's, nigga," said Poo-Poo.

"Hey you better take your fat-ass with me, 'cause look like you need some tennis shoes, bastard!"

"Come on ya'll," I pleaded. "Cut it out."

"Ah, sis, we just kickin' the game," said Poo-Poo.

"I know, but sometimes kicking the game can lead up to something."

"Okay. We'll stop."

I handed Bippy the money and they went out the door talking to each other.

The phone rang and it was my uncle: "Hello, San?"

"Yeah."

"Julio is here now and we are headed you way so get you money together. We will be there in about 15 minutes."

"Okay."

"Bye."

"Bye." I hung up the phone, put the cocaine in my pouch, and the cut and the triplebeam in the cabinet. I ran upstairs to count the money. Let me see: I figured that I owed him $6000. I decided I'd use some of my money to pay it off. The knock was at the front door, so I ran to Harry's room to look out the window. Man, is them already! I turned around and swallowed hard, then I ran on down the stairs to open the door. "Hey! What's going on?" I asked while motioning them to come inside. Once inside, I closed the door and offered them a seat.

"We'll sit in the kitchen," Julio said. We all walked in the kitchen and sat down. I said, "Here's $6,000," I said, handing him the money.

He looked at me in an eye flinching way. He said, "Sam! You have really been working. I wanted to know where were you living. This is why I'm here. I brought you six more anyway; whether you moved the first or not ...but goddamn!" He and my uncle laughed.

The telephone rang. "Hello," I said.

"Hello, sis-in-law. What's going on?"

"Nothing much. What can I do for you?"

"I got some people in town and they want an ounce. They will be here in about 20 minutes."

"Okay, well as soon as they get there, call me."

As soon as I hung up the phone, Big H said, "Who was that?"

"Ah, that was just somebody that wants an ounce."

"Damn, Sam, we were here on time."

"Look, I thought you said that I was to get something else, Big H?"

Big H looked at Julio. Julio said, "I got it. I just wanted to see if you would ask for it." I smiled. Julio said, "Hey, listen, Sam. I want to have a long talk with you, but it can wait. I don't want to hold you up. Here. I brought you this," he said, handing me another oz for myself.

I smiled and said, "Thank you ...oh thank you so much."

He said, "Thank you. I have something else for you 'cause you will need them." He went into the little case and pulled out a gun. I paused for a minute, but I didn't get scared. I took a good swallow.

He said, "Here," handing it to me, "this is yours and here's another one for you."

"Wow," I said in amazement. One was a blue steel .38 and the other one was a .45 automatic.

"Now one day next week we will go to the shooting range."

I thought—shooting gallery ...

"I'm gonna teach you how to shoot both of them; especially the automatic. Well, Sam. We got to move on a little further. Hey. I'll be looking to hear from you, okay?"

My uncle didn't do much talking. He just sat there. They both got up and went back out of the front door.

The phone rang, again. It was my half-sister. She was a bull-digger (lesbian). She is about five feet one inches with a pop gut and wears men's clothes all the way to the underclothes. She had gold in her mouth and she was dark-complexioned. I had forgotten all about her. She had been to prison ...for drugs. She also was a junky and knew a lots of people. When I answered the phone, I heard her on the other end: "Hello! Big Sis."

"Damn, if it ain't Lil' Man," I thought. That's what we usta call her. "What you doing? Where you been?"

"Nothing but getting high ...you know me."

"Well, what made you call me?"

"Well, I was just thinking about you, me and my wife."

"Oh! Let me tell you this ...well guess what? You ain't gonna believe me. You gotta see for yourself."

"What? Tell me what's done happened?"

"Honey, I got some cocaine."

"What!! You a damn lie, girl ..." she said, laughing on the phone.

"I'll tell you what ...get a ride and come over."

"Shit! I ain't got no money, plus everybody over on this end is gone."

"Well, get a cab."

"For real, sis?"

"You heard me."

"Okay. I'm coming, but I know you are telling a lie. I know you've got some shit up you sleeves."

"Okay. Wait 'til you get here."

"Let me call a cab. I'll be there in a minute."

I got off the phone and took my cocaine upstairs and put it in the pouch. Then I said aloud: "Now! Let me count my money." When I figured profit, it was about $5,000. I couldn't believe it was that much. I said aloud, "Woo-wee, good God almighty. Let me call Mama and tell her I'm going to bring her some money to go to town!" I picked up the phone to call and my little sister answered. I said, "Hey! Where's Mama?"

"Who is 'dis?"

"Girl, put Mama on the phone."

"Wait a minute."

"Hello," said a "mama voice" on the other end.

"Hey, Ma, I'll be down there this tonight or in the morning. I got a thousand dollars for you—plus, I want to tell you about something. Okay?"

"A thousand dollars ...Lord, have mercy. What are you doing?"

"Look, Mama, I'm not stealing; I'm not robbing and you know I'm not picking nobody's pocket. Now, I'll see you later. Goodbye."

As soon as I hung the phone up it rang again. "Hello?"

"They're here, now," said a voice on the other end of the line.

"Who is this?"

"It's Will."

"Oooh, okay. Why don't you bring them over?"

"All right. We'll be there in a little bit."

"Okay. Hey, hey ...are you sure they want just one ounce?"

"Yeah, that's all they said."

"Okay, then. I'll see you when you get here." I hung up the phone. I started back talking aloud: "Damn. I've got to put me on some clothes." I looked in the closet then I looked in the chest of drawers and pulled my faded blue jeans out, laid them on the bed, and started to iron them. After I ironed them I looked in the dresser drawer and got a white sweatshirt and ran the iron over it a little bit. I got a bra and drawers out of the drawer. Just then I heard this "knock knock, knock." I looked up and went to the window to open it. I yelled out, "Hold on, Lil' Man; how much is the cab fare?"

She yelled back up to me, "Three-eighty."

"Okay, I'll be right down." I closed the window, opened the dresser drawer, and got a $5 bill. I ran downstairs to the patio door and gave Lil' Man the money. I then ran back upstairs to get the little cocaine that Bippy was using. I knew Lil' Man couldn't wait to 'see' what I had.

Lil' Man came back in from paying the cabbie and anxiously yelled, "Where's the cocaine, hoe?"

"I got it, motherfucka, I got it!" We always carried on like that—joking like.

"Look here," I said, waving the bag in front of 'him.' He looked down and pulled her pants leg up and go his 'tools':he had a shoestring and a drink top with the cotton already in there—plus, he had three works.

Lil' Man said, "Well, here honey, put some in there and let me check it out."

While putting the cocaine in the top, Lil' Man got a cup full of water and put the needle in the water to draw some of it up. I was curious: "Let me see ..." He looked in the top and said, "How much you put in there?"

"I don't know ...what you think?"

"Oh, it's about a 30 cent piece (meaning $30). Let me put 50 of water on it." He put ten more line of water in the syringe. He squirted the water on top of the cocaine. He turned his needle around and stirred it up. Then he put the work in his mouth to see how it tasted. He smacked his lips and said, "Damn! It tastes good as hell!"

Then he started to draw the cocaine up in the needle; his eyes were opening wide because the dope had made 20 more lines instead of 60. It was 80.

While thumping the needle, Lil' Man said, "Woo baby, this has got to be some badass cocaine."

"Why you say that?"

"Shit! Look at the goddamn work ...I put 60 of water and the motherfucka went up to the 80's." Anxiously he started turning his arm ...getting ready to really check it out. "See Sam, good 'caine makes water. Now, go on in the front room—leave me alone."

"I want to see."

"What? Ah, girl ...well it don't matter with me. Huh, I been shooting dope a long time."

He got a hit right as he ran half of it in. His lips turned white. He started tooting his nose. His lips were hanging open. He snatched the needle out of his arm and went to the bathroom and threw up. I ran behind him and asked, "What's wrong, Lil' Man? You all right?"

"Yeah," he answered and it sounded like he was gasping for air. He was spitting. "Woo wee!" I noticed his eyes were running water. "Sis, you got a asshole kicker, girl! This mother fucka' will knock you dick in the dirt."

"Well, ain't you gonna shoot rest?"

"Wait a minute. Let me handle dat. Just don't fuck with it, okay? Sit down somewhere."

"Well how you gone shoot it with the blood still in there?"

He walked fast in the kitchen and said, "Damn! I hope this shit didn't gel." He held the work up and shook it.

"Shake it," I said.

"Goddamn." He was standing with his hand on his hips.

I walked in the kitchen and said, "What?"

"Lookat... Damn...gotdamn... "

I watched him closely. He took the inside of the work out and tried to pour the blood and dope out but it was like jelly.

"Lil' Man!" I yelled.

"What!" he yelled with frustration.

"Well, hell ...I ain't done nothing to you. What 'cha mad at me for?"

"Oh, I ain't mad ...'cause I just know you got some more ..."

"But what if that was all?"

"Why I'd be trying to un-gel the mother fucka' and put some water in it!" We both laughed a while.

"Guess what, Lil' Man?" He looked up at me while he was trying to clean the work out. He said, "What it is?"

"Bippy and Poo-Poo is over here."

I smiled and Lil' Man smiled. He said, "What! Where they at?"

"They went to the mall to buy some clothes."

"Oh yeah. Where in the fuck Bippy get money from?"

"From me, of course," I said with my eyes bucked.

"Oh! So, Bippy been helping you?"

"Uh uh."

"Well listen at this. Why don't you bust some of those sacks down and let me take them to Hunter Street and Auburn Avenue and sell them for you?"

"What you mean, bust 'em down?"

"I'm talking 'bout make some quarters and fifties. Shit, I can knock out a thousand a day! I know."

"Well, Lil' Man, I don't know 'bout dat 'cause I've been doing it the other way and it's easy."

"Listen. It's a lot of work but you can make much more money, plus deal whatever you and Bippy is doing. Come on, Sis, please let me go to work. I won't fuck you up. You know if I sell for another nigga and he don't pay me shit—I can sell for my sister for nothing."

"But I wouldn't have you working for nothing. Just let me think about it. But you know what? I don't know how to bag 'em up."

"Well, didn't Bippy tell you how to bag with 'seal-a-meal'?"

"Yeah, but I told him I didn't want to use it 'cause I want my thing to be different."

"Well, hello Big Cocaine Lady," he said shrugging his shoulders up. "So what you gon put the stuff in?"

"Some baggies—sandwich bags."

"Well you can tear the corners off of them and make me some of them."

"We will see 'bout it. Oh, wait a minute—here comes my car. Bippy and Poo-Poo are back. Get the door, Lil' Man, while I clean up. I ain't gon let you throw my shit away." I laughed.

When I got done, I went to the door to see what they had got from the mall. Poo-Poo yelled, "San! Guess what? That crazy mother fucka speaking of Bippy went and bought seven packs of goddamn candy."

"CANDY! Bippy why you eat so much candy?"

Poo had noticed Lil' Man and before Bippy could say anything, Poo said, "Lil' Man, what storm brought you over?"

"What you thank ...the cocaine, man! Bippy, I know you dun tried some."

"Ah, man," said Bip, "ain't that some badass 'girl'? Woo wee! That mother fucka' had my bad ass."

"Man, you should have seen me. I snatched the mother fuckin' work out and throwed up."

Everybody started laughing.

Bip asked me, "Can I get a hit now? Shit, I need one."

I said, "Okay. Wait. Let me look at your clothes, first." I pulled some out the bag and said, "Oh! These are pretty. What kind of shirt you got? Let me see ..." I said as I was searching through the bag. "Woo, I like this. It's pretty, too."

"Yeah, I got some underwear. That Poo-Poo's a mother fucka, San! You know that same bitch did?"

"Naw ..."

"That motherfucka played with his dick and pointed it at all the white girls down there." Poo-Poo laughed and said, "Ah, hell! But look at what HE did ...he went over and talked to a white girl ...told her that I wanted her." I laughed.

Lil' Man said, "Man, ya'll niggas know better! Dekalb don't play that shit. Niggas fuckin' with their white women. You are insane. Ya'll better cut that shit out. All the bitch had to do is call the cops ...San would have been getting ya'll out of Dekalb."

"Ah, fuck that," Bippy said. "San, put it in here," he said, referring to the cocaine I pulled out.

Lil' Man reached in his sock and pulled his tools out and said, "Wait, man. Use this top."

So Bippy put the spoon back.

Poo-Poo said, "Ya'll shoot too much dope. Why you have to keep going back and forth? Damn! Look like you veins would get tired. Here my arm," Poo-Poo stretched out his arm toward Bippy, "hit me. Gimme some, Bippy."

"Man, fuck you. Leave me alone. Go drink that cough syrup you stole out the groceries store."

"We drank it on the goddamn way back, Uncle Tom mother fucka... "

"Naw," I said. "Poo-Poo, you still like that cough syrup?"

"Yeah."

"But you had enough money to buy it but you stole some?"

Bippy said, "The bastard just like to steal!"

Poo-Poo said, "Ah, go to hell, sissy!" All this was going on while Bippy and Lil' Man fixed their cocaine up. They compared their works to make sure that they were getting the same amount.

Poo-Poo said, "Look at how Lil' Man think you got more than he got." Still playing around, Poo-Poo kept talking, "Gimme that shit, nigga."

Bippy said, "Man you can have my woman, but don't fuck wit the dope. Now quit playing."

Poo-Poo said, "Oh, sissy-ass nigga ..."

"Damn!

"Okay, man ...go 'head. Do your stuff ..." Poo-Poo just laughed out loud and kept talking: " ...big stupid-ass bastard."

Bippy: "Fuck you, Poo-Poo. Damn, San. You got a crazy son of a bitch for a brother. Where in the fuck your mama get him from?"

Poo-Poo started to walk out of the kitchen into the living room. He looked back and said to Bippy,

"Looka here ..." Poo-Poo made a real ugly face at Bippy and went on up the stairs.

Bippy said to me, "You brother is insane. That cough syrup got the best of his big funky ass. Come on, Lil' Man, go on and hit yourself so I can use your tie."

"Wait a minute, funky junky!"

"Bitch, you are fucking your goddam self ..."

"Who you calling a bitch ..."

I jumped in, "Come on, ya'll!! Be cool. Go on and shoot that shit."

Bippy calmed down, "Come on Lil' Man. Stop fuckin' around."

Lil' Man did his. Bippy was peeping out windows ...going from one side to the other. Bippy whispered to Lil' Man, "Lil' Man ...Come here, man. What do you hear?"

"Oh, you see somethng out dare? Move over. Let me see." Lil' Man stepped on Bippy's toe trying to peep out the window.

Bippy yelled, "Get off my goddamn foot, man!"

"Sh-h-h-h-h. Be quiet. You talk too much."

Bippy and Lil' Man were peeping and walking. Lil' Man got hot and pulled his shirt off. He had on a T-shirt and an ace bandage to hold his breast down.

Bippy saw it and said, "Man, what in the fuck you got that shit on for? You ain't no real man, man!"

"Nigga, kiss my ass and 'real man that.' Don't fuck with me, Bippy. Keep on ...I'm gon' call Poo-Poo."

"Okay, okay ...don't call that dumb son-of-a-bitch."

"Well, you better let me go."

Realizing how much was left, Lil' Man asked Bippy, "Hey man, did you snort all yours?"

"Hell yeah. I can deal with it now."

"Well, honey, I can't. Gimme my strings back so I can shoot my other lil' bit."

The telephone rang. It was Will. He was up to the all-night store and had forgot how to get over here. Will: "Hello, San. I'm at the store on the corner. Which way from here?"

Me: "Come into the apt complex. I'm in the second building on the right: #3. You will see the car in front of the door."

Will: "Okay, then. Be looking out for me, here?"

Me: "Okay, boy. Bye."

When I got off the phone I said to Bippy and Lil' Man, "That was Will. Come on ya'll, let's clean up before he get here. Naw, I tell you what. Just take it upstairs. I can handle this down here." I gave Bippy the rest of the stuff in the little bag so that he and Lil' Man could stay upstairs. I was looking out for him through the window.

"Here he comes ...ya'll gone?"

They went on upstairs with cups and all their 'stuff'.

I opened the door while saying, "Hey!" with a big smile. "You got here at last, huh?"

"Yeah. I forgot where you live."

"This is ...well, come on in first. Have a seat. Everybody sit down at the table. Ya'll want something to drink? I don't have anything but some Coke ...naw ...make that Pepsi."

"Well, that's fine," Will said.

While I was getting the Pepsi, Will introduced me to Brass as being out of Detroit. Brass was half-black, half-Mexican. He was another six-ft fine curly headed nigga with a thick black mustache. His eyes were real dark. He was very hairy, thin build, but fine. He had on all black and looked good in it. As I was serving up the drinks, Will said, "Well, let him check out the stuff."

I noticed Will had on some khakis and a pleaded shirt. As for me, I still had on my same shorts. I went upstairs to get the ounce that he wanted. I brought it back down and passed it to Will. Will passed it to him. Will said, "Gimme a plate, San."

I went to the cabinet and got a plate for him. Brass opened it up and poured it out in the plate. He said, "Sandy!"

I looked up and said, "Huh?"

"Do you have a sifter?"

"Oh yeah. Let me look in the drawer."

I got the sifter and gave it to him. When he sifted it, the smell was very strong.

He said, "Sandy! Do you have a triple beam?"

"Oh yeah, just a minute. Let me get it."

Boy, I was glad he asked for it so I could see how to work it. I got the box out of the bottom of the cabinet and gave it to him—unopened. Smiling he said, "This is a new one. I know that it works right." Then he took all the rubber out. I stood right besides him and watched him close. I saw him put everything on zeros. Then he put the cocaine on there and it weighted 29 grams. He said, "Oh! You give an extra gram on the ounce, huh?"

With confidence, I said, "Yeah, sometimes." I was so happy to know what an ounce really weighs. I made a note to myself: Now all I had to do was figure out the eighths, quarters, and a half ounce. He put the cocaine back into the bag without even checking it. I guess the man knew 'good blow' by him coming all the way from Detroit.

"Well, baby. What do I owe you? $1500?" He was reached into his pocket and pulled out a diamond money clip and counted out fifteen $100 bills. He said, "Look here, Sandy! What would five ounces cost?" I looked at him in shock. I didn't know what to say. I was trying to think and talk at the same time. I had my elbow resting on the table with my hand on my chin. Then I said, "I will have to call and see."

"Will I get a discount?"

"I'm pretty sure you will if you buy five. How long are you gonna be here?"

"Just for a couple of days. But if the price is right, I can get the money here real quick."

"Well, look. I'll find out for you and let you know tomorrow. Okay?"

"Sure. So, what should I do? Come back here tomorrow?"

Will spoke up and said, "What you do is—call me and I'll get in touch with San."

"Yeah. That's cool."

Brass looked at me and said, "Will you give me a cloth so that I can clean the scale off?"

"Oh, that's all right. I'll take care of all that."

"You see, baby, where I come from, you don't leave shit like this laying around. You got to get up, clean up as you go."

I looked at him and said, "Thanks. I needed to be told that," I said smiling.

"I can tell that you are new to 'the game.'"

"Oh?"

"Not new ...but fairly new."

"I've been in for a minute." He didn't know that I meant a real-live minute.

"Well, sis-in-law," said Will, "we gone be taking off now. How 'bout letting us out? We've got to be moving on."

"Okay, then. I check you out tomorrow."

"Okay." The three of us got up from the kitchen table. Brass extended his arm out, took my hand, and shook it. We both said, "It was nice meeting you."

I let them out of the door. I went to the stairs and called Bippy and Lil' Man. By the time I got there, Bippy was already peeping at me. He scared the shit out of me! I looked up and said, "Damn, Bippy! You scared the shit out of me. That shit still got you peeping."

I had a little tape player/record player/radio in one. I turned on the music and started to dance...the Dance of Joy! I felt real good; better than I ever felt in my life.

Bippy saw me dancing. He was enjoying it. He called out to Lil' Man and Poo-Poo, "Hey ya'll, come here. Hurry up! Come see San." Bippy was saying it all to the rhythm of the music. "Get it. Get it. Work. Work. Look at the Go-Go." I stopped and all of us starting laughing. I forgot how tired I was. I said, "Let me clean that scale and stuff up. Look, Bippy, when I get finished, I'm going to take a bath then we gonna go down on the Avenue okay?"

"Sure baby." Lil' Man asked, "You gon do 'that' for me? So, what you gonna do, Sis?"

"Okay. I'll fix 'em. But I want to take a bath first. All right?"

"How many are you gonna fix me?"

"Don't worry about dat. Just wait and see. Hey, but you gon cut the bags up."

I cleaned up and took my bath and was ready to go.

"Come on, Lil' Man. Let me fix this up for you."

Bippy said, "What you gonna do?"

"Why you say it like that?"

"Oh, I just see all them corners. It look like you gonna make some quarter and fifties."

"I am ...for Lil' Man."

"Hey, baby, that's a good idea."

I put a little in the bags and showed it to Bip and Lil' Man. They looked at it and said that it was fat, but I should let it stay. I told them I would, but outsell all the pushers on the strolls.

"Well Lil' Man, how much money you want for your efforts?"

"How much you want to give me?"

"On no ...what do you think?"

"Let me see ...start me with about 25–quarts and 10–fifties. How that sound to you?"

"It's okay to me."

We fixed all the quarters up first. He showed me how to fold the tie. It was two laps over and tie ...two laps and tie. Struggling, I said, "Damn, Lil' Man, like dis?"

"Once you learn, you'll become fast. It just seems hard now 'cause you 'new to the game,' but in a little while, baby, you'll be the baddest bitch in town."

"I hope so. 'Cause I'm ready!"

Then we started on the fifties. We finally finished all the bags. Lil 'Man got all the bags up, threw them in the trash can I took I out to the dumpster. After Lil 'Man came back in the house, I said, "Are you ready to ride?"

Both of them said at the same time, "Yeah, let's ride then."

Bippy hold up and ran in the bathroom to slip his pants and shirt on. When he came out, he had on his brown pants and beige sweater shirt.

Poo-Poo said, "Ah, shit now! Look at the only whore in the brown. Bippy's pants fit his ass real good."

"Ah, you just mad 'cause my body is shaped better than yours."

"So what, motherfucka, your dick won't get hard?"

"Lay your fat ass down and see, sissy."

"All right, let go," I said.

We went out the door. Poo-Poo hollered out, "Will you be back, baby?" talking to Bippy.

"Go 'head, now. Let it go, chump."

We got in the car and Poo-Poo was still at the door. I got out of the car and told Poo-Poo, "If anybody calls, take a name and number. Oh, ah—look in my dresser drawer and get some money to get Harry and Cocoa some Red Lobster or something, okay?"

"I gotcha."

Bippy, Lil' Man, and I rode on off headed for the 'stroll.' I asked Lil' Man, "Where do you want to go first?"

"Hey, you can drop me off on Hunter Street and check back in about two hours. Yeah, that will give us time to check down on the Avenue to see who's down there."

We drove to the west side and let Lil' Man out up there by Pascals Brothers. He got out of the car and said, "Let me have about $5 to put in my pocket in case I have to make some change." I reached in my little pouch and pulled out a $10.

I gave it to him saying, "Listen. I don't want no shit out of my sister 'cause I ain't 'bout to be fucked nor am I gonna let nobody play on me. Okay, sis ...I mean, bro," I said smiling.

"Ah, girl, you know me better than that."

"I'm just letting you." We pulled off. Bippy said, "Hey, you don't think Lil' Man gon fuck you up, do you?"

"On no, but if he do, I'll turn that ace bandage into a hangman's noose," I said laughing.

We made a turn on the stroll (Auburn Ave). Bippy got out down by the rib shack at the corner of Foote and Auburn Avenue. He told me to go around and come back to pick him up.

As I was going around, I thought about the guns that Julio had given me. I saw a phone booth and got out to call home. Poo-Poo answered: "Hello."

"Hello, Poo."

"Yeah."

"Look in the kitchen and get those guns and put them up away from the children."

"You're late, baby. I already took care of that."

"OK, bro. I'll talk to ya' later."

4

I jumped back into the car and went down Auburn Avenue. I was at the light of Auburn Avenue and Piedmont when I saw a friend of mine named Shell. I pulled over to the side and got out to talk to her. She used to be a Textet dancer—with Joe Tex. She was about five feet and weighed about 110 pounds, was dark complexioned with short hair. She was real cute. I said, "Hey, Shell. What you doing down here? You ain't dancing no more?"

"Naw, baby. I had to quit. Mama needed me at home. You know she's been sick."

"Oh. I didn't know that. Well, what you doing now?"

"Oh, I've got a pretty good job at the factory sewing."

"That's good."

"Well, San, what you doing for yourself?"

"I just got fired from my job. So I ain't doing nothing now."

"Are you still playing ball?"

"Yeah, but I can't play basketball until next year."

"Why?"

"Because I tore my Achilles tendon. But I'll be able to play softball."

"I know that's right."

"Take my phone number down and call me, 'cause I know that you still have your entrance card."

"Yeah. I'm gonna keep that."

She wrote my number down. I got into my car and took off. I went down to pick Bippy back up. Bippy saw me coming down Auburn Avenue. He walked out in front of the car and jumped in saying, "Hey Babe. Let's go. Jeff wants to see you, so step on it."

We went straight over to Jeff's house, got out, and went in. I was feeling kind of at home when the guy opened the door this time. Bo said, "Jeff! San's here!"

Jeff answered back, "Well, send her back."

I could hear him real good. I walked into the kitchen. There he was with some Kelly Green on and didn't he look good! He had a bunch of hot clothes laying in a chair. Jeff said, "Sit down, baby. Hey, listen. Do you have an ounce on you?"

"Yeah. I got one."

"Well, here's your money—already counted."

I counted it over. He jumped up and got his working stuff then said, "What size clothes do you wear?"

"Eleven. Why you ask?"

"I just wanted to know."

"Well, if you want me, I'll be at home."

"All right, baby."

I started back out the door then I heard him say, "San!"

I walked back to the kitchen. When I got to the door, he threw me a beautiful royal blue leather coat. I asked, "What is this for?"

"Just try it on."

My eyes bucked. The jacket was a perfect fit and I liked it very much. He said that it matched my car. I blushed, "Oh, thank you. Thank you very much."

"Now go on 'head home. I'll call if I need you."

"Hey, do I owe you anything for the jacket?"

"Girl, get out of here."

"Thanks again."

I walked out of the kitchen into the living room and out of the door. Bippy said, "What ...where you get that coat?"

"He gave it to me."

"Ah hell, don't let that nigga play on you—'cause baby, wit what you got, you can get any motherfucka you want. You know that, don't you?"

"Uh-uh."

"Well you can. If a motherfucka know you got the sack, hey baby, they gon' try to play. So don't fall for that, San! You're already a pretty girl, fine ...plus you got nerve. Just wait and watch. All the niggers you deal with will try to catch; even your step daddy might try."

I looked at him with my nose tooted up and said, "For real?"

"Yeah. But I know my baby sis gon' handle it. Right?"

"Yep. Damn, Bippy! We got to go check on Lil' Man. It's been too long. Let me call home."

We went to the corner and called. Poo-Poo answered and I asked, "Hey, Poo. Did Lil' Man call?"

"Yeah. He's here now and got a pocketful of money."

"Okay, bye."

I jumped in the car and went down the expressway flying. When we got in the house, Lil' Man met us at the door saying, "Look, San! Don't get me started and not finish."

"I'm sorry. I really forgot."

"You got to take care of business better than that," Poo said. "And what's that fucka been doing (referring to Bippy)?"

Bippy said, "None of you damn business."

I said, "Come on, ya'll. Help me fix some more up."

Bippy said, "San, why don't you fix me some, too and let me go to Auburn?" Lil' Man said, "Hey, that a good idea. Sh-h-h-it, we can kill two birds with one drop off and anyway, San, it's time for you to stay out of the way. You don't need no trouble, okay? Now, here's $970."

I took some short and said, "Woo-wee! Come on, ya'll. Help me fix it. Lil' Man, what do I owe you?"

"Don't worry 'bout it, now. Pay me when I get off. But you can give me a little bit though."

"Okay. Damn, Bippy. We gon' need some more cut."

"Give me the keys. I can catch them before the store close."

"No, wait. I still got enough for one ounce. Plus I got about four more eighths left, I think."

"Okay. That what you got will hold up. Now give me a little bit, too."

"Bippy, you should got you some boy while we were out."

"You know I got some boy. This here's the Bippy."

Lil' Man said, "Let me speed ball with you."

"I bought enough for you nigga, but you gone give me half of the money I paid for it."

"Okay, man." I said, "Let's get through. Poo-Poo, don't let the children come down." Poo-Poo was in the living room watching my little portable TV and said, "I gotcha."

This time I had to fix up 50 quarters and 20 fifties. I was hoping that Bippy wouldn't fuck me 'cause I would have to get my brother to find him. I had a little trust when I should have had more because he's the one who helped me. Besides, if he did fuck me, I'd fire him. Let me stop thinking like that. He ain't going to do nothing like that. But the thought of him being a junky. Fuck it. You win some, you lose some.

Bippy yelled, "San, San! Where's your mind?"

"Oh, I was just thinking."

"Oh, baby, I ain't gon fuck you up."

"How'd you know that I was thinking that?"

" 'Cause I can tell. I understand, but I'm the one who's gon help you, watch out for them other niggers, baby. I love ya'!"

I smiled and said, "I love you, too, Bippy. If it wasn't for you, I wouldn't even be this far."

"Ah, just give us our stuff." I poured the stuff in a little bag and gave it to Lil' Man this time.

I said, "Okay, ya'll do that while I do this. I think I can handle it. I'm gonna make them fat anyway."

I sifted the four eighths that I had up. I cut bags, bags, and more bags. I fixed all the quarters first; laid them out until I finished putting cocaine in the last quarter, and then I started to fold. I folded so many that my speed beg on to pick up. I was rolling! I got two whole bags and put 25 in one; 25 in the other. Then I started on the fifties. I did them the same way: ten in one and ten in the other. I got the rest of the cut and weighed it up. It weighed exactly 16 grams so I took an unopened ounce and sifted it up. I took the rocks and laid them aside. I took the shake and mixed it with the cut. The shake weighed about 12 grams. I sifted it together. Then I added them up and it came to 28 grams .... Now I was lost ...I needed Bippy.

"Bippy, come here! Come here quick!"

"Damn, what you want? I was just about to get my hit."

"Look! I got 28 grams of shake and wait ...let me weigh the rock up."

I put the rocks on the scale and they weighed 17 grams. I asked him, "Now, how am I gon do this?"

"Let me see." Bippy studied the shit. You would have thought he was some kind of scientist. Then he continued, "Okay, put ten grams of rocks in and 18 grams of shake. That will make an ounce." He started back in the bathroom.

I said, "Wait, man. What about the rest?"

"What you should NOT have done was to sift up those rocks in the other eighths, but it's too late, now. Just make up you two eighths and save the rest of the shake for us to work with on the stroll. Yeah! That'll work."

"Okay. Gone and do your stuff. Oh, here. Try this." I put some cocaine in a bag and gave it to Bippy. "Give Lil'

Man some, okay?" "Thanks." I fixed the two eighths and put one gram of rocks in each eighth. I used the spoon for them. I put the rest of the shake in a bag. I got a pencil and marked on the rest of the shake so that I wouldn't forget it. Damn, I'm still way ahead.

I got up and cleaned up everything: put all the stuff up and was ready to take them to work. My job was getting to be exciting to me. I enjoyed every bit of it. It made me laugh, smile, and think positive about everything. We can eat. My mother can eat. We have it going on. I then went to the corner of the wall over by the cabinets, folded my hands to pray:

Lord Jesus,

Thank you. Thank you for being so wonderful to me. Thank you for helping me feed my children, my mother, and my sisters and brothers. Lord, thanks for not letting nobody steal from me and not let nobody hurt me because I know that I am a sinner and is doing wrong. But I don't have any choice right now. Please Lord, just keep watching out for me and my children. Thank you, Jesus, not for the dope but for your protection. Amen.

I looked up and smiled.

Oh, P.S., Please don't let the police get me.

I went into the living room to talk to Poo-Poo. I said, "Tomorrow we gon call Linda to see what the children want for X-mas." "Okay, but you ain't got to rush." "Naw, I just want to do that."

"All right then." "Oh! I forgot! I got to go down to mama's house. Let me call her. Naw, I ain't got to call. I did say I'd see her tonight or tomorrow. Hey! Ya'll 'bout ready." Bippy and Lil' Man were still in the bathroom.

"Yeah. We cleaning our mess up now. We'll be through in a few minutes."

Lil' Man came out first. I asked, "How was it?"

"It's the same to one. What you do?"

"Oh, nothing. I just had to fix some more up." When I saw Bippy come out, I said, "Oooh, let's ride, Bippy."

Lil' Man said, "Here I come."

We left again. This time I left my pouch at home. We were going out to work. I turned around while saying, "Damn! I forgot the stuff."

I tossed Lil' Man the keys to the car. I said, "Ya'll gon get in. I'll be right back."

I went in and gave Poo-Poo my pouch and told him to put it up.

"Here, Poo, put this up."

I got about $50 out of it then I went back out the door—flying. I jumped in the car and drove off.

"I got to stop and get some gas."

I pulled in a service station, got a Pepsi-Cola and some gas. Lil' Man got him a strawberry soda and Bip got him some candy. We went on down on Auburn Avenue first. Bippy got out way up Auburn Avenue by the fire department.

"Hey! Let's go to Summer Hill."

"You mean ...tell me, San, you ain't been over there yet?"

I just shook my head.

"Shit, Sis. You roots are over there. Girl, lots of niggers sell dope over in that area."

"Oh, don't forget Mexican Villa."

When we got over there I saw the Biggest Mouth in town and he knew a whole lots of people. We stopped on Georgia Ave. and I got out at the liquor store. Then I heard the Big Mouth.

"San, baby! You ain't playing basketball?"

"Naw, I'm waiting on softball season."

The Big Mouth belonged to Johnny, but everybody called him Meathead. He stood about five feet 11 inches and weighed about 165 pounds. His complexion was light brown.

"Well look, here. I heard that you lost your job." He talked a lot and heard just as much.

"Oh yeah? Man, news sho do fly, huh?"

"Well, what you gonna do, now?" I looked at him and said, "That's what I want to talk to you about. I got some cocaine."

"What!"

"Wait now, let me tell you 'bout it."

"Okay, go head."

"I have a lots of it and I need somebody to help me move it. Can you help?"

"Hell yeah. Fix me some bags."

"Look Meat, as many people as you know—black and white—I know you can do more than some fuckin' bags."

"Well, that's true. I tell you what, why don't you fix me some quarters and let me sell 'em. You know I ain't gon fuck up, 'cause I don't do nothing but snort. You ain't got no cocaine, now?"

"Ask Lil' Man. He's in the car."

He looked in the car and saw Lil' Man and he started laughing as he started talking, "Huh, huh, huh, huh, Lil 'Man, is San ..."

"Don't ask me motherfucka," Lil' Man cut him off. "Look here." Lil 'Man held the bag up so that he could see it.

Meathead looked at me with mouth wide open then I said, "Shit, me and my family can eat now."

"San, what your phone number?"

"555–4121."

"Oh, you still in Decatur?"

"Yeah. You know I like Dekalb County."

"When can you fix me some cocaine up?"

"It gotta be tomorrow now."

"Okay then. Gimme a sample."

"Wait 'til tomorrow, man."

"Well, what time?"

" 'Bout 11:30 or 12:00."

"That's good."

"I'll see you then. Look! If somebody wants some weight, let me know, hear?"

He nodded his head and said, "Gotcha. Later, babe."

I jumped in the car smiling from ear to ear. I went on over to the West Side after that. When we hit Hunter Street, niggas were waiting on Lil' Man. He said, "Let me out." He was opening the door while the car was still rolling.

I yelled, "Wait! Goddamn. You'll get there."

"San, they waiting on me."

"Well you still gotta let me stop the damn car." When the car came to a stop, Lil' Man got out and I said, "Look here, I'll check back in about two hours."

He said, "If you don't, I'll be back out to the house."

"Okay." Then Lil' Man hit the car and I drove on off.

I went straight back to the house. I opened the door and asked Poo-Poo, "Did anybody call me?"

"Naw."

He was laying on the sofa half asleep. He jumped up and said, "Oh yeah ...a girl."

"A girl?" I was looking surprised. "What was her name?"

"Let me see. Damn!"

"What did she say her name was, Poo? What Poo?"

"Wait, Sis. Let me thank."

"Damn, wonder who in the hell that was?"

"Oh, okay, it was Tonya. Yeah, Tonya."

"Tonya? Who in the hell is Tonya?"

"And uh, she sounded mad."

"Well did she say that she was gon call back?" Just then, the phone rang. Before he could get to it, I picked it up and said, "Hello."

"Is San there?"

"Yeah. This is San."

"Well, look. You don't know me but I got some stuff from ..."

"Wait a minute. Tell me this—how did you get my phone number?"

"I got the number from Jeff."

"JEFF! What in the fuck ..." I was patting my chest. "Okay, go 'head."

"Like I said, Jeff gave me some bad stuff and told me he got it from someone named San. You see, San, I don't want no trouble but I spend lots of money with Jeff. He buys a lots of pieces from me, but he did me wrong!"

"Well, what do you want me to do about it?"

"Look! I'm not asking you to give me nothing. I got some clothes that you might like."

"Where are you, Tonya?"

"I'm on Columbia Drive."

"Well, did he tell you where I live?"

"Naw, he didn't. I got some news for that motherfucka. Son of a bitch, I don't like that goddamn shit, a bastard-low-lifemother fucka... "

"Okay, okay ...let me call that bitch, here? Call me back."

"For real, San?"

"Yeah! I'm a woman of my word."

"Okay. What time do you want me to call you back?"

"In about three minutes. It won't take long to read that motherfucka."

"Okay, bye."

"Bye."

I held the phone in my hand. I hesitated a minute then I slammed it down. "Damn! I ain't even got the motherfucka's goddamn number. Ain't dis a bitch." I was nervous. I had to tell myself to "just wait."

Poo-Poo was looking at me and then asked, "What's wrong, Sis? What is it?"

"Nothing much, bro. I'll handle it."

"What? Somebody's talking 'bout fuckin' with you?"

"Naw. Nothing like 'dat. Woo-woo—that long punk-motherfucka ...I got something for his stankin' ass ...ah, bitch ..."

The phone rang, again. "Hello, Tonya?"

"Uh-huh. How do I get there?"

"First of all, are you by yourself?"

"No, my man is with me."

"No, no, no. You can come by yourself."

"All right, then."

"Go I-20 West. Get off at Candler, turn right. The first light, turn right. I'm in the second building on the right. I'm the first fenced in apartment. It's #23. You will see a blue and white T-Bird in front of the apartment."

"Okay. I'll be there in five minutes."

I hung up the phone. " ...ah long, tall son-of-a-bitch ...a no-good-dope-selling-motherfucka ..." Poo-Poo laughed and said, "San! You sell dope, too."

"Yeah! I know that."

I bust out laughing my damn self.

Knock. Knock. Knock.

"There she is." Poo-Poo got up.

"That's all right, Big Boy. Let me get this."

I opened the door. She was a tiny girl, about size five. She stood five feet tall with pretty black skin. She wore a wig, but it looked real nice around her face. She had on a burgundy leather suit with burgundy boots. She wore earrings, watch, and gold around her neck. I noticed she had a clothes bag folded over her arm. She spoke, "Is San home?"

"Yeah, come on in. I'm San. Look, girl. I ain't mad at you. I'm mad with that punk-motherfucka. He wasn't supposed to give nobody my motherfuckin' number. Excuse the expression, but I don't like that shit."

"I understand, but San, I'm tired of giving all my goods to a nigga and the shit he gives is bad. You're by yourselves, ain't you?"

"Yeah."

"I left him up on Columbia Drive, okay?"

"Let me see what you have."

She had some bad shit: double-breasted three pieces, blouses, and jackets. But the price tags ...wow! $100, $250, $300 tags. I thought to myself: Damn, how did this little girl steal all this shit.

"Well, Tonya, what do you want?"

"I just want to swop. I always get a third for my pieces."

"Well, how much is all of this?"

She went in her purse and got a pencil and figured it up. I checked out her figures and it came out to be $900. She looked at me and said, "It's $900."

"Well, what you want?"

"How much is your eighths?"

"They are $200."

Her eyes bucked and she said,

"$200? Is that all?"

"Yeah. What's wrong?"

"Jeff charges us $250."

"Well, you know he's got to put something on it. Wait a minute, let me get it."

I got it from Poo-Poo and came back in the kitchen. "So I owe you a eighth, plus $100." I handed her the eighth and the money and said, "Here you go."

She smiled and said, "Can I get my 'bag' back? I need it when I go to work."

"Oh, okay. Go ahead and get it."

"Well, San!! It was nice meeting you, but not on these circumstances. Can I call you instead of Jeff?"

"Oh, sure. I need to get some things anyway."

"What do you need?"

"I need some of everything. Do you get stuff for men, too?"

"Yeah."

"Well how about little boys?"

"What sizes?"

"About 12's." Tonya wrote that down then asked,

"Well, what size do you need in women's clothes?"

"I need from 7'sto11's. I need them some things for X-mas. Oh! My mama wears a 15/16. Get her a lot of stuff 'cause I want to make her happy. I want the best for her: shoes, if you can."

"Naw, baby. I don't get shoes. But if I run across somebody who got some, I'll let you know. Okay?"

"Look Tonya, if I'm not here, tell my brother, Poo-Poo. Oh, I'm sorry. I didn't introduce you all. I had that mother fuckin' nigga on my mind." Then I yelled for Poo-Poo, "Poo-Poo!"

"Yeah," he answered back as he sat up.

"This is Tonya, this is Poo-Poo."

Each of them said, "Please to meet you."

Then Tonya left. Poo-Poo said, "Damn, that's a pretty girl. Woo wee."

I went in the kitchen, grabbed the clothes to try them on. Poo-Poo said, "Take you ass upstairs. I'm tired of looking at your naked ass."

"Ah, shut up. All right, I'm going up." I tried on the white, first ...then yellow ...then green ...I tried on everything. It looked good on me, too! I thought to myself while looking in the mirror: "Now you need to shoes and hats to match ...how 'bout that?" I put my faded jeans back on and went back downstairs. I didn't even bother to hang 'em up.

"Damn, Poo-Poo," I said, "I forgot to tell her your size. Just what size do you wear?"

"Size 40."

I looked wide-eyed and said, "You wear a 40? Damn, boy, you better lose some weight!"

"What you talkin''bout? You're the one who's gained weight."

"Well, softball will knock it off me. Well, let me go and check on Lil' Man and Bippy ...naw, naw, I better fix some more quarters and fifties up before I leave. What you think? Come on, brother, you better come help me. This time I can tear them. You get the plate and sifter for me. I'll be tearing the bags."

Before I finished fixing the cocaine, the phone rang. It was Bippy telling me that he was out of quarters and had only four fifties left. I told him that I was fixing them now and that I would be about 20 minutes and I'd be there.

Soon after I hung up the phone, I heard knocks on the door. I looked at Poo-Poo and he looked at me, shrugging our shoulders. We were both wondering, who could that be? "I'll be damned ...." I told Poo-Poo to check through the peephole. Before he could even get to the door, we could hear voice from the other side, "Open the door. It's Lil' Man."

Poo-Poo said, "Ah, it's that little mother fucka." I laughed and said, "Who?"

"Lil' Man."

Poo-Poo opened the door and in came Lil' Man. What an entrance he made: twisting and carrying on ...flashing money while saying, "See, baby! Get me ready. I can't wait on you. I got to take care of my job. San, baby! I know you just leaving, but baby you got to step up a little bit 'cause you ain't fast enough for me. Have Bip called yet?"

"Yeah, he just called. He only got four fifties let. I got to get back down there."

"You see what I'm talking about? We got to work something out by tomorrow. You need to sit down and fix up a whole ounces and make quarters and fifties out of it."

"You right. I got to get some cut in the morning then we will take care of that."

"Well, honey, fix me up."

"How much is that?" Lil' Man was handing me the money.

"$900. You know I got to let some credit go. When a nigga buy three or four bags and come back for credit, you got to give it to him."

"I ain't said nothing."

"Well gimme my shit and let me ride."

"How you get here?"

"Oh, I got friends."

"Don't you think you've done enough?"

"Honey, let me work. This is my job. I ain't just started selling. I been selling dope."

"Okay, okay ...You see I'm over here taking care of my business. I'm almost finished. All I got to do is tie the quarters and fix up the fifties."

"Well, tie my 25 up and start on my fifties. While you do dat, let Lil' Man get a hit." He went in his socks and got his tools. I gave him his stuff and he went in the bathroom.

I was glad the kids were asleep. By the time Lil' Man got through looking ugly, I was just about finished. Then the phone rang again. I told Poo-Poo to answer it and that if was Bippy, tell him that I pulled off about three or four minutes ago. I'll be damn ...Poo-Poo answered and sure enough, it was him!

I told Lil' Man to get his shit and let's go. As we were hitting the door, the phone rang again. Poo-Poo told me that it was Duey while he covered the mouthpiece of the phone. I took the phone to talk to him, "Hello, what's going on?"

"I need to see you."

"Look, where you at?"

"Right here off Glenwood exit."

"Well, just wait there. I be there in about a minute. What you need?"

"Bring me two balls, okay, San? Hey San, it ain't gon take you long, is it?"

"Naw. See you in about two minutes 'cause I'mon myway out of the door headed that way, anyway."

I gave Lil' Man his and we were out of the door together. It didn't take long to get to Glenwood; Duey was there at the service station by the payphone booth. I pulled up beside his car. He gave me the money and I gave him two eighths and said, "See you later." He said, "It's the same thing, isn't it?"

I was backing up and nodding my head yeah. He said, "Later, baby."

I wasted no time, I headed straight for Auburn Avenue. I got off at Edgewood and Bip was standing there. I saw him and stopped and he got in. I asked him, "How'd you know that I was coming this way?"

"I didn't. Say, you got me ready?"

"Yeah. Here you go."

"Drive on down to Piedmont so I can get out. Oh, and here is all the money but for two fifties, okay?"

"Lay it on the seat."

"I can get out right here."

I stopped and he got out. Then I said, "Hey, guess what Jeff did?" Bippy looked back in the car and I continued, "That fucker gave my number to a girl named Tonya."

"Oh, Tonya? Man, that's a bad bitch. That hoe can sho' nuff steal. She's bad."

"I'm gon let you go for now, but I'll tell you 'bout it when you get home, okay?"

"Okay. See ya' later, baby."

I went back home and as soon as I got in the door, Poo-Poo said, "San, Jeff just called."

"He did. What did that son-of-a-bitch say?"

"He gon call you back."

"I'll damn sho'll be glad when he do 'cause I got something for that ugly fucka ...that black bastard ...woo ...just wait."

"I told him that you will be right back."

"Well I'm god damn sho'll gon wait on his stankin' ass ...young punk." I went to use the bathroom and while I was still there, the phone rang. I ran out of the bathroom to get it. I didn't even wash my hands—thinking this could be that ..."Hello," I said real mad like.

"Hey pretty ..."

"Pretty! Pretty, my ass. Nigga, why in the fuck you give that bitch my fuckin' phone number? You know that shit ain't right! I thought that you was better than dat."

"Naw, see ..."

"Naw, my ass."

"What I'm saying is, baby, please, don't do me like that."

"You know that I didn't know that girl."

"But she's cool."

"How was I suppose to know? You didn't even have the decency to call and let me know that you did it."

"Okay. I'm sorry. Will you accept my apology?"

"Yeah, but you know that was wrong. Please don't do that no more."

"All right, baby ...well, look here. I need two ounces."

"Okay. I'll be here."

I slammed the phone down while saying—"Ya stupid son of a bitch." That shit pissed me off. Back to the matter at hand ...I just realized and still talking out loud, Damn, I ain't even got no cut, dog! I ought not sell him nothing. Ol' punk motherfucker! He really has made my ass want to do the "Apple Jacks." Poo-Poo just fell out laughing.

I said, "Dat ain't funny, nigga, shit! Hell, I'm gon' take a bath 'cause I'm tired." Poo-Poo said, "When?"

"Damn! I got to pick up Lil' Man and Bippy. Dog, Poo Poo, you need to learn how to drive, man. You know what? These mothafucka's gon' make or break me!"

"One thang about it, Sis." He raised up. "They ain't gonna hurt you."

"I know that's right."

So I ran upstairs to take a bath. I was so tired 'til I went to sleep in the bathtub. It wasn't until I heard knocking that I woke up ...Poo-Poo was on the other side of the door, "San!"

"Huh, who is that?"

"Poo-Poo. Hey, Jeff is downstairs."

"Okay. Damn, I fell asleep in the fuckin' tub. Tell him I'll be out in a minute."

I dried off, went into my room, grabbed some shorts & shirt and ran downstairs. I kinda rolled my eyes at him with a smile and said, "I've forgotten about that, okay?" But please don't do that anymore."

"Okay. I promise. Here. Count your money. I'm kinda in a hurry."

"Gimme that, Poo-Poo." I went into the living room and got my pouch. I walked back into the kitchen and said, "Here you go."

"Thanks, babe. Well, let me run. I got to take care of some people. Hey, ah, when's Aunt Hazel coming home?"

"Sometime next month. I don't know exactly what day," I said.

"Ah yeah?"

"Uh-uh."

Jeff headed for the door and told Poo-Poo, "Let me out, Poo-Poo." Poo-Poo got up and let him out.

When Jeff left out, I looked over at Poo-Poo and said, "Look, Bro. I'm gon' go to bed 'cause I'm tired."

"Well what you gon' do 'bout Lil 'Man and Bippy?"

"Shit, they'll call or come."

"S-hi-t, you better put on something and go get your money!"

"Shit, I don't feel like drivin'."

"Hey, Sis. You got to make your own bed."

I stomped the floor saying, "Shit, I'm tired. I don't wanna sell no quarters and fifties. Shit! That's too much work ...people get on my nerve ..."

"Well, Sis, you got to get tough, kid. From what I've seen, you gon have to ride with the 'rosco' wit as much money you be handling."

"Well, let me ride one more time. I know one thing, if they ain't through, they gon' half to wait til' tomorrow 'cause I ain't going back down there. And I'm going just like this ...I ain't puttin' on no clothes. I'm gonna slip on some shoes and coat and I'm goin' on down there." I did just that.

I got Lil' Man first then we headed for Auburn Avenue. Lil' Man asked, "Damn, Sis, why you pick me so quick?"

"Shit, I'm tired and you need a break anyway. I'm gon pull over and you gon drive 'cause I'm beat."

We pulled over by one of them colleges. I laid my head back on the headrest and said, "How many did you do?"

"I did 'bout three quarters and five fifties. It done got a little slow, but I coulda did more if you hadn't pick me up."

"Yeah, I know." I dozed off to sleep. The next thing I knew ...Lil' Man was shaking me saying, "Wake up, San. I don't see Bippy." I jumped up and said, "Damn! 'Wonder where he's at?"

"S-h-i-t! Bippy may have don fucked up."

"You think so?"

"I don't know ...but might be. I could have told you dat that's why people won't give him no more work ...he fucks up a lot. I'm gonna go up by the shooting gallery to see if anybody seen him."

Lil' Man got out by the rig shack and went upstairs. When he came back he said that girl Betty said that Bippy was gone ...he had got a cab. I said, "Well, wonder where he lives?"

"Shit, who you asking?"

"I don't know. Well, let's go. I ain't gonna miss 'that' anyway?"

"Oh, you gon' just let him go like that? You're crazy!"

"Naw, no I'm not. Bippy's the one who introduced me to a lot more than that. Anyway, he might not be don' messed up."

"I hope not. But keep in mind ...just 'cause you're a female that don't mean that niggas can fuck over you."

"I know that, Lil' Man. Let's just wait and see."

"Okay, Ms. Patient." I could tell Lil' Man was mad. He scratched off and I said, "Damn, nigga. Don't fuck up my car tires."

"Hell, you're my sista and I ain't gon let no nigga fuck over you!"

"Forget it, Lil' Man." We headed home. I broke the silence and said, "Listen, I'll see you when we get to the house, okay? And if you want, I'll drive home 'cause I'm really tired and ain't no cab this time of night ...not out there. Okay?"

When we got home, Bippy was already there. I started in on him trying to figure him out, "Man, you had us going all the way down there and here your ass is here?"

"It got hot down there."

"Well, that's good. Hey, let me pay ya'll 'cause I'm tired and I want to go to bed. Here Lil' Man ...here's $200 and Bippy's here's $200 and a gram of the 'pure,' okay? What I'm gonna do is buy ya'll a car so I won't have to run like this."

Lil' Man said, "Yeah, I know what you mean."

"San, you've been good to us already—ah, that's all right," said Bippy, "What I'm gon do from now on is give you half of what you sell, okay?"

"Naw, San!" said Lil' Man. "They don't pay us like that."

"Well I'm not 'they,' and that's that. Now here, let me give ya'll the cocaine so I can go get some sleep." I gave them the dope and went upstairs.

Poo-Poo said, "I'm going up too, 'cause I don't want to be here with ya'll speeding ass."

"Oh, give me the rest of the sacks, ya'll," I said and they handed them to me and I went upstairs and went to bed. I was fast asleep and it seems just as soon as I fell asleep, here comes Lil' Man yelling, "San! San!" He was shaking me real hard.

I answered, "Uh, what?" I must have been talking in my sleep.

"San, wake up! Bippy need some 'boy.'"

I opened my eyes and said, "Uh?"

"Wake up, Sis! Bippy need some 'boy.'"

I jumped up and turned the light on saying, "What's wrong?"

Lil' Man seemed panicked while saying, "Come and see! He need some 'boy'! Hurry up! Lord, have mercy. What done happened? Come on, please hurry up!"

"I'm coming. Gimme my shirt on the dresser!" I had shorts on. I slipped it on over my head and ran downstairs. Bippy was breathing fast and hard. He could barely speak, "Gimme some boy. Please hurry up, San. I need it."

"Well, where I'm gonna get some 'boy' from?"

"On no. Please get me some."

I was scared and walking in circles. I asked, "Lil' Man, where can I find some at this time of morning?"

"I don't know, but let's ride."

I told Bippy to come on with us but he said, "Naw, I gotta stay here, 'cause I'm scared."

"Come on, Lil' Man, somebody on this side of town got to have some." Lord Jesus, please don't let nothing happen ...on no, what would I do? Please keep him, Lord, please. I started to cry 'cause I was very scared. I started back talking to Lil' Man, "Come on, Lil' Man, Let's go. What you waiting for?" We got in the car and went over two or three houses and couldn't find nothing. "Lil' Man, what we gon' do? Let's go to the grocery store and get some cough syrup and let him drink the whole bottle. That will bring him down."

"Okay. We can stop at KK's."

We stopped at KK's on Candler Road. Lil' Man got out and went in. He brought back two bottles of NyQuil. We headed back home. When we got there Bippy was in the window just shaking. I said, "Bippy, we couldn't find no boy so you are going to have to drink this cough syrup."

He snatched the bottle out of Lil' Man's hand and swallowed it down in seconds. Then he gulped down the second bottle.

"Lil' Man, that ain't going to hurt him, is it?"

"Nah, it will just level him off."

"Boy, he done scared the hell out of me. Well, what happened? How he get like this?"

"He tried to shoot a whole fifty and damn near went out."

"Dog. Mama always told me: God takes care of old fools," I said. I looked up to the ceiling and said, "Thank you, Jesus. Lil' Man!"

He looked at me and answered, "Oh, I think he's going to be all right ...yeah, that greedy fucker gonna be all right."

"You really think so?" I asked, because he really didn't look he was going to be all right.

"Yeah," Lil' Man spoke with authority, "If he was gonna die, he'd be dead now."

"Really?"

"Look, San, when cocaine take you out, you're sho' nuff out. See, it will burst your heart."

"Boy, you can bring 'em on back ...look a there ..." I said, amazed as Bippy opened his eyes. I said to him, "Go on back to bed."

"Lil' Man, what did you do with my work?"

"Look at him," I said. "What do you want it for?"

With dragging speech, he answered, "I'm ready to do my other stuff and god damn. That shit done al ..."

"...almost killed your ass and you want some more?"

"I thought you gave me that, Bippy," said Lil' Man. "Man, you got to be crazy. Ain't no way in the fuck um gon' give you my shit."

I shook my head and said, "I don't believe this. Yeah, he's all right. I can tell now. That fucker is asking for some more ...Ya'll crazy."

"And I'm go be crazier than that if Lil' Man don't gimme my shit."

I shook my head. I guess I just didn't understand. Then I said, "Give it to him; go on and give it to him, Lil' Man. I'm going to bed and I'll see ya'll in the morning."

Bippy looked pleased to hear that then he said, "Go on and get some sleep, here? 'Cause we will. Good night."

"Yeah, good night." I went on upstairs.

5

It was morning; the sun was shining through the window even though it was kinda cold outside. The phone rang and I answered in a sleepy voice, "Hello?"

"I have a collect call to anyone from Aunt Hazel."

"What? Okay, okay, put her on ...hey Aunt Hazel. How you doing?"

"Fine, now that I made parole."

"What!" I was smiling and blushing my eyes. "When you coming home?"

"Well, I come home for Thanksgiving—leave—and I go back that Saturday—and back home that following Monday. So what I want you to do is pick me up."

"Okay. I will. Look here. What time can you leave?"

"We can leave at 6:00 A.M. in the morning, so please be on time."

"You know what I told you about that 'thang'?"

"Uh-huh, yeah."

"Well, I'm rolling with the punches. How 'bout that?"

"Well, did Bippy help you?"

"Yeah, and Lil' Man, too."

"What? So you straight then? Goddamn, then handle it, baby. Take care of your business."

"You wanna talk to them now?"

"Naw. I'm gonna let you go."

"Okay."

"So, I'll be looking for you Thursday morning."

"Right, right."

"Bye, baby."

"Bye, Aunt Hazel."

I hung the phone up and ran in Harry's room and woke Poo-Poo up. Man, was he excited as I told him the news, "Poo-Poo, Aunt Hazel will be home for Thanksgiving. Then she will be out for good on Monday."

"What? I know she glad 'cause she been down for six years."

I ran out the room downstairs and woke up Bippy and Lil' Man. "Wake up, ya'll, wake up!" I pulled the covers off Bippy and Lil' Man. Lil' Man had made a pallet on the floor. "Git ya'll asses up!" Bippy was pulling the cover back on him and over his head but saying, "Okay ...okay ..."

Lil' Man looked at me with this real ugly look on his face. I didn't mind them ...I kept saying, "Hey, ya'll! Aunt Hazel will be home Thanksgiving and she will be out Monday after Thanksgiving." Then the cover came off Bippy's face. He jumped up, got a cigarette, lit it and said, "Well, well, well. The Queen Bee will be back on the street. Did you know how strong Aunt Hazel was with that 'sack?'"

"Naw."

"I didn't find out until she was a junky ...I mean a stone junky ...shit, Aunt Hazel was the best dope seller on Auburn Avenue. Everybody knew Aunt Hazel. She had the 'boy' and the 'girl.' And believe me, San, she sold more dope than five or six motherfuckers put together."

"What kind of bags did she use?"

"The boy was in the little bags you buy from the record shop and the cocaine was in the seal-a-meal bags. And I'm telling you, she didn't get busted until she started shooting that shit. Hell, she'd been selling dope for about four or five years before she started shooting it. The nigga she was wit turned her out. But baby, Ms. Hazel was a mean number. Niggas from all over town came to her ...even to her house."

"Damn!" I said. I didn't know that she was that bad.

Lil' Man jumped in, "You remember when we were in the state pen together?"

I said, "Yeah."

"Shit, Aunt Hazel was getting dope in there. We stayed fucked up. Honey, we had a good time 'til they built that new prison."

"How was the new one?"

"How in the hell I know? I left the motherfucker before they finished it."

"Well, time to go to work, ya'll. What time is it?" I asked.

"Oh yeah. We got to get some more cut."

"Yep," Lil' Man said.

I told them I'd cook some breakfast if Bippy go to the store. Then Bippy finally answered my earlier question, "It's 10:30."

"Damn, it's 10:30 already?"

"Yeah. So gon 'head and give me the money so I can take care of the business."

"Look-a-here. Let Poo-Poo kick it wit ya''cause I want to send some money to my mama .... naw, that's all right. I'll do it myself." I ran upstairs to get some money so Bippy could go to the store. Handing him $50, I said, "Here Bippy. This is for the cut."

"Listen, San! If your people got this kind of 'girl' why don't you ask him for some cut?"

"You think he may have it?"

"Hell yeah. If he got that much blow, he's bound to have some cut."

"I'll ask him the next time I meet with him."

Bippy went to the store while Lil' Man cooked and soon after we ate. I cut the cocaine: I made some ounces, half ounces, quarter ounces, eighths, small quarts and fifties. I was at it!

After a while, Lil' Man asked, "What time is it now?"

Bippy looked at this watch and said, "Goddamn, San!"

I said, "What?"

"We were suppose to meet Meathead over in the Summer Hill."

"Damn! Sho'll was. Come on! He might still be over there."

"Well, let us get a little hit before we go, okay?"

"Ya'll gon and hit and I'll go to Summer Hill, okay?" I gave them a fifty a piece. I headed for the door and realized I didn't have my keys. "Look in there on the table and see if you see my keys." We all looked on the table and on the counter. They weren't there so I went upstairs. They were still looking for them downstairs. I yelled, "I got 'em."

I left the house going to Summer Hill. I was hoping Meathead was still there. Bullseye! There he was on the corner.

He saw the car and flagged me down. He got in and said, "I thought you wasn't gonna make it."

"We almost forgot. Here. Here's 25 quarters and ten fifties and $10 to make change and get you something to eat."

"Okay, then. Look here, where can I get in touch with you when this runs out?"

"Just call home. If I'm not there, my brother will be there."

He got out of the car and I drove on back to the house.

When I got home there was a yellow '98 in my parking space. I muttered, "Damn! I wonder whose car is that?" I got out and went in the house. It was Tonya. I greeted her, "Hey girl, what you got?" She pulled out clothes. As she pulled I started figuring who was gonna get what ...that would fit mama ...and that would fit my sisters. She had $175 worth. I let her get the eight and I owed her $25. As she was going out the door she looked back and said, "San, I wish you would meet my man."

"Naw, Tonya. I don't want to see nobody else right now."

"Okay then. I'll be seeing you."

Bippy and Lil' Man was in the upstairs bathroom. (I asked Poo-Poo where they were.) I went to the bottom of the steps and called them. "Lil' Man, Bippy, com on ya'll."

The telephone rang. They answered back that they were coming. I looked over at Poo-Poo to see who the phone was for. He was handing it to me. I asked, "Who is it?"

"I don't know."

"Well, ask who's calling."

He asked and said, "It's Will."

"Will!" I yelled all gay and shiny eyed. I wanted to talk to him.

"Yeah!"

I grabbed the phone and said, "What's up, brother-in-law?"

"Looka here. I talked to Brass and he will be over here in an hour. He wants three ounces of the same stuff."

"Okay. Just come on when he get there. I got to run off for a minute, but I will be right back."

"Okay. I'll talk to you then."

I hung up the phone and I was jumping up and down. I went to the stairs to call Lil' Man and Bippy, again. "Hey! Is ya'll through yet? Come on now."

"Okay. We coming. Hold up."

Poo-Poo heard me say, 'What kind of shit is this?" "You got to sit them down and tell them what you expect them to do," Poo-Poo said.

"Well ain't no sense rushing. I got about an hour before the people will get here. Damn, let me call Big H to see if he got me ready 'cause I'm gon need to see him before the night is over." I dialed the phone. "Hello, is Big H there?"

"No. He's not here right now, but he will be back."

"Okay. Tell him to call San. It's very important."

When I got off the phone Lil' Man and Bippy were coming down. I said, "Come on ya'll. I know it don' take that long." We went on out the door and got in the car. I took off for Auburn Avenue. While riding, I asked them, "Listen. Why do it take ya'll so long to shoot cocaine now?"

"Honey our veins had frozen up."

"Man, you're a lie. If your veins freeze up you'd be dead. I might not know much 'bout cocaine, but I do know about the freezing of the veins." We all laughed.

We were on Edgewood. We saw ambulances, police cars, and the fire dept. Bippy was in the back. He sat straight up and said, "Wonder what's done happened?"

"I don't know, but I want to see."

When we turned on Bell Street I hadn't given Bippy his stuff yet. He told me to let him out so that he could see what had happened. I parked in the parking lot, got out and walked down by the cafe´. I saw Fat Man and asked him what was going on.

He said, "Lots-of-mama had O.D.-ed."

"Well what did she O.D. off of?"

"Some 'boy.' They got a motherfucker running around here with some dope that turns green when you cook it up and it ain't nothing but kidney pills and too much rat poison."

I looked at him and said, "You mean that they put rat poison in 'boy'?"

"Hell yeah. Especially if a bitch or motherfucker don snitched on someone; and that whore was good for turning a motherfucker up. I'm glad the bitch is dead."

"Woo wee, Fat Man, you shouldn't even thank like that."

"Why not? If a nigga is that low down, he or she need killing. Well, look here, the talk is out that Aunt Hazel's niece has a sack now."

I fucked up and said, "Where did you get that info?"

"Never mind where you got it. So, what the deal is?"

"I don't know what you talking about."

"Ah, come on, San. I buy cocaine myself. Shit, I much rather buy it from you than somebody else."

The streets were very, very crowded. Police were all over the place. I asked him, "Well, what you looking for?"

"I'm just a little bitty nigga and I want nothing but a half of an eighth."

"A half of an eighth? Naw, naw. I don't have it that small."

"Shit. You got Bippy working quarters and fifties. I know you can come up with a half of an eighth."

"Well the best I can do is an eighth ...and it cost $200."

"Two hundred dollars! Ah hell, I can get that. So ah, when can I get it?"

"Let me see. I got to go to Hunter Street after I leave here, then I'm going out to the trenches."

"Where is the house?"

"I'm in Decatur."

"Oh! You still live in the same place in the townhouses?"

"Yeah. I ain't going nowhere no time soon."

"Well how 'bout one and a half hours?"

"Okay. That will give me enough time to take care of what I gotta do."

"But listen to this. Is the thang straight?"

I looked up at him and said, "It must be. You've heard about Bippy's blow; and Bippy's blow is my blow, right?"

"Ah, go 'head on with that fast talk."

"That ain't fast talk; that's fact. Let me go. Here comes Bippy. I'll see you when you get out there."

"Look. Give me your phone number."

He handed me his pen and a card. I wrote the number down for him and gave it back. He said, "All right, baby. I'll check you out later."

Bippy walked up to me and said, "What that fat-ass motherfucker want?"

"Some cocaine."

"Well. Well. Well. Come on, San, give me my shit and let me O.D. a motherfucker."

"Ah, nigga. You wouldn't do that."

"Let's go back to the car." We walked back to the car and I gave Bippy his pack and money then we left.

Lil 'Man said, "What was all the policemen doing down here?"

"Somebody O.D.-ed down here named Lil' Mama ...Lots-of-mama ...something."

"Oh no!" he said. "Well that's one more snitch gone."

"Oh, you knew her, too?"

"Shit ...who didn't know that old fat nasty bitch? That motherfucker will tell on her own mammy. See, you really need to stay from down here 'cause it's some low down dog ass niggas out here, San! They will fuck you up, baby. I mean, fuck you up, bad!"

"I'm gonna stop coming just as soon as I get my shit together. All right?"

"I'll see. You better listen to somebody who knows what the deal is, 'cause that jail thang ain't no fun. When you get behind bars every motherfucker in the world forget about you. Your own family will turn their back on you."

"But if anything should happen to me, I don't think my family would turn their backs on me 'cause I'm gonna try to give them the thing that we have never had. Hey let's get off that jail thang. Let's talk about the money we gonna get. Here you go ...where you gonna get out at?"

"You can let me out right here. I'll call you when I'm just about done."

"Okay."

"Just have mine ready. I'll come and get it."

"Okay, baby."

"I'll check you out later."

I went on back to the house to wait on Will and his friend. I called Big H back to see if he had gotten back yet. He hadn't. "Damn, Big Boy. Wonder what time he gonna get back? I sure need to see him."

Poo-Poo answered me, "Take your time, Sis. He'll be there. You know what?"

"What?"

"You beginning to talk like you know what you are doing, huh?"

"Yeah. Wouldn't you if you had this kind of money?"

"I guess so."

"Shit, nigga. You know damn well you would enjoy ever bit of all that money."

"But money ain't everything."

"Oh, baby, but you can't live without it. Can you?"

"Yeah, I can."

"Bullshit! Tell me how?"

"Keep on living with you and mama."

"Ah, boy. I ain't talking like that. You know what I mean."

"I was just kidding. Look, there's a car pulling up."

"What color is it?"

I stood up to look myself and saw that it was Will. I said to Poo-Poo, "Get the pouch for me."

I opened the door and Will said, "What's happening?"

"Nothing much. Ya'll come on in. I got you ready."

That nigga Brass was sharp as hell. He had on a pinstriped blue and gray double-breasted suit with a turtleneck sweater. The sweater was gray. Brass said, "I got to catch a plane so would you kind of hurry up?"

"Oh, okay."

Poo-Poo walked in and handed me the pouch. I went to the counter, got the three ounces out, turned right around and gave it to Brass.

He just smelled the bags and said, "Here, baby! How much do I owe you?"

"I'll let you have them for $1400 a piece."

"Okay. Cool."

He counted out $4,200 and said to Will, "Let's ride, man."

They got up to go out the door. I called Will, "Here, Will. Thank you for being nice about bringing me customers." I gave him an eighth.

He kissed me on the jaw and said, "Thank you, San. Thanks a lot."

"Oh, you are very welcome."

As they were going out of the door, once again, Brass said, "Listen. I'll be in touch with you, okay?"

"Maybe the next time you're here, we can go out and have a drink."

"Okay."

"I'll be here." I closed the door and locked it. Then I went to the phone to try Big H on the phone again. He still wasn't there. I told Poo-Poo, "I know what I can do."

"What?"

"I can go down to my mother's house."

I took out about $700, put it in a bag and headed for my mother's house. When I got there, Mama was upstairs asleep. I went up, kissed her on the jaw and she woke up. She started to get up and I said, "Naw, Mama. You can lay on down."

I sat on the bed beside her. I went into the bag and came out with the money. I said, "Mama, here's $1,000. Take this $5,000 and put it up for me."

"Baby, oh baby. What have you been doing? Lord have mercy ..."

"First let me finish. Take the other thousand and go X-mas shopping." She started crying. I kept talking, "Ah, ma. Don't cry. You deserve the best. I mean the very best of everything. I just hope one day you will be in your own home."

"But where did it come from, Sandra?"

"Well, it goes like this: Big H introduced me to ...well ...some dope."

My mother sat straight up in the bed and before she could say anything I kept on talking, "Wait, Ma. Let me finish. I'm not using it for myself."

"But, baby, you know how that stuff is. You might go to jail or somebody might kill you for that stuff. You know what happened to my sister Hazel."

"But Mama, it ain't gonna be like that. She was dealing little bitty pieces. Plus she was using it. Mama, just say that you'll be my side."

"Baby, I'm your mother. I'll always be by your side."

"Okay, Ma. Just trust me, okay?"

"Okay."

"I love you. Lady, can't you see that I'm gonna give you what all black people want? And that's money with love. I love you. Now stop crying. I'm gonna be all right. Don't worry. Poo-Poo is with me."

"That's why you wanted him over there?"

"Yeah."

"Then you lied about the rich man, huh?"

"Yeah. I'm sorry. Will you please forgive me?"

She gave me a big hug and said, "You know that I'll forgive you."

"Now Mama, I'm gonna work and save some money, get me a business and let it go."

"For real?"

I nodded my head yes as I said to her, "Well listen, girl. I got to go now and I'll bring you some more next week, okay?"

"Just be careful, baby. I'll pray for you."

"Thank you, mama. I love you. See you later."

I went downstairs happy 'cause my mother was on my side. When I got outside I looked up to the sky, threw my hands up and said, Thank you, Jesus. Thank you for Mama. I went to the record shop and bought a tape by Lenny Williams and played it. I went on to Summer Hill to collect from Meathead. Time was flying by. I went over to my uncle Big H's house to re-up.

Every day, all day they were coming through picking up cocaine. It was getting close to Thanksgiving. It was about the 25th day of November and I was to pick my aunt up. On that same night, Tonya came by. I heard the knock, knock, knock. I opened the door and greeting her, "Hey girl."

"Happy Thanksgiving, San. I got something I want to show you, but it's not mine alone. Part of it belongs to my ol' man and he's mad at me. But he wants to meet you 'cause he seems to think that I'm beating him."

"Well, okay. Bring him in. I'm in a good mood." She went to the door to get him. I was sitting down in the living room with a yellow light on. Tonya came right back and he was right behind her. From the moment I saw him, I could not take my eyes off this man. He was so fine; I mean FINE! He stood six feet 3 inches and weighed about 170 pounds. I sized him up ...he wore about 40 long suit. He had a gold on the right front tooth.

His complexion was medium brown. He had on a rust-colored Dashiki V-neck type suit made from ultra suede. His hair was styled slick down ...going to the back. He spoke first, "How are you doing? I'm pleased to meet you. I've been wanting to meet with you for some time, now."

"What's your name?"

"Ray."

"Why don't you have a seat?"

They followed me into the kitchen and sat down. I mean, this nigga was finer than all the niggers I had met ...all put together. Ray began to speak again, "This is what I wanted to show you, San." He pulled out a mink coat. I looked at it but I made sure he could not tell that I was impressed; not with the coat nor him.

Nonchalantly, I said, "What size is it?"

"Oh, it's your size."

"How would you know?"

"My lady told me what size you wear."

I figured that much from when I gave her all the sizes I was interested in but I wanted to hear him explain. I played it off with a smile and said, "Oh, that's right. Well, to tell you the truth, I really don't want a mink coat. Do ya'll have anything else?"

"Naw. We ran out of time."

Then Tonya spoke up, "Well, San, will you just hold it for us until we turn some of the cocaine?"

"No. I don't want to hold anything of that value, but I'll let you get an eighth on credit."

"Oh, would you?"

"Yeah. Hold on for a minute. I'll be right back."

I went upstairs to get it for them. "Here you go."

"Well, I can't promise we'll bring the money back tomorrow, but I will have it to you the weekend."

"Okay. That's fine."

"Thank you, so much."

"It's okay. I understand." I was speaking to Tonya but I found myself looking at Ray. He watched me as much as I watched him.

Tonya looked at him and said, "Are you ready to go?"

"Yeah, baby."

They put the coat back into the bag and left.

Bippy and Lil' Man were at work. I was getting tired of being in the house all the time, so I decided to go to a basketball game. Just as I was about to make my move, the phone rang. I answered, "Hello?"

"Hey there, pretty lady."

"Well, hello. What's going on?"

"You are on my mind right now."

"Oh yeah?"

"Can I come over?"

"Sure. What you want?"

"I'm not buying this time. I want to visit with you."

"Really, Jeff?"

"Why not? I don't have anything to do tonight. How about you?"

"Well, I wanted to go to see the Hawks play."

"Can I go with you?"

"Yeah. I'm not dressing up though."

"Oh, baby. Anything that you wear will be all right with me."

"What's wrong with you?"

"Does anything have to be wrong with me to want to be with you?"

"No, I guess not."

"Well, tell me baby, what are you wearing?"

"A warm-up suit and tennis shoes."

"Wear your hair down and put on a little makeup."

"No. Not this time. Maybe when I go out."

"Well, listen. Lou Rawls is in town. Why don't you come and go out after the ball game?"

"No, that's too much in one night for me."

"Come on, San. Baby, you need to get out."

"All right. I will, but you promise to bring me back soon after the show is over?"

"You got a bet."

"Okay. What time can I look for you?"

"It's 6:25. I'll be there about 7:45. Is that enough time?"

"Yeah. I'll talk to you when you get here, okay? See I gotta go and fix my hair."

"See you later, baby."

"Okay, Jeff. Bye." I jumped up and said, "WOW! He wants to take me out!" I ran upstairs to look in the closet to see what I was going to wear. I pulled out three outfits: a yellow one, a lavender, and an orange. I held each up against me and looked in the mirror to see which color looked best for my first date with him. The orange pantsuit looked best. It was a pantsuit with a top that pulled over with a belt. I really didn't want to be bothered with my hair, so I jumped in the car and went to Rich's in South Dekalb Mall. I bought a beautiful orange hat with a gold chain going around the top of it. I bought some orange shoes, too. After I got my accessories, I headed back to the house. I took a bath and combed and brushed my hair; I put my hair in a pony tail because the hat would cover it. I made some side curls and a few in the back. I put on some false eyelashes and my makeup. Time was passing. There was a knock on the door. I yelled, "Who is it, Poo-Poo?"

I ran down the stairs saying, "Damn, where's your key?" I opened the door even though I was still putting on my clothes. Poo-Poo whistled and asked, "Where are you going? To the beauty show or something?"

"I got a date."

"With who?

"Jeff's going to take me to the Hawks game and out to a club."

"That's nice, but don't get involved with him 'cause the word is out that he's fucking up. He done started using too much dope."

"Oh no, brother. You don't have to worry about me. Okay? I can take care of myself. I can take care of all these jive-ass niggas."

"Boy! You look pretty!"

At the time, there came a knock at the outside door. Poo-Poo went downstairs to answer. "Oh ah, somebody's at the door."

He went to see. Then Poo-Poo yelled back up to me, "San! Jeff's here."

"Okay. Tell him I'll be right down."

I looked over at my cocaine and started not to take any with me, but I did. I got an eighth, put it in my purse alone with my makeup. I only took about $50 with me ...just in case something went wrong.

I walked down the stairs with my hat on. Jeff was in the living room. He stood up staring at me. Then he said, "You are beautiful. I can't believe my own eyes. San! I don't even know what to say. Hey baby, you look wonderful." He looked at me from one side to the other and said, "Where are you earrings?"

I felt my ears and said, "Thanks. I left them upstairs." I went back to get them. They were kind of big gold ones. I came back down. I began checking him out. He had on an eggshell, double-breasted suit with an eggshell turtleneck sweater. He wore a pretty gold chain that had his name spelled out in diamonds around his neck. And his rings and that watch, bad, just bad. I looked at him and said, "You look good to look at every time I see you."

"Well, lady ...what can I say. Come on, let's ride."

"Okay."

We started out of the door and he said, "Wait a minute. Where's your coat? It's cool out and it might get cold."

"I ain't got nothing to go with my outfit; nothing but my white moa hair."

"Get it. It will look good with that orange. Besides, we kind of matching; don't you think so?"

"Yeah, if you say so." I went back up to get my coat and soon after, we left in his Cadillac.

We took off for the ballgame and then to the club. I was hoping that someone would see us and want something, but nothing was kicking. We went to Underground Atlanta. We had a nice table for two. He had already made reservations. I didn't know what to order other than a fruit punch. I really was enjoying the show. Just as the lights went down, up popped the question. "San, I know that you don't have a man, but I feel like you are dealing with some lucky guy. Are you?"

"No. Why do you ask?"

"Well, San. It's like this: you are a good strong woman. Every man need someone like you. Not for what you can get, but for the strength that you hold. You see, behind every great man, there's a great woman. You are a great woman ...but where's the great man?"

"I don't know. Men to me, so far, are just after the cocaine that I can get, not after me. I want someone who's gonna want me for me, not for the cocaine. If I didn't have that sack, would you be interested in me?"

"No, because we wouldn't have been seeing each other."

"You are a nice guy, but you're not the one for me. You see, because of the thing you do and say."

"What do you mean by that?"

"The last time we talked, you said you want to sell dope until you die. Well, I don't. I want just enough to get me and my mother a house, a legitimate business, and peace of mind."

"But what's wrong with me?"

"Nothing as far as I can see. I'm one who like to feel the fire. I can tell when a person really likes me for me. I would love to be just your friend, but not you lover."

"You can't blame me for trying."

"No, I can't and I won't."

"Will you get mad if I keep trying?"

"No, not unless you get on me nerve."

"No, baby, I will never do that to you. San, I want you."

"Jeff, I really appreciate your wants, but I'm looking for someone who really needs me."

"I really like you, girl. And I've got to have you for my woman."

"Tell me, Jeff. Tell me the truth. Is it really me or the cocaine?"

"To tell the truth. Right now, it's both of you."

"Oh, I see. But if I didn't have the cocaine, would you still want me?"

He leaned over and kissed me once, then he kissed me again and said, "Yeah, baby. I would want you. Are you ready to go? The show is just about over."

"Yeah. I guess so."

"Are you hungry?"

"No, not really." His kisses went all through my body. I really enjoyed them, but I didn't want to show it. The man had chill bumps crawling all over my body, and little did he know, I was enjoying all of it.

"Well, okay. I'll take you home."

While walking though Underground Atlanta, we took pictures, bought balloons, and gave the monkey some money. We took pictures with an overlay of Bonnie and Clyde. He had me holding the two machine guns. Jeff took the picture and said, "San, this is the way you should be."

"Why do you say that?"

"Because I know you carry just that much weight."

I was getting tired. The night was very nice. It wasn't cold, but the wind had it crisp and cool. My feet were tired and I pulled my shoes off as we went to the parking lot. I realized we were walking holding hands.

When we got to the car, he unlocked my side and started to open the door, but instead he tugged my coat pulling me closer to him. With just the right grip, Jeff had me where he wanted me. He kissed me so tenderly, yet with enough passion to make me drop my shoes and my purse. My hat fell off my head and I went with the flow. I wrapped my arms around his frame. It was like I had wanted to grab on to him since the first time I saw him. He knew what he was doing. It was like science. He kissed my ear, my neck and then, he kissed my much-anticipating lips. Just as I was really getting with it, he whispered, "We better go."

He opened my door and I got in. Jeff gathered my things and placed them in my lap while looking dead in my eyes as the lights glistened through the pitch-dark sky. I watched him walk to his side of the car and I caught my breath, re-grouping before he got in.

Jeff played some Teddy Pendergrass. And after few moments, he said, "San, I've been doing a lot of fucking up lately. I mean I've really fucked up. I usually don't let shit go out on credit. But I have and I shouldn't have."

"What do you mean, Jeff?"

"I need someone like you to be by my side; to help me out."

"I don't know about that because I have lots of things on my mind—"

"Look, baby. If it's all right with you, I would like to bring all the cocaine customers that I have to you because I've been fucking up too much, San."

"Okay. I can go for that. Then you can make some money off of who you bring, that is, if it's some weight."

"Oh, yeah, baby. That's all I'm gonna bring you. You know better than that. Looka here, San. When I get to you house, I want to buy a gram of personal for myself."

"I brought a little with me. You want a hit?"

He had a big smile on his face and said, "Yeah. I need a hit bad."

He opened the bag up and got a card out of his glove box. That was it. He snorted some and offered me some. I shook my head, no. That didn't seem to bother him. He drove me on home and when we got the apartment, he said, "Would you like for me to come in?"

"Yeah."

"I still want to get that gram from you, okay?"

"Okay. Let me get my keys out first." I opened my purse and got my keys. I went into the house and as I was walking in, I was pulling off my coat. Then I said, "Would you like some orange juice or soda?"

"Just give me a glass of ice water."

We both went into the kitchen. I fixed the water as he sat down at the table. He snorted some more and said, "San!"

I looked at him and he continued, "Would you please give me a mirror or a saucer?"

"Um-huh."

He put some of the cocaine on the saucer. He looked at me and said, "Here. Try a little. It won't hurt you."

"No, no. I don't think that's for me. Anyway, what does it do for you?"

"Nothing but fuck me up. Make you feel real sexy."

"Yeah?"

He put it up to my nose. The way he looked at me, I went on and snorted and got some up my nostril. It stung a little bit. I did it again, and again, and again. I wasn't feeling any different. He got up and said, "Well, baby, let me get that gram and ride."

"Okay."

I picked a bag up off the table and said as I handed his to him, "You can buy this."

"This is more than a gram."

"Yeah, but take it anyway."

"All right, baby. Here's your money." He counted out $100 and handed it to me. He kissed me on the cheek and said, "Talk to you tomorrow, pretty."

"Okay," I said real mellow like, "Good night."

I let him out the door.

6

The next day was good. Jeff brought several people over. Duey came. Fat Man, Brass, and Meathead all came by. I sold about $10,000 worth of cocaine in weight. Lil' Man and Bippy sold all together about $1,500 worth.

It was time for me to ride down the highway to pick up Aunt Hazel. I called Sugar to see if she would ride with me: "Hey, Sugar. Will you ride with me down to the state prison to pickup Aunt Hazel?"

"Yeah! When are you leaving?"

"In the morning, about 4:00. She can leave at 6:00."

"Okay. I'll be ready."

It was about midnight. I had my brother to take my children down to my mother's house. I was in the house alone. I went up stairs and opened my cocaine bag. I found myself getting some rocks out and mashing them up with a card. I snorted, and before I realized I had snorted more than I thought. I started sweating. I mean really sweating. I felt very hot. I ran downstairs and got a Pepsi Cola and a glass of ice. I went back upstairs and snorted even more. I started to like the way my mouth was feeling. I ate some. It was good. I looked at the clock and it was 3:25 A.M. I said to my self, "Damn! I got to get ready!"

I thought I heard somebody. I got the .38 blue stretch gun and put it under my arm and starting walking. I didn't see anybody. I went into the bathroom, looked out the window and shut and locked it up. I was unaware of the effects of cocaine. I didn't realize it had me going through some changes. I found myself just walking in circles. I said to myself: "I got to go."

I went back to the bathroom and washed my face. I went back to my room and found myself snorting some more. I got dressed and packed an eighth with me, then left. While driving over to Sugar's house, I was looking through the rearview mirror. It seemed that somebody was following me. I pulled the car over to the side to let the one behind me pass. I thought it was the police. I said, "Damn! What's wrong with me? I'm talking to myself."

I opened the little bag of cocaine and snorted some more, using my finger. It was all over my nose. I finally reached Sugar's house. I blew the horn. It seemed like I was afraid to get out of the car. I was looking back, forward and to the sides. I said to myself, "I know this cocaine ain't doing this ...O well." I blew the horn, again. I said, "Here she comes."

When Sugar got in, I noticed she was laughing. I said to her, "What are you laughing for?"

"You got something all over your face."

I looked in the mirror. Cocaine was all over my face and in my lap. She asked, "What is that?"

I thought I might as well tell her, "It's cocaine."

"Where did you get it from?"

"Oh. I didn't tell you, did I?"

"No."

"Well, it's a long story. I'll tell you about it sometime. Have you ever had any?"

"Yeah. Meathead gave me some."

"Oh! You want some?"

"Yeah. Let me try it."

"Here. Get what you want." I cranked the car up and left headed to the prison. We were snorting and talking the whole way there. Sugar even smoked some reefer. I looked up and realized that we were practically there. We could see the sign that read, STATE PRISON. I said, "Well, Sugar. We are here." I looked at Sugar and burst out laughing. Her face had more cocaine on it than mine had earlier.

"What's so funny?"

I pulled the sun visor down so that she could look in the mirror. When she did, she busted out laughing. I said, "Girl, we don't even know what we are doing."

"I tell you what. My false teeth are frozen."

We busted out even harder. "Wait. Here's the turn," as I almost missed my exit.

We went on down the road to the prison. We could see all the people getting ready to leave. It was 6:05 and believe me, Aunt Hazel was ready to leave. We didn't even wipe our faces and got out to help Aunt Hazel put her bags away in the trunk. She looked at both of us and said, "Ya'll better get your asses back in the car. Dope is all over both your faces."

We started laughing at each other as we wiped our faces and got in the car. Aunt Hazel put the rest of the bags in the trunk. Sugar got in the back.

As soon as Aunt Hazel got in, she said, "Let's go. Get me away from this place." She kissed the both of us and said, "Drive the car, San! What's wrong with you? Ya'll speeding like hell." We laughed again. Aunt Hazel went on to say, "Give me some (referring to the cocaine). I go home Monday, anyway. They ain't gonna check me when I get back. I sure wish I had a work with me."

"Un-un," I said. "You gotta snort with us."

"Okay. Give it here."

Sugar passed Aunt Hazel the bag. She hit it and said, "God-damn!" She was holding her face. "Girl, this motherfucker is raw! How long ya'll been snorting?"

"We just started."

"Ya'll nose gon be fucked up!"

Sugar asked, "Why you say that?"

Aunt Hazel looked back at Sugar and said, "Ain't no cut on this, I mean none. Good god almighty! Woo-wee!" She hit it again and kept on talking, "Stop by the store so I can get something to wet my mouth."

We stopped by the first store we saw. All of us got out and went in. I got me my favorite soda: a Pepsi. And I bought a cup of ice. Aunt Hazel got pop, also. Sugar got strawberry or grape soda. We were on our way back to Atlanta. Then Aunt Hazel asked me, "Well tell me how you been doing with the dope?"

Sugar looked shocked because she had no idea and I had not told her about my "business."

I responded to Aunt Hazel and said, "Honey, I've been rolling!"

"Did Bippy take you to the right people?"

"Yeah! I've met lots of big people. I mean big. I done saved about $10,000 already."

Aunt Hazel looked at me and said, "What!"

"Un-huh. I'm gonna buy me my dream furniture to put in my dream house one day. That is if it's the Lord's will."

"You just be careful out there. I'll be home Monday and I can help you."

"No! I don't you to mess with it anymore. You just stay back so you won't get involved with it no more."

"I ain't gonna shoot no more; I'm just gonna snort."

"Okay. Snort. We gon see ..."

We were back in Atlanta. The first place she wanted to go was to Auburn Avenue. We got out, went up and down all over the whole strip. She lived on Eugenia Street over by the stadium. She finally got ready to go home. We went to her house and no one was there. She checked for the key she usually kept under the porch mat. Sure enough, it was there. We opened the burglar bar door. A crying dog greeted us. He was happy to see his master. We sat and talked for a while and snorted for a while. I gave her $100 and left her a hit of cocaine. I told her that we would be back later on. Aunt Hazel said, "Come over to Eloise's house. That's where everybody will eat."

"Okay. We'll be over."

It was about 11:00 A.M. I wanted to get a little sleep so we went on to Sugar's house. When we got there, we couldn't even go to sleep at all. So we sat at the table in the kitchen and drank Pepsi and orange juice for a while. We started to look tired, but wasn't. Time was passing on by. I said, "Let's ride."

"Where are we going?" Sugar asked.

"Let me tell you about these two fine niggas. One's named Jeff and the other, Ray. Jeff sells a lot of cocaine and heroin. He's good looking; tall and fine but the other one: Ray ...that nigga left me with my mouth wide open. He's just that fine, girl. I think I like him the best 'cause he's different. He's more of a gentleman than Jeff."

"Where did you meet him?"

"Girl, all of the pretty niggas buy cocaine."

"I sure want to see them."

"Well, when you're not working, you ought to come over. Come on, let's go. You drive this time."

"Okay. Give me the keys."

We got in the car, stopped over to Sugar's mother's house and ate a little, then we headed for my Aunt Eloise's house. When we got there, everybody in the family was there. We talked, ate, told lies, and jokes. It was getting late. I said to Sugar, "Come on. I'm ready to go get some more stuff, ain't you?"

"Yeah."

On the way out the door, I saw Big H pulling up. Aunt Hazel stayed there. Big H. spoke out, "Hey, what's going on?"

"Nothing much," I said.

"I see you got your partner with you," he said, referring to Sugar.

"Yeah, well, we'll talk to you later. We've been riding all day and we're tired."

"Okay, San. Check you later."

As we were approached the hill, he yelled out, "Come by the house tomorrow!"

"All right!"

We got situated in my house in Decatur. Sugar and I listened to some music. Then the phone rang: "Hello?"

"How are you doing, baby?"

I put my hand over the mouthpiece and whispered to Sugar that Jeff was on the line. "Would you hold on, please?"

"Yeah."

Sugar had been trying to tell me, "I want to see him."

I went back to my phone conversation and said to Jeff,

"Hey, listen. What are you doing?"

"I need to come see you. I want to come get one of those things."

"Okay, baby. I'll be here waiting for you." I hung up the phone, clapped my hand together and said, "Guess what, Sugar? He's on his way here."

"For real, girl?"

"Um-huh. You'll see. I wish you could see the other one."

"What's the other one's name?"

"Oh! It's Ray. He's a bad number, baby. I mean bad."

Just then there was a knock at the door. I told Sugar to get it. Sugar was speaking through the door, "Who is it?"

"Jeff."

While opening the door, she said, "Come on in. She'sin the kitchen."

"How are you doing, lady?"

"Fine, and you?"

"Oh, I'll make it."

I entered the living room and said, "Excuse me. Sugar, meet Jeff. Jeff this is Sugar."

They both nodded their heads to each other. Then Jeff said, "Sugar, are you as sweet as your name?"

"I would think so."

"I like you friend," he said referring to me, "but she doesn't seem to think nothing of it."

I said, "What can I do? All I can say is—just keep trying."

"Okay, baby. Now let me get that and ride."

"Hold on for a minute. Let me go upstairs."

I went up and came back down with the cocaine. He had the money all laid out on the table. I gave him the cocaine and then he left. I said, "Lock the door, Sugar, and help count this money."

"Girl! That's a lot of money. Is it yours?"

"Some of it."

"You gonna be big time, huh? Let me work with you after work."

"Okay if you want to."

"Shoot! You know I need something to do. You meet a lot of people, don't you?"

"Yeah! You want another hit?"

"Naw. We better go to bed."

"Okay, 'cause I know I'm tired."

"All right, let's go."

We walked up the steps and went into my bedroom and talked for a while. We eventually talked ourselves to sleep.

The next morning Sugar woke me up, "San! San! Girl, you sleep too hard. Honey, wake up, San."

I opened my eyes, looked at her and said, "What is it?"

"The phone's been ringing."

"Ah, shit." I turned over and put the cover over my head. "I thought it was something else. I'm sleeping. Why don't you go back to bed."

"You better wake up! It's 11:30, anyway."

I snatched the covers off my head and said, "You've got to be kidding." I was thinking—I should have heard from Tonya by now.

"Damn! We got to get busy. Remember your uncle wants you to come by there."

I sat on the side of the bed rubbing my head and then I said, "Wonder where Lil' Man and Bippy are. They should have called by now."

"Who is Bippy?"

"Oh. He's somebody that sells small packages for me. Lil' Man sells for me, too."

"You're on the ball, huh?"

"I hope that it gets better. What we need is another car. Let's go to the auction tonight. I'm going to buy a car."

"Okay, but let's get started on what you got to do today."

"Right."

I went on and got washed and dressed to leave. As soon as we hit the door, the phone rang. I picked up,

"Hello?"

"How's your Thanksgiving?"

"Oh, hey Tonya. It was so-so. How was yours?"

"We went over to my mother's house."

"Well, what's up?"

"We'll be over in a few minutes, okay?"

"You've got to hurry 'cause we're on our way out the door."

"Don't leave. We will be there in 15 minutes."

"Okay. I'll wait 20 or 25 minutes and I'll talk to you later." I hung up the phone and explained to Sugar that we were going to wait a few more minutes for Tonya and Ray ...they were on their way over.

"Good. Now I can see who's the finest between him and Jeff."

"I need to let my hair down, huh?"

"Ah, honey, you still gonna look the same way ..."

We both laughed. Then she said, "Girl, that man don't want you."

"Sh-it! Just pay attention at the way he looks at me."

"Look! Here they come."

"Sugar, you want a little hit before we go?"

"Yeah! But don't we need to eat first?"

"That's why your ass so big, you wear a size 11 just like me. We both done got too fat. Open the door, Sugar." They both had bags in their hands. Sugar watched the man all the way in. She even looked at his ass. I saw the way she was watching so I had to get her attention. I spoke up, "Tonya and Ray, this is Sugar. Sugar I want you to meet Ray and Tonya."

They greeted each other. Tonya and Ray went in the first bag that Tonya was carrying. It was a lot of things for my sisters. The other bag was stuff for my kids.

"Well, what you want for all of it?"

"We got about $1200 worth of merchandise," Ray said.

"So, how do you want to do this ...I'll give you a quarter ounce and $100 ...that's all right?"

His fine tall ass said, "Yeah! That's a bet."

I went upstairs to get the cocaine to give to him. I handed him a $100 bill, too.

"Look, San, why don't you and Sugar come over to my apartment next Sunday. I'm going to cook out."

"Cook out? Don't you think it's a little too cool outside for a cookout?"

"Yeah, but we will eat inside."

"Oh, all right, then. What time do you want us to be there?"

"Tonya will pick ya'll up around noon. How about that?"

I had my personal bag of cocaine with me. I offered them a little hit. They looked at each other and they both said to me, "I thought you didn't fuck around."

"I didn't when I told you I didn't. But now I do a little. Here!"

I moved the clothes out of the way and motioned for them to sit down. Ray helped me move the clothes from in the kitchen to the living room. He looked at me so hard I felt the vibes going through my body. I looked at him dead in his eyes and said, "Thanks."

We went back into the kitchen to sit down.

"Anybody want some orange juice?" I offered.

They all answered, "Yeah."

I fixed everybody something to drink then we snorted for hours. Everybody was speeding. Tonya asked Ray, "Are you ready, baby? My heart is about to jump out my chest."

Ray stuttered, "Th—th—thi—this cocaine is, is damn ggggoood!"

"Well, San, it was nice, but we got to go," Tonya said as she looked at her watch. "It's 7:00. We need to make a move."

"Okay, ya'll. We'll be seeing you, here?"

"Wait a minute," Tonya said, "I need to use the bathroom."

"Go ahead. It's right as you go up the stairs."

She walked out of the kitchen. I could feel Ray staring at me. Even Sugar saw it. I felt very uncomfortable because of the way he looked at me. He said, "Are you married, San?"

"Nope."

"Do you have a man?"

"Nope."

"Well, I know that you have somebody that you want to be with."

"Nope. Why are you asking me all this?"

" 'Cause I want to know. Since I've been coming here, I have never seen you with anyone."

"I know. But you need to have somebody."

"Yeah. Every woman needs a man."

I could see Sugar laughing inside.

"Haven't found one yet. How about that?"

Now Sugar's laughing out loud. I asked her, "What'sso funny?" Then I offered Ray another one and one. He said, "No, you hit it. I like the way you look when you hit it ..."

Just then Tonya entered and said, "I'm ready." She hit the cocaine that I had on the card.

I got up to let them out. They both thanked me, again. I said, "I'll see ya'll Sunday." Then I let them out.

I turned around and looked at Sugar just as she opened her mouth to say, "San! You know what? That nigga got eyes for you, girl. It's written all over his face. And another thing he can't even hide it. The look that's in his eyes ...woo-wee!"

"Let's ride, Sugar. But you know what? I keep feeling these vibes coming from him. What does that mean?"

"That means that you like him and he most certainly likes you. It's obvious."

"Well, what am I gonna do?"

"Nothing but go eat Sunday."

We laughed. "Remember, San, you don't know nothing about Tonya—plus, she shops at your dope store."

"I know ...

"Ah honey, let's just go. We will be here talking about that nigga all night if I don't get you out of here."

"Okay."

"Let's get your things and take them upstairs before we leave."

We took the clothes upstairs and left going to Aunt Hazel's house. We first stopped by Georgia Avenue to see if we could see Meathead, but we didn't. Then we went by Aunt Hazel's house. There was a note on the door that read: WE WILL BE BACK. I said, "Sugar, let's ride to Hunter Street then to Auburn Avenue and don't forget to stop by your uncle's house."

"Oh, yeah! I almost forgot."

Sugar drove up and down Hunter and Auburn Avenues. There was no sign of either one of them. Then she asked, "You think that they might be together?"

"I don't know. But if they have fucked up, I know a trick."

"Well, they ain't nowhere to be found."

"Let's go on to Big H's house."

"No, let's stop by Aunt Hazel's again, first." We went by and she still hadn't returned. So we went on over to Big H's house. I got out of the car and said, "Come on, Sugar. Ain't you coming in?"

"I thought that you wanted me to wait out here."

"Naw, girl. Come on in."

We went in and all the way to the back. Aunt Hazel, my uncle, and his wife were all back there snorting cocaine like crazy. I knew then that Aunt Hazel had told them about me. He and Aunt Hazel were talking their asses off. Then he said, "Come on. Join the party."

I looked and saw about an ounce laid out on the table. They were snorting rocks. I mean some of the rocks weren't even crushed. I put my hand on my hips and said, "Damn! Ya'll noses gonna fall off."

"Naw," said Big H, "it ain't. Julio told me what to do for it."

"Oh yeah? What did he tell you?"

"He told me to put some Vaseline on it. Shit, we ready."

My aunt was sweating like it was the first time I hit them rocks. Her name was Mina and she had a twin name Nina. Just then, Mina said, "Grab a chair, ya'll. Come on, baby. Let's get it on. This is some good shit. I like it, San! Do you ...do you like it Sugar? Where ya'll been? We been waiting on ya'll. Come on, girl, get some."

Mina snorted 50's, one in each nostril. Her mouth was twisted. Then Aunt Hazel said, "Mina, you are wide open. Let somebody get a word in."

"Naw, I ain't." She then turned to me and Sugar and continued, "What'sya'll problem? You scared?"

We laughed because we knew that the cocaine had all of them. I then said as Mina was trying to snort more, "Wait a minute, Mina. Let me mash them up."

"That's the best way to do it; put the rocks in your nose."

Everybody started laughing. Then I said, "No-o-o, Mina. I like mine crushed up. I can't put them rocks in my nose."

"Well, here. Put this tiny winy one in there."

"You crazy! I can't put that cocaine in my nose like that. What's wrong with you?"

"What's wrong with ya'll? Ya'll look like ya'll done gone crazy to me."

We laughed. Then I said, "Well let me do mine the way I like to do it, okay?"

She handed me the card and said, "Here! Go on and it the way you want to then."

It was getting late and Aunt Hazel had to be back in Hard-wick by 6:00 the next morning. I said, "Aunt Hazel, what time are you gonna pull out of here? You know we only got about six more hours before we leave. You've got to get your things ready."

"My things are already packed and ready to go."

Handing me a key, she continued, "Go over to the house and get my bags. They are in the hall on the floor all ready to go. Just put them in the car and bring them over here. We can leave from right here."

"Let me get another hit before me and Sugar go."

I passed the card to Sugar when I got done. She hit it and then we left them the same way we found them ...snorting.

While driving, I said, "Sugar! You see how much shit they snorting?"

"Un-huh. They gonna be up all day long. Boy, they can snort, can't they?"

"Hell yeah. They better cool out before their noses fall off." We were at the house. "Come on, Sugar. Help me get these bags right quick."

We jumped out the car and ran up the steps. I opened the door and we got all the bags. Once we packed them in the car, we headed back to the killing ground. As we got out the car, Sugar said, "You hear something coming from those bushes?"

I stopped in my tracks, then I said, "If it is, I ain't going over there to see. You look."

"Hell no! Let's get in that door." We both ran up the steps, scared as hell. We busted in the door and didn't even lock it because it was unlocked in the first place. I mean they didn't even hear us bust up in that mug. They were still getting busy and talking. I heard Mina say, "Why ya'll staring at me? Do I look funny?"

Everybody in there laughed because she was really tripping. Aunt Hazel said, "All them damn rocks got you thinking like that."

"Rock, hell. I know I can see and hear. Ya'll laughing and talking about me. I ain't no goddamn cartoon ...ya'll motherfuckers look more like the cartoons than I do. And Big H, I don't know what you laughing for with your sick ass."

We laughed again. She got up and walked out talking. She looked back from the doorway and yelled, "All ya'll, just kiss my ass."

We laughed even harder. Sugar said, "What's wrong with Mina?"

"Nothing but that cocaine got her and she don't even know it," Big H said while laughing. He then looked at Aunt Hazel as said, "Gimme a cigarette."

She looked in her pocket and pulled out a pack of Kools. Mina walked back in and looked at all of us and said, "Ya'll some ugly motherfuckers." Then she stuck her tongue out and left back out. We all noticed that she was peeping in, though. I laughed and said, "Mina, come here. Ain't nobody talking about you."

"Yes ya'll is, and I don't give a damn. Just keep on laughing ...I'm gonna throw some water on that shit."

Big H looked up and said, "If you do, I'm gonna beat your goddamn ass. Now come on in here." He stood up and repeated, "Bring your goddamn ass here and stop acting."

"Come and get me, big bad motherfucker. Come on." He started towards her then she said, "Okay, okay ...I'm coming."

"You just want to be petted. Sit your goddamn ass down before I knock it down."

She came on in and sat down, then she said, "I'm sorry ya'll. Forgive me, hear?"

I said, "We forgive you, Mina. Here." I put the cocaine on the card up to her nose. We snorted for about 30 more minutes and then I said, "Well, well, well, ya'll. It's time for us to make a trip down the highway."

Everybody got up from the table. We all went to the door. Aunt Hazel kissed her sister, Mina, and said, "I'll be home for good on Monday. We can have a ball then, all right?"

"Yeah," Mina said.

"Hey," Big H asked, "why don't you help me through a 'Coming Home Party' for Aunt Hazel?"

"We'll do just that," I said. "Well, what night you want to have it on?"

"Shit, the same one she gets back on."

"All right, then."

"We'll get it together when you get back from down there."

"All right. Let's ride ladies."

Aunt Hazel and Sugar were waiting outside. Aunt Hazel yelled back to the house, "See you later, Big H."

We got in the car and headed back for the prison. When we got there, we took the bags out. I said, "Aunt Hazel! Do you think that they will check you for drugs?"

"Hell naw! They wouldn't think that I would do a stupid thing like that so close to getting out ...hell, I'm out of here for good on Monday."

We both broke out with a big laugh. She kissed Sugar and me on our foreheads. As she stood there, we slowly pulled off while waving goodbye. Aunt Hazel yelled, "Don't forget: 6:00 A.M., Monday morning—"

"We'll be here!" Sugar yelled back.

On our way back, we noticed a little cafe´. We stopped and ate. After eating, we went into the bathroom to snort some more cocaine. We needed it to open our eyes because we were exhausted from running since that morning. And eating didn't help any; we really felt tired. We both washed our faces after the hit, thinking that the cool water would refresh us. I asked Sugar, "Do you mind driving?"

"Hell, naw, girl."

"I see two highways. That sunlight is really fucking with my eyes. Come on, let's stop next door and get us some sunglasses. We need to fill up the gas tank, anyway."

Sugar went to get the glasses while I filled the tank. Once we got back situated, I felt somewhat revived. I went ahead and drove back.

After many miles, we noticed a road sign: ATLANTA 10.

"Damn, San! You really put your foot in the tank ...you know you can drive if you don't know nothing else."

"You know, it seems like I drive better since I got into this thang. Hey, let's stop by Big H's house to see what's going on"

When we got there, Big H and Mina were still getting down by themselves.

"Goddamn, Big H, ya'll gon kill yourselves? I know you got to be tired."

"Naw, baby," Mina said, "We go all night long. Come on. Get ya'll some more."

"We just gonna get a little hit and then we got to get some rest. I got to get up with some people."

Big H said, "Look here, San, Julio will be over here later on tonight. So get your money ready for him, okay? He's got to go out of town to get us some more."

"How long will that take? We are not out, are we?"

"Naw, but he's gonna leave about 16 ounces."

"Oh, damn. I thought we were going to be out for a while."

We left and went looking for Lil' Man and Bippy. Then I said to Sugar, "Fuck it. They're the ones who will lose out 'cause they could have gotten more."

"Well, what did you give them?"

"About $1,000 worth, each. Anyway, I really don't need them because I like selling big pieces. So, what you got to do the rest of the day?"

"Nothing but call my mother to check up on my daughter."

"Let's go back to my apartment and do that. While we there, we can take a bath and put some more clothes on."

"I ain't got no clothes there."

"We wear the same size, girl. You can put on one of my warm ups. And I got some new bras and underwear. Why don't we just go by your mama's house, instead of just calling? But then again, she might look at us like we crazy or something. You better call."

We stopped at the next phone booths. She called her mama and I called mine. Everything checked out concerning our kids.

We went on to Decatur. As soon as we got in the house, the phone began ringing. It first was Duey. I took his order and got on off the line with him. Then Jeff called: "Hey, baby. I've been trying to get you for five hours. I got someone who wants three ounces."

"Okay, sweetheart. I'll be here. I just got back from taking Aunt Hazel back."

"I'll be right over."

Next, Fatman called. He wanted something. Then it was Will. He called to let me know that Brass was on his way back. I just took the phone off the hook so that I could at least get these orders ready before taking anymore. Sugar said, "Were all those calls for cocaine?"

"Honey, yeah! We got to get rolling. Shit, we've been fucking off for two days and now it's time to work. Let's fix the cocaine first then we'll take a bath if that all right with you."

We got the scales, the cut, the bags and went to work. We made up all that I had. I just felt like it was gonna be a good day. I had gotten very fast and very good weighing the cocaine and bagging them up. Sugar watched. Then she said, "Girl, you are really fast with that stuff."

"Yep. But I need to be a little faster."

Then they started coming in ...one by one. The last person was Jeff. We sat and talked a while. We snorted for a while. He pulled out some heroin. I thought then, if he offers that to us, he's not our friend and sure enough: he did just that. "This is some boy. Ya'll want some?"

Sugar didn't know the difference, so I hurried and answered for the both of us, "Ah, no. We don't want no habits."

"Anything you do, baby, becomes a habit if you do it long enough."

"Maybe so ...but that's one we don't want. So you just go on and enjoy yourself and let us enjoy ourselves." That really pissed me off, but I didn't let it show. I was thinking all that time how he calls himself trying to catch and got caught. Shortly after that, I said, "Well, Sweetheart, Sugar and I have to make a run. We're not rushing, but we've got to take care of some business."

"Okay ...so where is the crew?"

"Hell! I don't know. I haven't seen them in two days. It doesn't matter 'cause I don't need them anyway."

"Well! All right, then, let me go and I'll call you later on. Maybe you want some company?"

"Nooo tonight. We're beat from this weekend with Aunt Hazel."

"I see ...take care and I'll talk to you later."

I let him out and closed the door real quick like. I couldn't hold back, "That mother fucker's got nerve! He offered us some 'boy.'" I hit the cabinet. "That low-life-death-dodging-graveyarddigging-son-of-bitch ...he makes my ass want to do the Applejack." Sugar just laughed then I laughed along with her. "Naw, baby. San can't fuck around like that. You know what?"

"What?"

"He's a real punk. So I guess he wants me to be a punk bitch, huh?"

"I know that my best friend can handle it, huh?" "Oh yeah. I'm gonna show that bastard how to play games and get paid all at the same time."

"Well what are you gonna do?"

"I'm gonna take every customer that he has."

"Whoa, San. You can't do that. That nigga might try something bad."

"Who gives a fuck? I don't. Do you?"

"Well I'm with my sista all the way."

"We are gonna sell cocaine day in and day out. I'm gonna go over there every time somebody wants some. I ain't gonna let him come too often. Watch me smoke."

Time was going by. We went to look for Lil' Man and Bippy again. I found Lil' Man at home. I knocked on the door real hard he came to the door, "Hey, big Sis. I got robbed."

"Bitch, I don't want to hear that shit! Where is my motherfuckin' money? You gonna give me something!"

I reached at him. Sugar grabbed me and said, "San! This won't get your money back!"

I struggled away from Sugar, grabbed Lil 'Man in the collar and said, "I'm your sister and I want everybody in my family to have something. And you do me like this? Naw, naw ..."

At that time his wife came in saying, "Ya'll got to go out of here with all this shit up in my house 'cause I ain't gone have it. If any ass kicking gonna be in here, I'm the one."

"Bitch," I said. "I'll beat your god damned ass! Who in the fuck do you think you are? Bitch, you ought to be the fucking man with your bald-headed ass ..."

"Get out of my house, San!"

Sugar was holding my arm as I was steady talking and trying to get to either one of them, "Put me out, hoe-bully-bitch. Come on, put me out. I'll kick you and Lil' Man's ass."

Sugar was still trying to calm me down, "San, San, come on now. You wrong for that."

I didn't care ...I was truly upset. "Fuck it! Fuck it! Ya'll be back ...Let's go, Sugar."

While walking, I was still talking,

"The stanking mother fuckers ...they both can kiss my ass. I might set the goddamn house on fire—old ugly bitch ...with her funny made ass ...old all out-of-shape bitch." I stood by the car looking at the window and patting my feet. Then I said, "Let me go back in there ..."

"No, San! If that woman kill you in her house, won't nothing be done about it. So let's just ride."

"But did you hear that old raggedy mouth whore?"

"Let's go."

I got in the car and burned rubber out from there before I truly had a change of mind. Then I said, "Old bald-headed bitch ...Sugar, that makes you want to do something to a nigger."

"I know. But just let's go. Just like you said. She'll be back."

"You know what, Sugar? I'm gonna start carrying a gun with me. I'm gonna learn how to shoot whoever gets in my way. I ain't gonna be fucked over by nobody. If I come up short, which I'm not, that Italian might shorten my fucking life. They say a nigger will make or break you, and I will be damned if I'm gonna let the bitch break me. Kiss my ass."

"Let's call Mama."

"That's my mama, not hers. Old bull-diking whore."

I then went over in Summer Hill to check on Meathead. He was on the corner. I jumped out of the car and said,

"What's happening?"

"I'm mad with your slow ass."

"What?"

"I've been out of cocaine since yesterday."

"Damn, Meat! I'm sorry. I had to take Aunt Hazel back to the farm."

"Yeah, well, you got me ready now?"

"Yeah. Get in the car."

"Who is that with you?" he said, looking at Sugar. Before I could anything, he realized who it was and said, "Sugar! What's happening, baby? Y'all taking care of it, huh?"

"Trying to," Sugar answered.

I said, "Come on, Meat, get in."

He opened the door and got in. He gave me $900 and I gave him $200 and an eighth, plus the $1,000 worth.

"What's the eighth for?"

"For you. It's a bonus."

He leaned over, kissed me, and said, "Thank you, San. Thank you. I can really pay all my bills now."

"Okay. Now. Let me and Sugar ride, babe. I'll be home. If I don't answer, just come out there. I'll be there sleep."

"Okay, then. I'll talk to you later."

He got out and we took off. Sugar had been watching me all the while, then she said, "You really made Meat happy, San."

"Shit. That's the way I did Lil' Man and Bippy. They ain't gonna get another break like that." As we were riding along, I noticed Burger King and said, "Let's stop by Burger King."

"We can go over to my mother's house and get some hen and dressing. Richardson Street, here we come. The Whopper ain't got nothing on your mama's dressing." Sugar's mama really fixed us up nice. We ate and went on back to Decatur.

"Well, Sugar, we got to get some sleep. We got to leave going back to get Aunt Hazel ...Damn! We were suppose to stop by Big H's, but I left the money at home. We'll see him when he gets over Big H's house. I'm pretty sure that he will call." We went in the apartment, took baths and went straight to bed. Sugar slept in my daughter's bedroom. She set the alarm clock. She knew that I wouldn't be up in time without some help.

The clock went off about 5:30. Sugar got on up and came running in to make sure I was up, "San, San. We're gonna be late. It's 5:30. Girl, get up."

I staggered around the room and mumbled, "Sugar, get the cocaine out the dresser drawer. Come on, we got to wake up. Hit this. We have got to get moving."

We put on our warm-ups. I had on a white one and Sugar was sporting a gold one. I grabbed our little personal bag and ran out of the door. I said, "Damn! Aunt Hazel's gonna be made with us."

I first stopped by a service station. We stopped and got gas, cigarettes, and soft drinks. We were at the Madison exit (we were almost there). When I saw that State Prison sign, I put my foot in the tank. There was nothing but silence until we got there. Then I said, "At last, Sugar. We made it. What time is it?"

"It's about 7:45."

"Damn!" All I could hear was Aunt Hazel telling me NOT to be late and that she would be ready to walk at 6:00 A.M. "I can just hear her mouth now ..."

We didn't see her so we got out and went to the office to find out whether she had left or not. I asked the lady and I was hoping that she didn't tell me something that I just didn't want to hear ...like she left already ...then I heard the white lady say as she looked up from her stack of papers, "She gets out today. It looks like it will be another ten minutes before her release."

Sugar and I looked at each other and laughed. After all that worrying and breaking all kinds of speeding records, we still had to wait.

It was 8:00 and we noticed three ladies coming out from behind the glass caged doors: one of them was Aunt Hazel. Her eyes were glowing. We all glowed. Aunt Hazel saw us and as she hit the outside she said, "Good-bye, State Prison. I hope that I don't have to see you no more!"

We got in the car and headed for home. Atlanta, GA—here we come. Sugar fired up a joint and passed the cocaine. Aunt Hazel said, "I want to shoot mine." I reached for the needle and Aunt Hazel said, "Oh no, baby.

I don't need to shoot none right now." "I know, but ..." "Hey baby, just wait. That shit makes your pussy wet." "Wow-wee, Aunt Hazel!" "That's the truth. It will make you skeet all over yourself." "Well, I don't want to try that needle if it will do all that." Sugar said, "I don't want to try it either." Aunt Hazel said, "Yeah, well, baby. I want to get wet between my legs." "Well, this is Atlanta, Georgia, and we will be home in a minute," I announced. "Are you going in the house, Aunt Hazel?" "Yeah. Take me home and let me get off." "Get off with who?" Sugar smiled and asked. "My man, of course." "Oh. Excuse me, Ms. White." "Now don't forget to come back by here later." "We won't. Remember we are going to have a party for you." "Yeah, hurry home, Aunt Hazel," I said. We got out and took all of the bags out of the trunk and took them in the house for her. I gave her $200 and about one gram of cocaine. I really didn't want to leave her much because she probably would have gone out and bought a needle.

"Are you ready to eat?" I asked Sugar as we started rolling away from Aunt Hazel's. I noticed a McDonald's and pulled up to eat breakfast. We left there, headed to Decatur. We went to the apartment; all tired and beat. Sugar said, "Well, San. School is tomorrow."

"That means work for me in the morning. Poo-Poo is going to bring the children home for me. So all we got to do is get your daughter Ann's clothes ready, huh?" I explained. "Mama will probably do that. Let me call Big H to see if Julio has been over there."

"Hey! What's happening?" I asked the man on the phone. Come to find out it was Big H.

"I've been trying to get you all morning."

"Man, you know that I had to go and pick up Aunt Hazel. Well, look here. He will be here in about 20 minutes. Can you get here?"

"Yeah. I'm on my way."

Sugar helped me count the money I owed the cocaine man. She asked, "Do you have all of it?"

"Yeah. I ain't thinking about that. I'm thinking that I got to get there before he leaves town. Let me get the money."

I went upstairs, got the pouch and returned to hand Sugar a bundle. "It's all ready ...hundreds first. Just count up $6,000 and the rest is mine."

"Here you go, $6,000."

"Look, I'm gonna make a run over there. Count the rest and hold on to it until I get back. Lock the door behind me."

I drove the car as fast as I could. Julio and I got there about the same time. He asked, "How are you doing, San?" he asked as we walked together up to the house.

"I'm doing pretty good."

"Big H tell you that I was going out of town, didn't he?"

"Yeah."

We went straight to the back. I handed him my money and he gave me six ounces and said, "Now listen, San. I'll be gone for about two weeks, so take it slow because you will only have 10 ounces left. So don't sell too many ounces at one time. You see that's gonna have to last you for two weeks or maybe even three. You got that?"

"Yes, I got it."

"Oh well. I guess I'll be going. I have people waiting on me. When I get back we going to the shoot range. You need to know how to shoot a gun."

"Believe me, I am ready to learn."

"Why? Did someone bother you?"

"Nothing that I can't handle."

"No, no. You tell me and I'll take care of that for you. I want to keep selling your cocaine. I have people for that line of work, all right?"

"All right," I said. "Okay. I'll check you out later, Big H."

I went back to my apartment. Sugar was there watching T.V. I spoke, "Hey. I got it. The man said that he will be gone for about three weeks. He left 16 ounces for me."

"Well! That's good."

"I've got to take it slow because it may take longer than that, but I hope not."

"The children are upstairs."

"Oh yeah. So where's Poo-Poo?"

"He went to the store."

"Sugar, you can drive home if you want to and come back tomorrow when you get off because I ain't got nothing to do."

"Okay. I'll do that. Here's your money, San. It's $7,000 ...even."

"On your way home, will you stop by Mama's house and give that to her?"

"You want me to ride with all of that?"

"Yeah! Won't nobody know that you have it. Go on and take it to Mama. Take Mama $6,000. You keep $200 for yourself, plus 20 to get some gas."

"Thank you, sister." She smiled.

"Next week sometime, we will go to get some three-speed bikes for the children."

"Yeah? Ann sure wants one. Okay, San. Let me ride."

I opened the door and let her out. I watched her pull off. I said to myself: "I'll fix my packages tomorrow." I got ready to go upstairs for bed when someone knocked on the door. I asked, "Who is it?"

"Ray," he answered in a low-toned voice.

"Ray!" I was more than glad to bypass my sleep. I was anxious to open the door, but I knew I had to take care of business, first. I said, "Hold on a minute." I ran upstairs to put the money away. When I returned I opened door for "them"—Ray came on in and I was expecting Tonya. (It was like if Ray came by, Tonya was right there with him.) Ray asked, "Why did you leave the door open?"

"Isn't Tonya coming in?"

"Not this time, baby. I'm alone."

I locked the door and asked him to have a seat. I went on, "I'm all out of orange juice but would you like some Pepsi Cola?"

"Yes. Would you put some ice on it for me? Just a little Pepsi because I brought something for you to drink."

I looked at him and said with a smile, "Oh yeah?"

I fixed a second glass with a little Pepsi. While opening a bottle of cognac, he said, "Excuse me for coming over without calling?"

"Oh, that's all right. I wasn't doing anything but getting ready to go to bed."

"Well if you're getting ready for bed, I'll just drink up and leave."

He looked at me with his sexy eyes. I was mesmerized and tried to speak. "I'm not sleepy (not anymore) I was just going to lie down."

"So, you don't mind staying up with me?"

"No, I don't."

"Here." He handed me some cocaine. "I brought us a little blow to do."

"But I have some."

"That's all right. You're always giving. Allow me to entertain you tonight. Oh, and I brought some music to play for you."

He had three albums: Patti Austin, Denise Williams, and Lenny Williams. He played Patti Austin's "Havana Candy."

"This is dedicated to you, San, so listen closely."

We snorted and drank while the moody music played. He asked for some more Pepsi. I went into the kitchen to put more in the glass. I closed the refrigerator door and there he was standing there like something to eat. He took the glass out my hand and leaned down to touch my lips against his. I looked up into his eyes ...speechless. I couldn't say a word. I was startled ...well kind of. I walked away. He put the glass on top of the refrigerator and pulled me close to him. This time it was a real kiss. Real smoothly, he removed the clamp from my head and freed my hair to land softly on my shoulders. I gently put my arms around him while he ran his fingers through my hair. He kissed my neck and ear. Then he looked at me while touching my hair and said, "San, you are even more beautiful than I thought. Why don't you wear your hair down?"

"Because I'm tender-headed."

"Are you sure that's the real reason?"

"Yeah, that's it."

"Well you know what I think?"

"What?"

"I think that you don't like the attention that you know it would draw from all the men. I mean you would have them drawing to you like a magnet. But you know what? You can't hide behind all your beauty that's stored up inside you." He leaned towards to kiss me again. He said softly, "San? I want to be the man you need. I really do care for you. Will you say that you will be mine?" I looked in his eyes—from one to the other and tried to answer, "But—"

He only interrupted.

Automatically, our lips gravitated to each others'. "Look what you're doing?" He was looking down at his penis. He got the Pepsi off the refrigerator, took my hand and led me back into the living room. We sat down and he poured himself another drink. Then he asked as he looked deep into my eyes, "Tell me what's on your mind right now?"

"You are."

"What do you think about me?"

'I'm wondering if you are for real or not."

"Look, baby. Don't give me an answer right now. I want our relationship to be real, not just an in and out thing. I want you to need me; to grow to love me, and most of all, to trust me. I want to be your man. I want to put dresses, heels, stockings, and diamonds on you. Take you to the best places in town. Will you do something for me?"

"What?"

"Let me take you to the beauty shop to get your hair done. I want to see you all dressed up."

"Why are you telling me all this?"

"Well, at first it was just business and believe me, I've been trying to stay away from you. But now I can't. San! The feeling that I have for you is indescribable! There's something on the inside that won't let me go."

He reached out for my hand and continued, "Please, San, just think about it. I don't want you for what you have. I want you ...for you. Try to feel my feelings, baby. They are real."

"Well what about Tonya?"

"Tonya has been with me for a long time, but there has never been any real love there. I care, but I don't love her."

"Well you don't love me either."

"No, not yet."

"Well, what makes you think I'm the one for you?"

"Listen, baby. You are a very brave woman and very strong. Tonya is good to me but she is very weak. I've tried to make her strong, but I couldn't. Plus, she doesn't trust me."

"Let me think about it. I just need some time to think. Wait. Let me get some rocks to snort."

I went upstairs to get them and come right back down. I handed them to him he mashed them up and mixed it with his shake.

"You know I can't wait until you and Sugar come over to my apartment."

"I can't either," I replied.

"Well, baby. I've got to go now because it's getting late. But I do want you to think about me, okay?"

"Here. Take this with you."

"No, leave it here for the next time I come over."

He got up and pulled me up with him and said, "I'm gonna put something on your mind."

I looked up at him real puzzled because I had no idea where he was going. He started to unzip his warm-up jacket. My eyes bucked as his mouth got close to my breast. I could feel his warm breath released from his seductive exhales. His moist lips gently kissed my left breast, then his tongue rolled round and round on it. Goose pimples were all over my body. I put my hands on his head guiding him back and forth. He looked up at me and kissed my lips, again and again. He stopped and looked at me. After taking a deep breath, he said, "San, I've got to have you, girl. I'm going to do everything I can to make you mine. Let me out. I've got to go."

Coming out of a daze, I said, "Okay, Ray. When will I see you again?"

"Real soon, baby, real soon. I won't make love to you until I'm sure that you want me. And when we do make love, I want you to see the stars."

"How about the moon?" I said, laughing.

"Well, we will just have to see when that time comes. But for now, I got to go, baby. Lock the door behind me."

I did just that as I was thinking: "I really enjoyed him. And like he intended—he really put something on my mind. He did just that." I thought about him until I fell asleep.

7

The next morning I was half asleep as I heard my children getting ready for school. I could visualize Ray and myself in the bed making love. Then the phone rang. It snapped me out of my ...I yelled, "Ah shit!" as I picked up the phone, "Hello?"

"Good morning. And who are you mad at (laughing)?"

"Oh, it's you. Ray? You won't believe it, but I was just thinking about you."

"You know what? You are not going to believe this, but that's the reason I called you so early. I had you on my mind. San, can I please come over?"

"When?"

"Right now."

"But I'm in the bed ..."

"—and that's just where I want you: in the bed."

"You know what you said about last night?"

"Yes, baby."

"I remembered and I feel like you want me as bad as I want you."

"Well I don't."

"Um-huh, well, I'm on my way."

"Ray! Ray! Wait Ray!"

He had hung up.

I jumped up and ran into the bathroom; I washed my face, brushed my teeth, and took a douche. I made the bedroom dark and put on a little makeup. It was such a little bit that I knew that he would not have been able to know I was wearing any. I went downstairs to unlock the door. I left it cracked so that he could come on in. An hour had passed and he still had not shown up. I turned on the radio and had started drifting into a sleep. I caught myself and I sat up in the bed. I looked in the mirror to see how my hair was looking. It was okay. I laid back down with only a towel wrapped around me. I dozed off. The next thing I remember is that I could feel something in my ear. It actually tickled. When I opened my eyes, Ray had taken off all his clothes. I looked scared—just a little bit. He said, "Don'tbe frightened, baby. I'm gonna make it good to you. Here, take a one and one because I want this to be long and good day for you and I." We both took a good one and one. Then he said, "You know, baby it only takes a little cocaine to bring all the freak out."

"Oh really? I don't think I need it then (laughing)." My laugh was cut short when he put the move on me. We made love for a long time and it was good. I didn't see the moon, but I did see a rainbow; colors were bright and beautiful. We went to sleep in each others' arms and woke up just to do it all over again. He enjoyed talking while making love and I enjoyed his sexy voice.

"Talk to me, baby. Tell me that it's good to you. Do you like it? Tell me."

Then I said in a soft whisper while looking him straight in his eyes, "Yes, baby. I love it."

"Well will you be mine?"

I was about to reach my climax and he could tell. He said, "Are you ready, baby? Tell me, do you want more? Come on. Turn over and let me get it from behind." I turned over and put two pillows under me.

"Now baby, take all of it. It's yours," he said.

I started to moan. He said, "Come on, baby. Tell me. Talk to me."

Then I said, "Give it to me baby. Give it to me. I'm ready."

"Oh, San! It's coming—"

"—me too!" I screamed.

"Come on, baby, come on. Oh, god damn, girl ...ooh shit."

He fell on the side of me and was all out of breath. I said, "You may not believe me, but I have never been fucked like that; out of all my days of lovemaking."

"Did you enjoy it, baby?"

I looked at him with a smile and said, "Yes. I enjoyed every bit of it and you know it. What time is it?"

"Why? Are you ready for me to leave?"

"No sweetheart. I'm going to cook breakfast for you."

"Well let me help you. Come on, let's shower."

"Okay. I'll go first. I won't be long."

"Oh no, baby. We're going to take one together ...like at the same time."

He got up and pulled me up. Then we went into the bathroom to take a shower. While in the shower we talked as the water fell on us. Then he said, "Hey baby! When are you going to let me meet the kids?"

"You will get a chance."

"Okay."

"Let's get out of here."

We got out and put on our clothes and went downstairs to cook and eat. The telephone rang while preparing breakfast. "Hello?"

"Hey, baby."

"Are you straight?"

"Yeah. But I'm, I mean, I have company."

Ray was saying in the background, "Let whoever come on. You still got to work." (I had my hand over the phone). I spoke back in the phone, "Where are you?"

"I'm pretty close to you."

"I'll be there in a minute. Get me ready."

"Okay."

I hung the phone up kind of slow. Ray said, "Who's that?"

"Oh, it's Jeff."

"Well, well. Wait until he sees me. I know he ain't going to like this, not one bit. You see, baby, he's talked about you so much that's why I did my damnest to meet you and I'm glad I did because I really do care. You and he don't have anything going on, do you?"

"No, but I did go on a date with him one night."

"Was it serious?"

"I thought that it could be, but he's not the one. He loves that heroin and plus, he offered it to me."

"He did what!"

"Yeah! To me and Sugar. Ain't that nothing?"

"May I get the door?"

"Why?"

"To let the nigger know that you have a man."

"Wait, baby, not yet. Please, I'm not ready to tell it yet."

"Okay. All right. You hold the shot cards."

Just then, there was a knock at the door. Ray was cooking the eggs while I opened the door. I yelled as I approached the door, "Okay. I'm coming." I opened the door and asked Jeff to come in.

He said, "How are you today with your hair down?"

"I just got out of the shower and I got it wet. Just have a seat and I'll get the package."

From the kitchen, Ray said, "Come on in, man."

Jeff looked in the kitchen and said, "Goddamn, man. What are you doing in the kitchen cooking?"

"I asked San if I could help her fix breakfast and she said yes. Is anything wrong with that? Has she chosen you?"

"No, not yet, but it's in the making."

Ray was smiling and said, "I really like the lady, man. I don't want to use her. I want her for who she is."

"What you think I'm doing?"

"I don't know and don't really care."

"Well, may the best man win, and I'll keep coming back. Anyway, you already spoken for, nigger, and by more than one woman. So we will see."

I had re-entered in the room and spoke, "Here you are, Jeff. Two ounces."

"Here, San, $3,000."

"The food really looks good," I said. "Jeff, would you like to have breakfast with us?"

"I sure would," Jeff said quickly while looking at Ray.

The three of us sat down to eat and talked about much of nothing. Ray asked Jeff, "So, what's going on, on the other side?"

"Nothing much. Just trying to make it man. How about yourself?"

"I'm trying to save enough money to open up some kind of a business."

"Those police are rough out there, huh?"

"Ah, man, they are on a nigger's ass like white on rice. Thanks goes to the Lord for letting me stay free from the jail because I've got to be out here for the holidays."

"I heard that."

"Look here. I'm having a cookout Sunday. You are welcome to come."

"Okay, man. I'll do my best to be there."

"San and Sugar are coming."

"I know that I'll be there for certain. Come on. Let me out, baby. I got to get to work."

Ray said, "Go ahead and finish eating, San. I'll let him out."

Ray laughed at Jeff, again. Jeff asked, "What's funny, nigger?"

"You are. This time I'll be funny, but the next time you will be funny to me."

"Yeah, we will see. Bye, nigger. See ya' Sunday."

"All right, man. Check ya' later. San! I got to go to work. I will be calling you."

That Sunday, Sugar and I went to the Ray's cookout. His apartment was beautiful. His color scheme was beige, brown, and rust. His living room had a beige pit group in it. The carpet was beige with a mink throw rug. He had mirrors everywhere. The walls spoke with fine art: paintings worth thousands. As for his windows, they were draped from tailored fabric. And to add to the de´cor, crystal was tastefully placed in all the right spaces throughout. His dining room had the same colors. He had a beautiful $600 Swede picture on the wall. His kitchen was black and white. The bedroom was royal blue, baby blue, and gold. It was breathtaking. While eating, I said, "Ray, you have a beautiful place. I love it."

"Thanks, San."

Time had flown by and Sugar and I decided to leave. Amazingly, no words were exchanged out of the norm.

It was December—close to Christmas. I sold cocaine every-day—all day—up until December 24th. The only reason I stopped then was because I ran out. Julio hadn't gotten back in town yet. I had about one eighth left. I was saving it for the New Year. We celebrated X-mas at mama's.

New Year's eve I was home alone thinking that I would be at home alone. But it really didn't bother me because I was use to it. Then the phone rang. "Hello? Who is this?"

"Damn, baby. Ray has made you forget about me?"

"Jeff! Hey, how are you? Happy New Year."

"The same to you, baby. What are you doing tonight?" "When midnight hits I'm going to be on my knees praying and thanking the Lord for letting me see the New Year come in." "Can I come over and bring it in with you?" "No, Jeff, not tonight. I really don't feel too good." "If you get lonely, feel free to call me before 10:00. Okay?" "All right, goodbye." "Later, baby." Ray didn't call all that day or night. I had him on my mind at all times. It was count down time; "10-9-8-7-6-5-4-3-2-1 HAPPY NEW YEAR, RAY." I got on my knees to pray:

Lord,
Thank you for letting me be here for the New Year 1978. Lord Jesus, thank you for shielding me and protecting my family. Thank you for the things you have done for me. And a special thanks for understanding me. Lord Jesus, thank you for being you. And thank you for not letting the devil trick me. Thank you, Jesus.
AMEN

I got up off my knees, got my cocaine bag, and went down-stairs to play the records that Ray had left over here. I snorted cocaine and listened to some music. I then got up, took that album by Lenny Williams off, and put on New Birth's "How Can I Live Living Without You?" I fixed me a drink of cognac and Pepsi with a little lemon. While sipping and relaxing, I heard the door knock. Damn, who could that be? I ain't got no cocaine.

I asked, "Who is it?" No one answered. I asked, again, "Who is it?" Still no answer, I said aloud, "I bet it's nobody but Jeff." I opened the door and didn't see anybody. Maybe I'm hearing things. As I was closing the door, I heard, "Happy New Year."

Ray was standing there with a bottle of champagne and a dozen of roses dressed in a tailored tux. He was very sharp. I grabbed the roses and put them in a vase. I smelled them. I ran over to him and kissed him. He popped the top, reached into his pocket, and came out with two champagne glasses. Champagne was everywhere. He said, "Baby, I want to take you out tonight."

"But Ray, I don't have anything to wear."

"Look, I know you have something to wear."

"No, I don't anything to match a tux."

"Now I can see that you don't have plans of going out because you have your hair in rollers."

"Oh how I wish I had something nice to wear."

"Why don't you go upstairs, put on your makeup, fix your hair, and I'll check the car to get my other clothes. Because, baby, we are going out on the town tonight."

I went upstairs to do just that. Not long, I heard Ray coming upstairs saying, "Go on, San. Get finished. I'll be changing."

When I came out the bathroom, there was a gorgeous, fitted, black and while striped gown laying on my bed. He had bought me some black satin shoes with matching purse. The man had exquisite taste.

"Ray, you did this for me? I don't believe it. Thank you."

"Stop thanking me and go on and get dressed. Besides, you deserve every bit of it and more. I'll be waiting for you downstairs. Okay? And don't be too long."

I was amazed. I got dressed and that gown laid on me as if it was made just for me. Everything fit perfectly. I found myself walking gracefully down the stairs. It was like I was making an entrance—a private entrance. He watched me glide down and said, "San, I don't ever want you to hide your beauty again. Did you look in the mirror?"

"Yes, I did."

"Tell me, what did you see?"

"I saw a different person."

"Here, baby. Here's a matching coat. Put your arms in."

"Ray, you are such a gentleman. I just don't know what to say."

"Come on, let's go baby."

We went outside and I said, "Ray, where's your car?"

"There it is."

"Where? The only car out here is that new Lincoln."

It was a Mark V, blue with a cream top. As he led us to it, I asked, "Is this yours?"

"This is why you haven't heard from me ...I've been trying to get this."

"Oh, it's beautiful."

He opened the door to let me in. He walked around to the other side as I watched him in amazement. All of this seemed like such a dream. I still couldn't believe it.

"We will take some pictures. How about that?"

"Where are we going?"

"My lady, your wish is my every command."

"Wait, Ray. I left the cocaine in the house."

"I'll go. You wait. Where did you put it?"

"It's on the table in the living room."

"Okay. Give me the keys."

"Oh, here you go!"

When he came back out, he also had the champagne and glasses. He said, "Here baby. We were leaving the champagne. Now where do you want to go?"

"Everything is so crowded ...I don't know."

"Well let me be your guide tonight."

"All right. Take me where you want to."

We went way out Peachtree Street to a club called The Rose. When we got there, it seemed like all eyes were on us. The hostess led us to a table for two. I noticed that it was carded "Reserved." I nudged Ray and whispered, "This table's reserved and there aren't anymore open."

He pulled out a fifty-dollar bill and while handing it to the hostess said, "No, baby. This table says, 'Ray and Family'"

After seating me, he leaned down and kissed me ever so gently. The club was beautiful. There were so many mirrors I could see myself all over the place. We had a great table. We drank more champagne than I had ever had and I was really feeling on of the effects: I got up to go to the restroom. When I got halfway there, I changed my mind and returned to the table. Ray asked, "What's wrong, baby?"

"Nothing ...it's just that I'm—"

"—shy and beautiful."

"It's just that it seems that everybody is watching me."

"Well! Look at yourself, San. You are something to watch. Go on to the bathroom."

"No. I can't."

"You want me to go with you?"

"No, no, no. I can wait."

We were there for about 45 minutes to an hour and then he said, "Are you about ready to leave?"

"Yeah, baby. I'm ready when you are. Now where to?"

"Well, how about my place?"

"I would love it."

We made it to his apartment. He went into his bedroom and got a Chinese smoking jacket for me. He said, "Here. Put this on."

I went into the bathroom, pulled my clothes off and put the smoke jacket on. He turned on some soft music. He turned all the lights down real low and asked, "Are you hungry?"

"Yeah, just a little bit."

"Well, why don't you fix us two T-bone steaks? They are all ready seasoned in the refrigerator."

"All right. I'll fix them."

I went into the kitchen and he yelled out, "I like blue cheese dressing and I bought you a large bottle of Pepsi since you like them so much."

I looked into the living room and saw him sitting with his head resting on the back of the sofa. I walked toward him thinking about how sweet he was. I got to him and straddled my legs over his lap and kissed him. I looked at him and said, "Ray? Ah, never mind. Let me go back and finish cooking these steaks."

"Tell me, baby. I want to know what's on your mind."

"No. I can't. Not right now."

"I think ...no...I will wait until you are ready to tell me."

Ray's phone rang. I could hear him, "Hello? Well not this morning ...I have company ...Would you call me back later? I don't know how much longer she will be here ...Look, I'll call you."

He hung up. The phone rang again.

"Yeah! I told you that I have company. Her name is Sandra ...Yes! She's a very special person to me. That's why she's with me on New Year's... "

I was straining so hard to hear until I almost burned the skillet ...

"Listen, I'll call you later, okay? I'm getting ready to eat." He hung the phone up, again and came into the kitchen where I was. He watched me prepare the steaks.

I said, "It's not ready, yet, but the salad is. Just sit down. You steak will be ready in a minute."

We sat and ate with dim lights. We finished eating and he smoked a cigarette. Then he pulled out the cocaine and said, "Here, baby. Take this while I roll a joint."

We went in the living room to enjoy the music. Then he said, "Just a little cocaine, baby. Okay? Too much and we will mess up our sex life."

After smoking the joint, he got real close up on me and said, "San? I have something that I want to tell you. I'm hoping that you will accept what I have to say. Please listen to me. I have more than just one lady. There's another one that you don't know about. I don't love her, either, but she's always there when I need her. I don't know what to do, but I do know that you really make me feel like I want to feel. You make me smile. You enjoy the things that I give you and I really like that. You are the one who really needs me. You see, San, I know for a fact that they will always be there for me. But you ...I'm scared."

"Why are you scared of me?"

"You are the type who might love me today and not tomorrow."

"No, Ray. Real love won't be like that." I got down on the floor and crossed my legs and I said to him, "Ray, I don't know what to say."

He got down beside me and said, "This is what I want you to know. I love you, San. I've been feeling this for quite some time. You can be all in one if you let yourself go."

He kissed me and we started making love on the floor. He said, "This is a night that you will always remember. I want you to relax and let all your feelings go ...just this one time. Don't be afraid, baby. Give yourself to me."

"I'll try, Ray."

I started to see the rainbow and its beautiful colors again. I moaned and said softly, "Ray?"

"Yes, baby? Tell me about it."

"I love you."

"Oh, San." He kissed me in my ear and on my neck and said, "Baby. Baby. Baby, do you really love me?"

"Ray? I'm ready!"

"Me too, baby. San! It's coming!"

"No, Ray. Not now. I don't take pills."

"I can't stop now. Baby, please don't fight it?"

"Oh, Ray!" I screamed out.

"Give it to me, baby."

"I do love you. I do."

We climaxed together. He grabbed my hair then he bit me on the jaw. He got up, went into the bathroom to get a towel, and came back and washed me off. Then he said, "Let'sgo to bed. I'm very weak. You've drained me dry."

I went to the bathroom and then to the bedroom. When I got there, Ray was knocked out. I got in the bed beside him. I leaned over and kissed him and said, "Good night, lover."

When we woke up it was 6:00 P.M. I said, "I've got to get home, Ray."

He was still tired and had a hangover. He said, "Take the car and go do what you have to do and come back to feed me."

I put my gown on that he bought me and went home to check on my apartment. I also checked to see whether Julio had made it back to town. I took a bath and put on a blue velvet warm-up suit. I made a call to Big H's. He had not heard anything. I called Sugar's: "May I speak to Sugar?"

"Hold on."

"Hello?" Sugar answered, "What's going on, honey?"

"Where have you been? I've been calling you?"

"I've been with Ray."

"What?"

"How about that?"

"How was it?"

"Girl, you would not believe it: he bought me some roses, took me out to a fabulous club and then you know what? Oh! He bought me a outfit that was sharp."

"How was it?"

"Girl, I think I'm in love ...no, I am in love."

"Ah hell. I've heard that before. So, you really had a good time, huh?"

"Sugar, it was like a dream. That man is bad, girl. But I got to hold back some of my feelings 'cause he's got two other women."

"Don't worry about them as long as he treats you right."

"Girl, he is so sweet."

"Julio hasn't gotten back yet. We've got to wait until he gets here."

"Oh, guess what? Ray has a new car and I'm driving it."

"You're lying."

"Okay. I'll be over to pick you up in it. I should be there in about 15 minutes."

I hung up the phone and rushed right over. I blew the horn and she came out laughing while saying, "Get down, Lil' Mama. He let you drive, huh?"

"Come on, let's go."

"Okay, but let me get my keys."

She went back into the house, got her keys and locked the door. I drove off. She started, "Girl, Ray really loves you."

"I don't know, Sugar. I can't really tell, right now."

"Why not?"

"I don't know. I just can't."

"Look. Did you take some pictures?"

"We sure did. I left it at the house. Well, where are we going now?"

' 'Let's go by Big H's house first, then back to my apartment. I got to go back over to Ray's house and fix him something to eat."

"Hum, I'm scared of you," she said while laughing. "You know that you like that nigga. In fact, you are in love and don't want to accept it. So, now give the man a chance. At least he's trying to show you that he really cares about you. Okay, so maybe he's playing a different way. Honey, just turn him a loose then you will see someone will have him before you count to 'three'. Ain't that what Joe Tex said? Yeah!"

"But I'm scared."

"Just take your time. He'll show and tell."

"Come on and get out and go with me."

Just as we reached the door Big H came out. I asked,

"Big H? What the deal is?"

"Where have you been? I just called your house."

"Is he here?"

"He'll be here in two hours."

"Let me go so I can call my customers to let them know. Let's go, Sugar. We've got to ride. So, Big H, call me as soon as he gets here, okay? I'll be waiting to hear from you."

We left and went back to my apartment. I made about 17 calls to let everybody know that I was in pocket. I then called Ray: "Hey, baby, I'm sorry that I haven't made it back there, yet. But my people are almost here so what I'm going to do is ..."

"Wait, baby. Just take care of your business and then come on to daddy, okay?"

"All right."

"I'm still tired and beat. Would you bring me some chicken noodle soup with you when you come?"

"What's wrong? Are you sick?"

"You should know. You did it to me."

"Okay, baby. As soon as I pick the thing up I'll be there."

"All right, love. I'll talk to you later."

"Okay, baby."

As soon as I hung up the phone, Sugar was on it, "So, what did he say?"

"He told me to 'take care of my business' then come."

"See, that's the kind of nigga I need."

"Come on, Sugar. Let's get the bags and cut ready."

While getting everything ready, the phone rang: "Hello?"

"Come on," Big H said.

"Okay, baby. I'm on my way."

"Bye."

"Sugar, finish this while I go get the cocaine." When I got there, I could see him pulling off. I ran in the house and asked, "Big H? Where is he going?"

"To the motel."

"Well, did he leave my stuff?"

"Yeah. He left you ten ounces this time plus your two."

"Wow! I'm going to roll now."

Aunt Hazel was in there ready to get down. She said, "Here, San baby. You want some?"

"Yeah. Give me a lil' one because I got to get moving."

I hit it and left. I stopped by the store and got some soup for Ray. Just as I made it to the apartment, I saw Sugar. She looked up at me and said, "Woo-wee! I ain't never seen that much dope in my life."

"Shit, me neither."

"What are you going to do? Are you going to fix it now or go over to Ray's house first?"

"I'll tell you what. We'll fix it when we get over there. Get the stuff and let's ride. Just put the cut and bags in a bag with the soup. I'll get the scale."

We went on over to Ray's house. I had the key so I opened the door and went in. I went straight to the kitchen, washed my hands, and fixed his soup. I took him a face cloth in the room so that he could wash his face. Then I said, "Come on, baby. Wake up so that you can eat your soup."

He groaned and stretched then said, "Okay, baby. Did you get straight?"

"Yeah. But I haven't fixed it up."

"Well, why don't you do it here?"

"I kissed him and said, "Thank you, baby. Let me get your soup, first."

I jumped up very quickly to get his soup. I served soup and orange juice to my patient. While handing him the soup, I said, "Baby? I brought Sugar with me to help. I hope that's all right?"

"You know that's all right, baby. Tell her I said 'hello.' What's wrong?"

"I told you. I ...well, it can'tbe 'that.'"

"But it is. You might be pregnant."

"Naw. I doubt that."

"You better check yourself, baby, because this my baby giving month."

"I ain't worried about that, all right?"

"You can't say that I didn't warn you."

"I ain't worried about that, all right?" I laughed and went back to the kitchen. Sugar and I fixed up all the cocaine. I came up with 20 ounces. I had 15 whole ounces, eight quarters, 16 eighths, plus an ounce of nothing but quarters and fifties for Meathead. There were a few rocks left. I kept them out for us to snort. We snorted and snorted. Plus, I still had my two ounces. I'll cut them up later. Then Sugar said, "We better leave. You know that you called all those people?"

"Yeah, let me tell Ray."

I went into his room. He was sound asleep. I went back into the kitchen and said, "Guess what, Sugar?"

"What?"

"Ray is knocked out cold."

"Well, we've got to go."

"I'll leave a note because I know that he don't feel like driving."

I left a note and some cocaine. The note read:

Baby, I went to take care of a little business. If you need me, please call. And don't snort too much of this blow."

We left and went straight to my apartment. Before we could get in the door, the phone started ringing. I ran in to grab it. I answered: "Hello?"

"Hey, it's Duey. Are you straight?"

"Yeah, come on."

"Later."

I hung up the phone and just moments later, it rang again. Niggers were in and out the rest of the night. We finished up around 4:30 that morning. Ray still had not called. I said to Sugar, "You can drive my car home so that you won't have to catch a cab in the morning."

Just then Jeff called: "Hello?"

"Baby, are you ready?"

"I guess so. I'm really tired. Are you coming right on?"

"I'm on my way." I hung up the phone and started back talking to Sugar, "Jeff will be the last because I'm beat." It seemed like it took forever for him to come. When he did knock, Sugar opened the door. I was all ready for him when he got there. I asked, "What can I do for you?"

"Let me get three ounces and owe you $500."

"Okay, you got it."

He gave me $4,000 and then left.

"Sugar, you can leave when you are ready."

"I think I'm going to leave here in the morning. I have got to pick Ann up on the way to work."

"Okay, then. Well, since you and Poo-Poo are here, I am going over to Ray's house. He will bring me back in the morning sometime."

"Okay," said Sugar.

I left and went on over to Ray's. When I got there, the note was still where I left it. I took a shower, got in the bed and went fast asleep.

I woke up about 12:30 the next afternoon. Ray was gone. I sat up in the bed and said, "Damn! He didn't even bother to wake me up."

I got up and washed my face and brushed my teeth, then I heard the bathroom door open. It was Ray with a lot of gold chains and watches. He even had some diamond watches. I still had the toothbrush in my mouth when I asked, "How in the hell ..."

"Just pick what you want."

"But Ray?"

"Will you do like I asked?"

"Okay."

I finished up brushing my teeth and marveled over all the gold and diamonds. I picked a little thin chain and a gold watch. "Is that all you want?"

"Yeah."

"Sit down a minute. Listen baby. With the money that you are making you have got to learn about quality, okay? Now here." He handed me a $1,000 watch and a $500 chain (they were tagged).

"Ray, this cost too much."

He looked at me and said, "San, nothing is too much for you. Take it. I want you to have it, okay?"

"Okay."

"Now, what I want you to do is buy the things of your dreams. You see how my apartment looks?"

"Yeah."

He held my shoulders and looked me straight in my eyes and said, "Hey baby, yours is suppose to look way better than mine. Take you money and use it. Get you what you want. Don't just sit on the money and wish for it."

I smiled and said, "Okay. I'm going to do just that."

"Now, are you hungry?"

"Did you bring something to eat with you?"

"No, but let's go get something. Then you've got to go to work and I got to get out and sell some of this jewelry."

I put the watch and chain on the dresser. He looked at me and said, "Now, baby. Come here. Hand that to me."

I gave him back the watch and chain. He turned me around and said, "You are wearing this." He locked the chain and turned me back around facing him. He kissed me then said, "I love you very much."

"I love you, too."

"Okay. Then wear this for me with your pretty self. Come on. Let's go."

He put the rest of the chains and watches in a bag then we left. He had on a pretty rose colored pants and shirt with rose shoes. I had on a beige warm-up suit. I had my hair back in ponytails. We went to the Lobster's and ate some red snapper. It was right around the corner from my apartment. We finished eating and he dropped me off back home. We kissed and said goodbye ...for now. The children hadn't got home from school and Poo-Poo was not there. The house was clean. I called Sugar to find out where she put the cocaine. It was under my mattress. The phone started to ring; it was Meathead. "Hello?"

"I'm ready."

"Okay, Meat. You've got to come my way because I don't have a car."

"I've got to get a ride, but I'll be there shortly so don'tgo no where."

"I ain't."

"Okay."

"Bye."

"Bye, baby, bye."

Will called. He wanted to get a quarter. Duey called and wanted to get a half ounce. My children came in. They looked at me and asked,

"May we go to the movies?"

"Yes, babies, you may go."

I asked what kind of movie they were going to see and they convinced me it was kids. I called a taxi for them and off they went.

I checked in with my mother. "Hey, Mama. What you doing, baby?"

"Nothing, just here."

"Mama! Guess what? I've met a man and he's very nice to me. I want you to meet him. He gave me a dress, bag, shoes, watch, and a chain to go around my neck. They are very pretty."

"He gave you all that?"

"Un-huh. Mama, you will like him."

"He ain't married, is he?"

"No, Mama. You know I don't like married men anymore."

"Okay, then. That's what I want to hear."

"I'm just calling to check on my child."

"I'm doing all right."

"Okay, honey. I'll talk to you later."

Shortly after I got off the phone with Mama, Ray called. "Hello?"

"Hey, baby!"

"I'm doing fine. These niggers got me working hard, real hard. Hey, I talked to my mama. I told her about you."

"You did?"

"Yeah."

"Well, what did she say?"

"She wants to meet you."

"Let's go over there now."

"Not now, baby. Let's go another time ...like when I'm not working."

"Okay then. Listen, I need to get a quarter. Tonya and I will be by there, okay?"

"Okay. Listen, does she know anything about us?"

"No. Does it matter?"

"In a way it does."

"Why?"

"Because she might get upset with me and put the police on me and you."

"Naw, she wouldn't do anything like that."

"You don't know, baby. Women are low down at times."

"Well, if she does find out about us, let me handle it. Okay?"

"Okay, whatever you say."

"See you in a minute."

"Okay, baby."

"Bye."

I ran in the bathroom, put on a little makeup; let my hair down so that she could see me in another way. It was strange. I wanted her to know about Ray and me, but I didn't want to tell her. When they arrived, as usual, I invited them in. Tonya said, "Girl, I didn't even recognize who you were. You are looking good!"

"Well, thank you."

I noticed that Ray was staring at me. I could actually feel it. Tonya continued, "Hey, I'm not trying to rush you, babe, but Ray and I have got to go."

"Oh? I'm sorry ..."

"Naw, naw, it ain't nothing like that. It's just that we have got to get out and sell a few things."

"Oh okay. Here's your quarter."

"Thanks, girl." They got it, paid cash for it, and left.

Moments later, the phone rang. "Hello?"

"What are you doing?" Sugar asked.

"Nothing. Ray and Tonya just left."

"Oh yeah?"

"Un-huh. Girl, he gave me a watch and a chain. They're really pretty."

"Girl, that's all right! And you say Ray and Tonya just left?"

"Yeah, but everything's still cool. She ain't got a clue."

"Listen, San. Are you going to play softball this year?" "You know damn well I am. The team won't be nothing without the clown."

"Well the coach called and said that our meetings will start next week. He wants your new number."

"Okay. Give it to him."

"All right. I'm on my way over there."

"Okay. I'll talk to you then." We hung up the phones.

Shortly after, Sugar was right over. Before she parked the car, the phone rang, again. This time it was my children.

"Hello?"

"Hello, San. This is Harry. We are ready to come home."

"Okay. Sugar will be right there. Ya'll wait for her, okay?"

"Okay."

"Bye-bye." I ran out the door to tell her to go pick up my kids at South Dekalb Mall. She got them and brought them home. I fed them and sent them upstairs to watch TV. Around this time, Poo-Poo walked in. "Good evening, everybody. What's up?"

"Nothing much. Look, brother, we have got to make a run. Will you hang 'til we get back?"

"What's what?"

"Remember what I told you?" I was looking over at Sugar. She knew and she responded while nodding her head, "Yeah."

"Well, I'm ready."

I dialed Jeff's number and asked, "Is Jeff there?"

"Yeah. Hold on for a second?"

"Sure."

It wasn't long and Jeff answered, "Yeah."

"Well what's going on?"

"I was just trying to call you. I got someone here who buys plenty of blow; I'm talking about sho' nuff, sho' nuff."

"So, ah, where are you?"

"I'm over in Ben Hill."

Sugar was right there, listening. I winked my eye at her while talking to Jeff. "So what do you need?"

"I need four or five ounces."

"Well you're on time, baby. I just picked up six ounces. "I'll be there in a few minutes."

"Bye."

I hung up the phone and said to Sugar, "Come on. Let's ride. We've got to go all the way to Greenbriar."

We got in the car and took off. While riding, I said, "I told you, Sugar, I've got to have all of his people nigger's got."

"Let's get him, sister."

"We're going to be tough when we learn how to shoot. Damn! I left them guns ...We don't need them right now, anyway."

We made it to the apartment and from my knock a voice from the other side of the door asked, "Yeah?"

"It's San. Bo, open the door."

He immediately opened and greeted us, "Hey! How are you ladies doing tonight?"

"Oh, just fine."

"You can go on to the back, San. He's waiting for you."

I walked in. There was a guy in there with a tuxedo on ...looking like a waiter or something. Then I heard Jeff's voice, "Hey, baby! This is Bud; Bud meet San."

"Pleased to meet ya'. Look here, Ms. San, I want to get five ounces if the price is right. How much will you let me have five ounces for?"

"Let me see .... Jeff, can I borrow your pencil?"

"Oh sure, baby. Here you go," he said as he handed me the pencil. I did my calculations; looked up and asked, "How about $6,500? That's $1,300 an ounce."

"It's a deal. Now let me check out the cocaine?" I pulled out one ounce, gave it to him, and he checked it. While Jeff was snorting, I was busy writing my number down for Bud. When Bud handed me the money, I slipped him my telephone number with the other four ounces. I gave Jeff a quarter for getting the sale for me. Bud looked at me and said, "Thank you, baby. I'll be in touch."

He left then I left. Sugar and I rode off, heading to Summer Hill. I couldn't wait to tell her, "Sugar, I slipped my number to that guy named Bud. Honey, he bought five ounces."

"Say what?"

"He sure did." Sugar just looked shocked. I noticed we had made it to Summer Hill and I went on to say, "Let's see if Meathead is over here."

We looked up Georgia Ave. There was no sign on Meat. Then Sugar yelled, "San! Keep on driving the police is behind you."

I looked in the rearview window and said, "Damn! I wonder where are they going? I'm turning down Conelly Street to see if they are following us." Sure enough, they turned too. The blue light came on. I said while taking my license out of the glove box, "What does he want?"

I eased my pouch under the seat. I pulled to the side and waited for the officer to come to the car. I could tell he was checking my tag number. After a few minutes, he approached the window and asked, "May I see your license and insurance card, ma'am?"

Somewhat, prepared, I handed over my license then said, "I'm sorry, officer."

I turned to Sugar and said, "Look in the dash and give me that insurance card." She went right to it; handed it to me and I passed it to the officer. "Officer, did I do something wrong?"

"No, but your inspection sticker has expired."

"Oh wow!"

"I'm writing you a ticket for your expired sticker. When you come to the court, just bring the receipt with you and you won't be charged." He handed me the ticket and continued, "Here is your license and insurance card, ma'am. Now, you be sure to get that sticker before you come to court."

"All right. Thank you, officer."

He walked away as I was rolling up the window. I cranked the car as I said aloud: "Thank you, Jesus."

"You know what, Sugar?"

"What?"

"We need to go to church."

"You are right about that."

"We really need to give the Lord some of our time and money. We need to think about going—real soon."

We went back to Decatur because that police made my last nerve bad. Time went by ...day by day ...everyday, all day, I sold eighths, quarters, ounces, and ounces. I rolled month in and month out: January, February, March ...

8

It was softball season. We had started practice. Niggers were meeting me on the softball field. One night after practice, I said to Sugar, "Come go to Hugh's Furniture with me in the morning. I'm going to buy me some new furniture. She looked at me and said, "What?"

"Yep. I'm ready to dress my living room and dining room."

"Okay. What time will you be leaving?"

"If you spend the night, we can get there when the store opens. I'm so glad."

"Yeah, that's sounds good to me."

The next morning we got on up and I put on some cutoff jeans and a vest with a red scarf on my head. I didn't even bother about putting on shoes. Sugar had on a jogging suit and tennis shoes. We drove all the way to Buckhead. Neither one of us knew where it was, but Sugar and I were determined to find it. We drove down the main street looking to the left and right. We finally spotted it. I said, "There it is, Sugar. Right there on the left."

I parked the car and we went in. The salesman was on the phone. He looked at us yet kept on talking on the phone.

I said to Sugar, "That motherfucker must think we ain't got no money ...coming in here dressed like this. Probably wondering why we came way out here."

He stayed on the phone for 30 minutes. That worked out just fine. I went ahead and picked out what I wanted. I strolled over to the desk where he sat (still) talking on the phone and said, "Hey! I'm ready to buy."

"All right, I'll be right with you in a minute."

I stood at the desk until he got off the phone. He asked, "May I help you?"

"Yes, you may."

While pointing, I said, "I want that pit-like sofa over there. That beige mohair, there ..."

"Oh, that cost is $3500."

"So. I want it." I went on walking and pointing,

"I'll take this pyramid table ..."

"That's $1,400."

"Thank you, sir. I want it, too. Oh, ah, let me get that glass table with the chocolate high back chairs."

He wrote it all up and I dictated. I didn't tell him I was paying cash. I let him write it all down on his finance company's application. He didn't even bother to ask if that was necessary. It took him about 20 minutes then he asked, "Your name, please."

"Susie Jones."

"Where should we deliver it, if it's approved?"

"23 Eastwyck Road, Decatur."

"Sign here, please."

I looked at him and said, "If it matters, I'm paying cash."

He cleared his throat and said, "What? You must be a bookie?"

"No, just 'nobody's average business woman.'" That furniture cost me $7000. I counted out every dollar to him. All he could say was, "Ma'am, this will be delivered on Wednesday if that meets your approval? Will anyone be at home?"

"I'll be there."

"Oh! Don't forget the interior decorator. The sign says it's free."

We left there and went to Sears. I bought a washer and dryer. We went to Radio Shack and I bought a stereo system. From there we went to Rich's and bought some drapes, curtains for the kitchen and patio. That just about rapped up the spree. We went on home. When we got there Sugar said, "Damn, San. You've spent $10,000 ...all in one day."

"I'll make it back. I've got to spend in order to receive. They will deliver the stuff from Sears tomorrow and next week the living room furniture will be here."

We put the drapes and curtains up. They looked great. So great until they made my carpet look bad. I called the carpet cleaners and made an appointment with them. They came out the next day and it had that Chocolate carpet looking and smelling like new. Between the carpet and the window treatment, it was laid out, even before the furniture arrived.

Ray was out of town. I wanted to surprise him on Monday when he was due back.

I got sick, feeling real lousy. I was throwing up all over everything. Sugar called and I barely made it to the phone because I was just that weak.

"Hello?"

"What's happening, girl?"

"Sugar, can you come over? I'm sick."

"I'm on my way."

"Please hurry."

I don't even know how or if the phone got back on the hook. It seemed forever, but Sugar did get a ride and rushed right over. She found me lying on the sofa. She took a look at me and asked, "Do you want to go to the doctor's office?

"No, just get me some soup."

After she fixed it, I ate a little of it and threw it right back up. I asked, "Damn, Sugar, what's wrong with me?" She looked at me and starting laughing, then said, "Shit, I ain't no doctor, but I'd say you are pregnant."

"Un-un. Bullshit. I can't be. I don't want no baby ...not now. I can't be... "

"You just might be."

"What am I going to do? I can't have no baby." I started crying.

Sugar consoled me, "Don't cry, just go to the doctor and get yourself checked out. Hey, I have been known to make a bad call but not often."

We got ready to go to see Dr. Jackson. After a few moments with him he said, "Ms. Whitt, I can tell right now that I'm going to give you a pregnancy test." While handing me a card, he continued, "You get in touch with this office on Monday."

"Okay, doctor."

It was Wednesday when they delivered my furniture. Everything was placed as I directed. It was such a transformation and it kind of made me feel better. I was home alone. Just as I was enjoying myself, I jumped up, ran to the bathroom and threw up again. Just as I was freshening up, there was a knock at the bathroom door. It was Ray. He took one look at me and asked, "Baby, what's wrong?"

"Ray, I'm sick. I've been sick for about a week."

"Hey, I've been sick, also. I told you, baby, on New Year's morning that you were pregnant."

"Ray! I love you."

He looked around at me and said, "Baby ...," He kissed me as he walked me to the living room. I stopped and said, "Thanks, for listening to me."

"Girl, you are something else. I love you so much."

Just then he focused on the table and then looked the whole living room over and said, "Wow! This is bad! What else did you buy?"

"A washer and dryer."

"That's the way you do it, baby. Now, back to you. What do you want to do? I'll agree to whatever you say."

"Baby, you and I are not ready for a baby. Ray, what do you want?"

"Baby, whatever you say, I'm for it."

"Okay. I want to play ball. I'm not ready for a baby."

"All right. But I want you to know that I am going with you."

I went to have an abortion. Ray not only went with me, but stayed and took care of me. He helped sell the cocaine because I was so weak. A month had passed; softball season was open. The only thing was I had to wait another two weeks before I could play. Ray was helping me with my children; he cooked for us; he waited on me "hand and foot." After my two weeks were up, I looked at Ray and said, "Thank you, baby, for being here when I needed you the most. I love you very much."

He looked back at me and asked, "You know what?"

I smiled and asked, "What?"

"If we get married, our understanding would be beautiful because you can deal with anything. San, I will always love you."

"Ray, you are one of a kind and I will always love you, too."

We kissed then he asked, "Are you taking the pill, now?"

"Yeah, baby, and believe me—I am ready for you."

We made love and this time it was better. It was like our love had grown deeper.

He rolled over and said, "Damn, girl. I don't know what I'm gonna do with you."

The phone rang. While I answered, he got up and took a shower. "Hello?"

"Are you going to practice?"

"Yeah. I'll stop by and pick you up, Sugar."

"Okay. Later."

"Later."

I got up and took a shower, also. While dressing Ray said, "I'm going to leave, baby, because I've got to take care of some business."

I opened my pouch, pulled out an ounce and said, "Here, baby. Get straight and pay your bills."

"Oh, baby, thank you. This one will lead to two. I'll be back. I've got to go, okay? I love you."

"Lock the door behind you."

He threw me a kiss and I finished dressing, then left right after he did. I picked Sugar up and we went to Pitt Park for practice. Duey met me out there to get a quarter. After the game, my coach, Sugar, and myself got fucked up. We snorted a while then we left. I went home. I was thinking about a girl that played left field with us. Her name was Diane. We called her Soul. I looked Soul's phone number up but couldn't find her in the book but I did find her mother's number. Her mother was a saved and sanctified woman of God. I called her because I couldn't find Soul's number.

"Hello?"

"Hello, Ms. Mae, how are you? This is San."

"Baby, I've been trying to reach you. The Lord came to me and told me to tell you to move, move!"

"Why? Where? What's wrong, Ms. Mae. What have I done?"

"Move, child!"

"How much time do I have? Where am I suppose to move to?"

"Baby, don't let the devil trick you. The police is coming."

"Okay. I will."

I didn't even bother to ask about Diane. I got off the phone and for one week, I looked for an apartment, but couldn't find one. I called Aunt Hazel and told her that I needed to move for a little while. She told me come live in her house with the children and she would get an apartment in the back.

I couldn't get in touch with Ray so I had called my brothers. They all came over to help me move. We got out of my apartment and had moved everything in the house in that same day— 257 Eugenia Street—my new residence. I had my phone transferred on the day that I moved. I had to go back over to the apartment to make sure that everything was out. Nothing was left unturned. I was back in my car pulling out, I noticed two narcotic cars coming down the street. I kept driving as if I didn't see them. A red traffic light caught me and I said aloud, "Thank you, Lord Jesus. Thank you." I smiled and went on home to my new quarters.

We gave the place a make over: the walls were painted beige, the woodwork chocolate. From the entrance, the living room was on the right, my daughter's bedroom was in the middle, and my son's bedroom was on the left, and my room was behind his. The kitchen had Old English brick walls. Its flooring was bricked with the same pattern as its throw rug. I found some curtains from Rich's that matched perfectly. I really fixed up the place.

All my people were still coming strong. It was like I hadn't moved; it didn't matter. I made even money. The money got so good to me until I broke down and started selling some fifties and grams myself.

Months went by and it was time for the school year to end on June 2nd. I allowed my children to go to my mother's for the summer. This way I could really sell some cocaine. I had a 24hour-a-day business right in my house. It seemed like people from everywhere came through.

I went to the plaza on Richardson Street. I notice that the cafe´ was going out of business. That gave me an idea. I went in and talked to the owners about their business. They gave me a lot of information. I went out to the leasing office and checked it out even more. I found out that the rent was $200 a month, and to get in you'd have to pay that plus one in advance. I got all the junkies together so that I could put them to work. We went to the restaurant supply store. I spent over $5,000 in cash. We then went to Color Tile where I spent over $1,000. We got paint, mirrors, glass, and more with $500. I spent at least $700 in Handy City for panel. The boosters got all my dishes and silverware. I stopped by the flower shop to buy some silk plants. My last stop was Rich's, where I purchased curtains.

The restaurant had yellow walls with brown tile. The bar was brown panel with diamond-shaped mirrors all over sides. The ceiling was yellow and the booths were orange and the tables were antique white. The countertop was white, too. We stocked the whole place up in about two weeks. There were his and hers restrooms. They were really nice. We sold everything except beer and wine. I had applied for a liquor license. I posted a NO DRUGS ALLOWED sign. Lots of work and money had gone into this place and everyone who helped was excited about the upcoming Grand Opening.

The Grand Opening was on June 30th. My Aunt Hazel, Aunt Sara, my mother, and Sugar all helped me run the place. We had a softball game that night. After winning the game, everybody came back to the restaurant. None of them wanted to buy anything, they were just being nosey.

That night I met a white girl who didn't want her baby. Her name was Sandra—she had red hair and blue eyes. She was a dancer at a topless bar downtown. We talked. I asked, "So, what are you going to do with your baby?"

"I don't know. I can't take care of it and my mother won't accept a mixed child."

"I'll keep him."

"Will you really?"

"Yeah. Bring him to me. You know where I live."

She got the little boy and brought him to me. He was loving. He was only four months old. To look at him you wouldn't believe that he lacked TLC. I knew that I would take good care of him. While dropping him off, Sandra said, "I will pay you every week for taking care of him."

"No, baby. You don't have to, that way. What I want you to do is help me with this cocaine that I have. I know there are plenty of people in that club that want it, huh?"

"Oh, hell yeah. I can sell a whole lot of grams."

"Well I'll start you with about ten a day, okay?"

"Okay, but I want you to know—I don't mess with no drugs."

"Damn, I didn't know that. That's good."

For about two weeks straight, Sandra sold plenty of cocaine. She brought all kinds of dancers to me—most of them were white girls and some of her white tricks. Just as we were on a roll, it happened. A nigger name Jack, a paid informant, came in the restaurant. He was a skinny little ugly motherfucker. My aunt knew him very well. He had a big nose, big lips, and a little head. He was about five feet ten inches and weighed 140 pounds. He knew me when I was a kid. He walked over to me and said, "Hey, Slick. I heard that you were taking care of plenty business throughout Atlanta. The word is out that you are the top dope seller here. They say that you got enough cocaine to supply ten motherfuckers with three ounces apiece. And that's not counting your small people. Let me get in on the action."

"Whatever I do is my motherfucking business; whenever and however I want to do it. It's my goddamn business."

"But I'm going to make it mine, too. You better listen to what I'm trying to tell you. You see, I know some people down at the law office."

"Fuck that law office, nigger. They got to catch me first."

"But baby, what I'm trying to tell you is they already know."

"Nigger, kiss my ass and get the fuck out of my face."

I had gotten loud because I was mad as hell.

"Well don't get upset," he said.

"Fuck you, you ugly fucker."

My aunt came over and said, "What's wrong?"

"THIS!" I said, pointing to him. "You need to talk to him because I ain't."

I started stacking dishes fast, throwing pots and silverware. Then I stopped and looked at him while he spoke to Aunt Hazel. She looked real scared, so I walked back over there and said, "Hey 'Jack,' get the fuck out, and I mean right now."

"Okay, baby, but I'll be back."

"You don't scare me, nigger. Go and get the goddamn police. I don't give a fuck ...and ah, bring your mammy ...you ugly son-of-a bitch. Suck my ass, you jive-ass bastard."

Needless to say, he left out. I turned to Aunt Hazel and said, "I can't stand him."

"San, you might need to talk to him."

"For what? I ain't about to kiss no motherfucker's ass to get along with him."

"But San, he can be a lowdown dirty motherfucker."

"I don't care. Let him do whatever. I don't care. He gets nothing here. Who does he think he is anyway?"

The next day he came back and said, "There's a warrant out on you and I'm talking a real live one."

My eyes opened widely at first then my second thought was that he was just trying to scare me. Then I said, "Well let them use it then. I ain't running. Tell them to come and get me."

"They want you to come to them."

"For what?"

"You'll find out. Why don't you just come and go with me. Maybe I can straighten things out."

"Why do I have to come with you? Why don't they come and get me?"

"If you turn yourself in, it will be better on you."

Aunt Hazel was there and she said, "San, go on down there and see what they want."

"Let me make a few phone calls first."

Then he said, "I'm just kidding."

"Look man—what do you want?"

"I need some work."

"Well, I ain't got none. Go get some from somebody else."

"Oh, you are just like that, huh?"

"Yep. Bye."

I turned to Aunt Hazel and said, "Damn, it looks like trouble with him, but I got something for his ass."

He left and didn't come back for three months. And when he did come, he wanted some cocaine. He had about $6,000 in cash. He asked, "Can you get me this much cocaine?"

"Hold on. Let me make a call."

I called Floridian Cubans that I knew. I gave them the low down on him. They told me to 'bring him on.' I went back to the asshole and said, "Listen, Jack. I can get you the cocaine only if we go to Florida."

"Okay. When?"

"We can leave tomorrow."

We boarded Delta's jet going to Miami, Florida. After getting there, I called to let them know that we had arrived. We checked into a motel and waited for my people. They came right over and brought the cocaine with them. One of the guys said, while looking at the 'asshole,'"No one fucks with San, man. I mean no one." They made the exchange and walked on out the door. Jack looked at me and said, " 'You are one dirty bitch. You brought me down here to be killed."

"What?" I asked with a grin on my face.

"I ain't going back with this shit, they are going to kill me. Here." He was trying to hand me the cocaine. "You take it back. I ain't going to get on that jet. You're having me set up. I'm going to call Aunt Hazel."

"Go on. Call her. There is nothing that she can do because see, big nose, they own this motel. Any call going out they will be on your ass like milk in ice cream." He pulled his gun out. I looked at it and him then said, "Do it, nigger, and you'll die, too."

"Bitch, you ain't shit. You are in the syndicate, you lowdown bitch."

"So what if I am, snitcher, what you got to tell? And if you do go running off at the mouth, I wonder what would happen to you?" I couldn't help but start laughing. I could see that he was the one that was scared this time around. I couldn't take it anymore so I said, "Come on, man. Let's go. Cut all the bullshit out. Let's ride."

"Are you crazy? Something might happen to me."

"No, you ain't done nothing ...yet."

"Well, before we leave, let me shoot some first."

He tied his arm up and shot some of the pure cocaine. He looked at me with this really strange look on his face. The next thing I saw, he fell to his knees and started looking under the bed, in the bathroom, out the window, and in the closet. He turned out all the lights and at that point, I said, "What in the hell is wrong with you, man? Turn those lights back on."

"No, no! Don't touch them. Somebody's coming. Be quiet."

I laughed for a while.

"Y'all trying to kill me," he said while looking out the window. "I've got to get out of here."

I had never seen nothing like this before. I said, "Jack, ain't nobody out there."

"Shut up. Be quiet."

I turned the lights back on. He looked at the door and asked, "Do you hear 'em? They are coming."

He threw the gun on the bed and got under it. That was some sho 'nuff funny shit. I started back laughing so hard until I cried. Then I said, "Come on out, you motherfucker, you. You so scary, motherfucker ..."

He finally came from under the bed and somewhat calmly said, "Let's go. You carry the dope."

"Oh, no. I ain't going to help you get the shit and take it back, too."

"Well, leave it then," he said.

"Damn, you really are scared. Come on, man, let's go. I've got to get back."

As I started to go out of the door I heard him say, "Close that damn door, fool. They might get you, too."

"Man! Go to hell. Ain't nobody going to bother you."

"Sh-h-i-t, let's wait a few more minutes."

Reluctantly I agreed to wait for what turned out to be 30 minutes. All of a sudden he said, "Let's go."

This fool was so messed up, he left his gun. But who knows, maybe it was intentional. He packed the cocaine in his jacket pocket. And off we were.

We boarded Delta on our way back home. When we got there, he was still scared. He said, "I need some cut and a place to cut it up."

We went over to Sugar's house. We had everything but the scale. He shot some more and started acting a fool, again. Sugar noticed him and said, "Damn, what's wrong with this nigger ...he's all up under my bed and shit. He has even turned the lights out."

I just laughed then Sugar and I talked him from under the bed. He started looking out the window and that's when I said, "Okay, let's go to the restaurant."

We left out and he had the dope on him. I got out of the car in front of the restaurant. He was telling Sugar to park across the street so the police wouldn't see us. I laughed and went to the corner to wait and see what he was up to. After they parked, they got out and he had given Sugar the 'bag.' I could hear him saying, "Sugar, you walk on the other side of the street and I'll stay over here."

Sugar crossed over and was nearly running toward the restaurant. He yelled to her, "You're walking too fast!"

Sugar came over to where I was laughing and said, "Don't you ever bring this mother fucker around me anymore. This nigger's crazy." I was still laughing when he approached us and said, "See, San's laughing, these motherfuckers out here don't be playing."

He was looking all around. I said, "Come on, let's go in."

We all went inside and joined Aunt Hazel. Then he said, "Aunt Hazel! These dirty bitches are trying to kill me. Tell 'em I was just teasing. Don't let them whores kill me."

Aunt Hazel, Sugar, and I just fell out laughing. We all tripped off him a little while longer then I checked out how everything was going. Everything was in order, so we decided to go on back to Sugar's house. This time, we bagged his shit up. Just as we were on the way out of the door he yelled, "Hell naw. I ain't going to let y'all leave me."

"Well your ass can go."

"I ain't going nowhere. You motherfuckers want to kill me, so you just going to have to do it here."

"Come on, man," I said. "It's late."

"No, no. Don't open that door. Don't kill me. Y'all can have the cocaine."

"Come on here. Just get in the car and you can look out the window all you want. Sugar, give me a sheet so I can cover up the window. You need to leave that sheet along, man."

"Just be quiet will you?" he asked.

We all sat and watched him go through all his changes. When he finally came down, he was ready to ride. So basically, he had brought us to the restaurant and when he was ready to leave, he left. He didn't even bother about whether we needed a ride or not. But it really didn't matter. He had done enough for one day/night. We were still laughing ...we all were in tears. Sugar and I went on still explaining to Aunt Hazel how his weird ass had tripped earlier. Aunt Hazel said, "I could have told ya'all how that nigger be carrying on. He's a real live nut."

"But Aunt Hazel," I said, "he actually got under the bed."

"Y'all need to see him when he barks like a dog."

We busted out laughing, again.

"I don't think I want to see that." Sugar said. "That nigger is scary, real scary."

"Honey, he was that way in Miami," I said.

"Well, we'd better close it on up. The crowd is thinning on out."

It was almost Thanksgiving, again ...Another year gone. I had planned to spend a nice evening at home alone because Ray had made plans to go out of town with his friends. Bud called: "Hello?"

"Hi, San. This is Bud. What's good for me?"

"Same ol' same ol.'"

"You still in that Atlanta spot, right?"

"Yes, I am."

"Well how long will you be there?"

"I'll be here the rest of the night."

"All right, baby. Check you in little while."

Bud came and left. I called Sugar: "Hello?"

"Hey, girl. What are you doing?"

"Nothing much."

"Are you having Thanksgiving Eve's company?"

"Not tonight."

"What about tomorrow?"

"I ain't got nothing planned."

"Well, let's spend the evening over to your house. Ray is leaving town tomorrow."

"Damn, girl, at a time like this? You're really lonely, huh?"

"Yeah. But we will have a good time tomorrow anyway."

The next day I went over to Sugar's house. She had dinner already prepared, well her mother had dinner already prepared. It was 7:30 and we had the music going and snorting cocaine, too. Just as we were getting down, we heard a knock on the door. We both looked at each other and I said, "I wonder who that is."

"I don't know," Sugar said, "I ain't expecting any company."

"Well open the door because they've already seen my car." Sugar opened the door to Ray. I had my back to the door when I asked, "Sugar, who is it?"

She didn't answer so I turned to see for myself, but before I got all the way around, he had made it to my face. Surprised, I said, "Ray! I thought you were gone."

"Your vibes wouldn't let me go. Baby, I brought some cognac." He led me to the couch and continued, "Baby, tell me something. Where would you like to go?"

"Let me think ...how about Tennessee?"

"Your wish is my command! Let's ride!"

"Well, can Sugar ride with us?"

"Yes."

I was so excited and happy. Ray really made my day. All the pain had gone all at once. We rode all the way to the Tennessee line then turned around. We went back to Sugar's house to get my car. He followed me home, but he didn't stay. We both agreed that tomorrow would be a good day.

Jeff called that night: "Hello?"

"Hey, baby, long time, no hear."

"Well I've been kind of busy. How about you?"

"Are you in the bed?"

"Not yet, but I'm headed there."

"Well, it can wait until tomorrow, or later."

"Okay, Jeff. I'll talk to you later."

I hung up thinking, "that was kind of weird," but I didn't think much else about it.

Thanksgiving was over and now it was X-mas time and another New Year's coming in. I sold cocaine real heavy in the months of

December, January, February, and March. I had made about $40,000 cash—clear dollars. Then we were out of cocaine again.

Big H called. He wanted me to come over because he had something very important to discuss. I left and went straight over. He said that he had talked to Julio. He wouldn't be supplying us anymore cocaine ...until May. I couldn't believe it. That was two months from now. "What?" I yelled. "I know but ...we can go to Miami and pick it up."

"Oh, that will work. When can we leave?"

"I've already rented a car."

"A car? No way! Let's fly."

"You mean in the air?"

"Yeah. It's time for you to take a trip in the air."

"Listen, Mina is going with us."

"Okay."

"And you can bring Sugar along if you want. There's one condition; none of you can tell a soul ...I mean no one, not even your mama."

"Okay, we won't. I'm going on now and ride to Sugar's house. What time are we leaving?"

"We can leave in the morning. We will make the reservations. I've got to get my things together."

"Yeah, me too. My brother will be with my children ...no I'm going to take them to my mama's house."

"Wait a minute. We'll only be gone for a day."

"Oh, is that all? Okay then, everything's fine the way it is."

"We will leave about 9:00."

"Okay."

I went over to Sugar's house and explained to her what was going on. She agreed to it. We got up the next morning and packed. We both had on blue warm-ups, tennis shoes, and carried tennis racquets. The plan was we were playing the role of tennis players. When we got there, we called a cab. The flight was scheduled to leave at 11:15, so we got to the airport at 10:30. We got our tickets and went on to the gate and waited for boarding. While on the jet, my aunt and uncle were a little scared, being that this was their first flight. It was Sugar's first, too.

We arrived in Miami about noon. Big H had all the information. We took a cab to the motel on the Cuban side of town. We were expected and the guy at the front desk gave Big H the key to our room. When we entered our eyes bucked at all the guns ...wall to wall guns: machine guns, cannons, and many others that I couldn't identify. No sooner than we shut the door, there was a knock on it. Startled, we all looked at each other. My uncle answered it. He told us that he was leaving, but would be right back. After he left, Mina asked, "San, do you think they are going to kill us?"

"For what?" I asked, "Hell, we ain't done nothing to them."

"So why did they take Big H with them but left us?"

"Maybe they are going to pick up the cocaine."

We turned on the TV to try to relax our minds, but that didn't quite work. That 'right back' seemed forever. All of a sudden, the door opened. It was Big H and Julio.

"Here," Julio said, "Let San check the cocaine."

He left back out the door. I hit it three times and went into the bathroom. It was about quarter ounce of cocaine. When I came out of the room, Mina and Big H had shooted all but a little. I said, "Damn! Y'all know we got to hit that jet. Y'all will be scared as hell. Drink some liquor so you can come down."

Mina was talking her ass off. Then the phone rang. Big H answered it. When he got off, he announced, "The cocaine will be here in minute."

Sure enough, Julio brought in a keyload of cocaine and some in a medicine bottle. There was a girdle with the cocaine in the ass of it. I put the girdle on. It made me look like I had a big ass. The other bag went into my Aunt Mina's bra and Big H had the medicine tubs. We left going out going to flag down a cab. I said, "Here's one."

The driver stopped the car and got out to load the trunk. He said, "My name is Harry. I'm just like the one on TV: Dirty Harry. I know it all: what do you need? Cocaine? Heroin? Speed? Whatever you need I know where to get it."

We all laughed and I said, "No thanks, Mr. Clint Eastwood. But tell me, do you know how to get us to the airport?"

We started to go the Miami Airport and just about halfway there I said, "No, cab driver. Take us to Ft. Lauderdale."

When we got to Ft. Lauderdale I instructed everyone that I was going through security, first. If it sounded, they were to turn immediately around. Big H agreed. I went through and nothing happened. Then it was Mina, Sugar, and Big H last. We all passed with no problem. As soon as we got through security, Mina went straight to the restroom with the tube of cocaine. I asked Big A where were Mina and Sugar and he said that they were in the restroom snorting. "What! Let me go get them."

When I opened the door, the medicinal smell from the cocaine was all over the restroom. I got some change and bought some perfume from the machine. I squirted everywhere trying to get rid of the smell. I called out for Mina and Sugar. When I found them, they had smashed rock up with their hands because they didn't have a card. They snorted and I told them that we had to get out because the smell was lurking everywhere. I grabbed the tube and left out the restroom. My aunt actually used the restroom and told me that I was rushing her. She got finished and loaded herself down with her shoulder bag, her handbag, and a little grab bag. I looked at her like she was crazy because she definitely looked it. We all left out.

Finally, it was time to board the jet. When everybody got settled, I leaned over to Big H and told him he'd better keep an eye on Mina because she would probably try to get to the rest-room so that she could snort some more.

"I doubt it," he said.

Sure enough, Mina got up and went straight to the rest-room. She stayed in there 20 minutes. I rang for the stewardess so that I could order another cognac.

She explained, "Sorry ma'am, only two per person."

"It's not for me, it's for my sister. In fact, she wants two."

"That will be $4.00."

She returned them to Sugar and I drank them both. Mina came out finally. I looked at her. She was wet from sweating. When she sat down, the cocaine was rising up. I noticed that the stewardess kept watching her. Doing her job, the stewardess approached Mina and put both of the air vents on her. When she left, I got up and pushed the cocaine back into her bra. The stewardess asked, "Is she sick?"

"This is her first flight," I explained, "and she's kind of nervous."

"We will be there in about 20 minutes."

I looked up at the ceiling and said, "Lord, have mercy. We are going to jail in the air."

"Remember what your mama said," Sugar said.

"And what would that be?"

"The Lord takes care of old folks and fools."

"You're right about that."

We both started laughing.

We finally landed and got down to baggage claim. We had been moving fast through the airport. I was walking so fast until every now and then I'd have to wait until they caught up. While waiting for a cab, Aunt Mina asked Sugar, "Have you ever been wrong and knew that you were wrong and knew that somebody was watching you?"

"No," Sugar answered.

Mina said, "Look at that old lady watching us."

I said, "Come on, y'all. Let's get home."

We grabbed the first cab to Big H's house. When we got there, the cab driver said, "Fifteen dollars."

"Goddamn," Mina said, "we didn't come from Macon. We came from the airport."

"Give the man the money, Mina," Big H said.

"I ain't giving him nothing."

"I'll call the police," the driver said.

"Well call them then," Mina said.

"Here!" I said, handing the driver $20.00. "Get out y'all, let's go. This has been a trip for me. I'm going to rest this weekend. You better believe me."

We went into the house and fixed up the whole keyload. Cocaine was all over my face and clothes. We put a one on all of it and came up with about 86 ounces. I grabbed 12 ounces and left. It was the weekend, but I was tired and I didn't want to be bothered. My aunt and uncle had worn me out. Sugar and I stayed at her apartment for three days and three nights. She didn't even go to work. The year was '79 and we started it off very good until Jack came back in the picture. I had been selling cocaine non stop. My mother kept the white girl, San's baby, through the week for me, but she was getting tired.

Jack came to the restaurant. It was July 1st. All the welfare-check customers had been by. I sold about $3,000 worth of the fifties and grams that day. Jack walked over to me and said, "San, GBI want to talk to you about the warrant that they have on you."

"Man, don't start that shit this year. You said that same shit last year."

"But this time, it is for real."

I looked at him and he did look very serious.

"Well, what are you going to do?"

"What do they want to talk to me about?"

"Just go with me, you will see."

I left with him and we went to the GBI building on the West Side. We rode the elevator and all the way up I felt more and more scared. I kept telling myself that they didn't have nothing on me. Jack told me to have a seat in the waiting area and he went into the office. Shortly after, he called me in.

"San," Jack said, "this is Mr. Brown and Mr. Jones."

"We have a warrant on you," Mr. Brown said, "for selling cocaine."

I looked up at him and swallowed hard. Then I asked, "Are you going to lock me up now?"

"No, not if you agree to cooperate."

"Cooperate?" I asked. "Cooperate to what?"

Brown looked at Jack and said, "You didn't tell her?"

"No, man. I wanted you to discuss that with her yourself."

"I just wish somebody would tell me what's going on," I said.

Mr. Jones said, "San, would you wait outside for a few moments. We need to discuss something."

Confused, I left out and waited. They talked for at least 40 minutes then Jack came out and said, "Let's go."

"Where are we going?"

"Home for now. I need to talk to you."

"What's going on?"

"Get on the elevator and I'll tell you all about it." We got in the car and while driving, Jack began, "They do have a warrant for your arrest. Now the deal that they want me to make with you is this: you sell cocaine for them."

"What? You got to be kidding? Me sell dope for the police? Man, you must be crazy. Don't you know that I would be hooked for life? Hell no. Ain't no way that I can do that. Why me?"

"Listen now. They know everybody that sells the shit in the first place. Your name has been ringing since the last part of '77 and you're made a sale to some agents. Now, to beat all that, they will destroy all the warrants on you if you agree to work for them."

"That's like selling my soul to the Devil. I ain't fucking with them white folks, not me."

"What's it going to be?"

"On no...I don't know....I got to think about it. God-damn! Ain't this a bitch? I got to sell dope to stay on the streets."

"Just think about it."

"But look at it from my perspective, Jack? If I sell dope for them and get tired, them motherfuckers will put me in jail or have me whacked off. Right?"

"Hell naw. They won't do that."

"How do you know? Is there some guarantee that they won't fuck with me after I'm tired?"

"No, but you won't have to worry about getting busted."

"S-h-it. They got some police that will bust the police."

"These men are the top of the line."

"Oh, I see."

"They call the shots."

"Yeah? Hmm-m ...take me back to the restaurant. I'll let you know something later, okay?"

"Don't make me wait too long, now."

I got out of the car and called Ray.

"Hello?"

"Listen, baby, would you please come over here real quick?"

"What's wrong?" Ray asked.

"Just come on, I need to talk to you. It's very important, Ray. Come on."

Ray came on over and I told him everything they talked to me about. Then Ray responded, "Baby, if they got a warrant, make them lock you up. Don't sell nothing for them dirty motherfuckers. I don't believe that they have anything on you. They probably want you to sell the dope that they have taken from some of the busts they've made. Don't worry baby. I'm on your side 100%."

"Okay ...that's all I needed to know. Well, look here Ray. If I should go to jail would you take care of my children for me?"

He leaned over to kiss me and said, "Baby, I can't love you if I don't love the kids. They are mine too, you know?"

I smiled and said, "Thanks, for being here with me at a time like this."

A week had passed and I hadn't heard from Jack nor had I tried to contact him ...until now. I went back to talk to the GBI agents Brown and Jones. I figured that I was not going to be dealing with no middleman (Jack). They had me wait shortly before I was sent back in to see them. When I walked in the office, I said, "I can't do that so just go ahead and lock me up."

"If you go to jail," Jones said, "you won't be getting out until you've done all of your time."

"Oh believe me, I'll get out."

"No, no," Brown said while smiling, "it doesn't go your way in the courtroom, honey. We call the shots and the bonds."

"Well, just go on and lock me up."

"Naw, naw," Brown said, "we don't want to lock you up. We want to work together. You need a little help anyway. So you just go on home and think about it some more. Okay, Sandra?" He was patting me on my back.

At this point I figured I wasn't convincing enough to this crooked ass cop so I just said, "I'll be back in a few days to let you know the real decision."

"Now that's the way you are supposed to talk," Jones said. I got up and walked out of the door into the waiting room for the elevator. I got into my car and said aloud: "They think that they really have me scared up. Let me go sell some cocaine. I've got to work now. I ain't selling nothing for them."

9

I sold dope all day and all night until Friday, July 13, 1979. I went back to the GBI office. This time I didn't wait until they invited me in ...I walked right past the receptionist and went directly into their office. Real boldly, I said, "Lock me up. I can't do it. I just don't like the way y'all are treating me. Lock me up. If you don't do it this time, I'm going to Dekalb County. They will lock me up."

"Listen, Sandra, no ..."

"Sandra, my ass! Put me in jail! I don't want to hear about it anymore."

Then they read me my rights. Afterwards, Jones said, "Since you are so smart ...I bet you that you won't get out. Let's take her down."

They took me straight to Fulton County Jail. The Grand Jury had already indicted me. Plus the warrant was a bench warrant. I called some of everybody. Ray got in touch with some lawyers. The lawyers come out to see me. Then they gave me the news: "San, we've tried and tried to get you a bond but the judge won't go for it."

"Well, can you beat this in court?" I asked.

"Sure. That's no problem. I just assumed that you wanted to get out real quick—like now."

"I do. I do. But I really want to know what's going to happen in the courtroom."

"Let me handle that. Trust me, you will be all right." My lawyers were Landrum and Blakely. They were two of the best in the South. They both were white and in their forties and had at least 50 years of experience between them. One of them had dark brown hair and the other one had brown and gray hair. It was quite distinguish looking. "Now. Tell me what happened?" asked Blakely.

"I really don't know. They said that I made two sales to some agents but that's a lie. I know everybody that I sell to."

"Tell me, San. Did you really make the sale?"

"No. I did not. They had a warrant."

"Well where is it?"

"I don't know. Look, I have never been to jail before. How would I know?"

"Well, listen. I'm going to have to leave for now. I'll go and get a copy of the warrant tomorrow to see whom you allegedly sold the cocaine to. Try to be patient for a little while, okay? I'll be in touch with you."

The matron escorted me back to 2–W-2 dorm. I went to sleep.

The following morning the matron called out my name: "SANDRA WHITT!"

I looked through the bars.

"Come on out here. There's someone here to talk to you."

She escorted me back to the attorney's booth. This time it was some white folks from Washington. The young guy introduced himself: "My name is J. Boggs. I'm an investigator from Washington, D.C. I need to know what kind of drugs that you were involved with. Were you forced to sell and has anybody threatened you?"

"Wait a minute," I said. "Hey, I don't know nothing. And I sure don't sell cocaine so you can get the fuck on."

I turned and yelled to the matron, "Will you please come and get me?" I turned by to Boggs and said, "I ain't got to talk to you. And I surely don't want to help you."

"I just—"

"My ass," I said. I walked on back with the matron. I was very pissed off. Those motherfuckers had called Washington,

D.C. My lawyer came back later that evening with a copy of the warrant. It read that I had sold dope to two agents on Peachtree Street. I said, "This is a lie. I haven't been on Peachtree St."

"You did not make this sale?" Blakely asked, "Is that what you are saying?"

"Right! I did not sell that cocaine to no one."

"Well the warrant was taken out in 1978. They say that they couldn't find you so that's why they issued the bench warrant."

"Bench warrant? That means dead or alive. What? Why did they do that? I didn't even do nothing."

"Don't worry about that. We'll take care of that, okay. You are scheduled for Judge Time's court in two weeks."

"What kind of name is that? I hope I don't get none?"

"Oh, you won't. We will be done at the courthouse tomorrow morning to see if he will grant you a bond. I've asked for $100,000 bond earlier, but he denied it. So, I'm going to try again."

"Hey Mr. Blakely, how much did they say I sold?"

He referred to the warrant and said, "Six ounces."

I just shook my head and said, "Thanks for coming."

Big H and Ray had taken care of the lawyer's fees. Mr. Blakely left and I was escorted back down to my cell. I cried and worried about my children.

I went back to the court to enter a plea. My plea was "NOT GUILTY." The judge set the hearing for the following month. My lawyer came back to see me and said that they still refuse to grant me a bond but that I shouldn't worry because I would be out after the trial.

I called Ms. Mae. She was a church lady that I knew. She recognized my voice off the bat and said, "Sandra! The Lord said penitentiary or death. The Lord said that you would be gone away for six months. So daughter, it is up to you to make the decision."

"Okay, thank you, Ms. Mae."

It was time for my trial. Everything was looking favorable towards me, then the judge asked, "Young lady, do you have anything that you would like to say at this time?"

' 'Yes, your Honor. I would like to change my plea to GUILTY."

My lawyers looked at me in amazement. The judge took his glasses off and started at me. I didn't move. I just looked at the judge. With tears in my eyes, I repeated, "Guilty, I'm guilty."

Mr. Blakely stood up and asked, "Your Honor, at this time may we request a recess to speak with our client?"

Everybody in the courtroom was talking ...no one was listening to nobody. Then I heard three aggressive knocks, "ORDER! ORDER! Order in the court," yelled the Judge.

"Ms. Whitt, did anybody threaten you?"

"No sir, Your Honor."

The district attorney stood up and said, "Your Honor, I recommend five years; four to serve and the balance suspended." The deputy took about ten other ladies and me back over to the county jail. I got a visit from my mother and children then I was sent to State Prison for Women.

When you first get there, they check everything ...we had to strip naked. They poured some stuff that smelled like roach spray all over my head and body. It was supposed to be something to rid lice and crabs off, if there were any. The prison was like a school for girls. You could go to school, work, and take up a trade. As for myself, I went to school. We dressed in uniforms, green or beige. You could even go to the dentist. I walked the line for about six months then my time came up.

One day on my way back from school, I could hear some of the girls talking about "going to the house." It was January 10, 1980. I stopped and asked one of the girls, "Hey, did you say that some people are leaving in the morning for the house?"

"Yeah, honey. They called about 20 girls' names to go to Atlanta's Halfway House."

"Okay. Thanks."

I started to walk fast to see if they called my name. I saw this girl named Judy. When she noticed me, she said, "Damn, San! They didn't call your name to go to the house, but I'm leaving in the morning. I'm sorry."

"I'll talk to you later. I'm going to check on this." I went into the dorm. Everything was kind of quiet when I walked in. Everybody knew that I had planned to go on this load. I had talked about what Ms. Mae said that the Lord said for me to ask the matron could I see my counselor? I approached the matron and did just that. The matron told me that I would have to wait a while before she could let me know. I waited and it seemed I waited some more ...but then that's all I had been doing was waiting. Finally, I was given the chance to speak with Mrs. Brown my counselor: "Did they call me for the house?"

"Sandra," she said as she stared at me, "I told you that you wouldn't be eligible for the house now. You have to have 12 months served."

"Okay thanks, but ...never mind."

I left out of there with tears in my eyes and I didn't think I had the strength to make it back to my dorm. I did all that I could not to fall out. I was truly puzzled and as soon as I reached my dorm, I fell straight down to my knees and prayed aloud through my tears:

Lord, you said that I would only do six months and this is my 6th month. Lord, please. There's not another load leaving from here until next month. I want to go home. Please, Lord, you said I could go.

I stayed on my knees crying until I heard someone say, "Sandra Whitt! Report to the chapel."

I got up and wiped my face and went to see who said what. I went upstairs. The guard said, "Sandra, you have to report to the chapel."

"Okay, but for what?" I was too late for the house now. Everything was closed. I couldn't even get my clothes so I couldn't imagine what was going on.

"I don't know, just go and see."

When I got there the chaplain called my name: "Sandra Whitt?"

I looked up and said, "I'm Sandra Whitt."

She smiled and said, "Pack your things, you're going to the house in the morning."

"What?"

My eyes bucked. I jumped, hollered, and screamed with tears of joy. I ran out of the chapel, jumping, skipping, and looking up to the sky saying, "Thank you, Jesus. Thank you. I knew that you wouldn't let me down!"

I was still crying and saying, "Ain't nobody got the powers that you have. I love you, Lord. Thank you!" When I got in my dorm, I screamed out, "Everybody! I'm leaving!"

All the girls ran down to see. They were just as happy for me as I was for myself. A lady named Mrs. Lois said to me, "Baby, you were being tested then. The Lord wanted to see if you really had faith."

"I know, I know. Thank you, Jesus."

I ran downstairs and got the things that I had there. I had 'til the morning to get the rest out of lock-up. The morning came and I got the rest of my things and all of us went to Atlanta. Most of the girls went to the Rising Sun Halfway House. The rest went to the other one. I went to school there. I worked and lived there. Eight months passed before I had met this white lady named Mary. We were about the same age and come to find out she was a millionaire. One day I heard the girls plan to set her up. They didn't like her because she was educated and had plenty of money. They planted some pills under her pillow and in her shoes. While they were gone to get the police (C.O.), I ran in her room and got all of the shit out. When the C.O. got there, they turned right back around with nothing but a "false alarm." No one had a clue that I was the one that moved the dope ...but she knew. She was very scared. From that day on, she befriended me. One day while eating, she said, "The day you get out, I got something for you."

"What?"

"Not now. Wait until you get ready to go home."

It was getting close to Halloween. All the girls in the house had planned a party. I went to work and came back to the house. This particular day I didn't feel well. As usual, as soon as I walked in the door I checked the parole notice board. My release date was posted: November 26, 1980—the day before Thanksgiving. Time was really dragging now, but at last we had the party. Ray visited me and took care of my children. Weeks had gone by. I was counting down the days, and now all I had left was a "wake up." It was November 26, 1980, at 8:00 A.M. Mary came to my room and said, "Here." Mary said while handing me a piece of paper with an address on it, "Go to this address for what I planned for you. It will be waiting there for you. Sh-h, don't ask any questions just do as I say." I took the paper and we hugged and kissed. She said, "Take care of yourself, Sandra. I'll be calling you."

"Okay, Mary. Thanks."

Sugar was out there waiting for me. as I walked toward her, I heard music blasting. It was Randy Crawford's "Street Life." Sugar and I hugged, then I said, "Sugar, take me to Marietta. I've got to do something before I go anywhere."

We drove around looking for this address. After about an hour in the area, we finally found it. Sugar parked and I went to the house alone. This white guy opened the door and said, "Hi, Sandy! Mary just called. She thought that you had changed your mind." Handing me a large box he continued, "Here."

"What's this?"

"You will see when you get home. I know you're anxious to get to your loved ones. Here, let me put it in the car for you."

We went outside and he put it in the back seat because my clothes and stuff were in the trunk. I got in the car and he closed the door. He said, "Call me when you get home. Here's the number. My name's Joseph, Mary's brother."

"Okay, I'll do that."

Sugar drove off. As soon as she got to the first red light, I asked, "What do you think is in that box?"

"Open it and see." I started to open it, the light changed and she pulled off. I fell back and said, "Damn, Sugar, hold on, kid. Let me check this out." I went into the box and yelled, "Sugar! Look, look, girl! This is a box full of reefer."

"What!"

She stopped the car to look. I put the music back on the "Street Life" track, because it was the only life I've known!

"San, are you going to get back into that?"

"Listen to the tape."

"Ah hell. I didn't buy it for you. I just bought it."

"Well it fits me, huh?"

I looked at her popping my fingers laughing. Sugar said, "You are crazy. I don't believe this. You ain't been out an hour yet and you got a bale of reefer." She shook her head.

I sang, " 'Money, money, money, money ...mon-ey! Some people got to have it. Hey, hey, and some people really need it.' You know that's what the O'Jays said."

She laughed and said, "Shut up. When do we start?"

I looked at her and we skinned, hitting each others' hand.

"Where's our first stop?" Sugar asked.

"Baby, you know where I want to go."

"Ray's house?"

"You said it right."

We went to Ray's new house that he had gotten since I'd been gone. He was really handling things. I rang the doorbell. He came to the door, picked me up, and kissed me. With a great big smile he said, "Come on in."

He took me on in and set me down. "Baby, baby, baby! Home free, huh? You look good, San. Have you been by the house?"

I could tell something was wrong when he asked that. In fact, I could tell that something wasn't quite right. "Oh, ain't nobody told you."

"Told me what? What's wrong? What are you talking about?"

He looked at me and Sugar, and she looked at me, then turned to Ray, and said, "You'd better tell her, Ray."

' 'What!" I yelled at both of them. "Will somebody please tell me what's going on?"

"Sit down a minute," Ray said.

I sat down and said, "Now ...I'm waiting. What is it? Ray come on now."

"Okay, baby, now don't get upset."

"About what?"

"You've lost your restaurant."

"What?" I stood straight up with my mouth wide open. I put my arm on the table holding my head. "What happened? Why? How could that be? I left money in the bank."

"There's no more money."

"What!" I quickly jumped back up and knocked the chair over, then I said, "Let's go, Sugar!"

Ray grabbed me by the arm. "Wait, baby. Let me finish."

' 'What's next? It can't any worse than this. Lord, have mercy. Why me? What have I done?"

' 'Your mama didn't want to upset you. Do you remember when you would get out on passes?"

"Yeah! What about it?"

"Well the reason I wanted you to put down my house or your mother's was because of what happened to the restaurant and the house on Eugenia Street."

"What happened over there?"

"The house was fire bombed."

"What! Who did that? Why wasn't I told this? Who was there? Was anybody hurt? Tell me!"

"No, baby. No one was hurt, plus your furniture was saved, also. The kids put it in storage."

"Where's Aunt Hazel? I called several times and no one answered. Y'all kept all this from me. Why?"

"San," Sugar said, "You would have gone crazy."

"I know that's got damn right. I'll be damned if it ain't one thang it's another. Who are my children living with?"

"Your mother."

"And they didn't say a word when I went down there on my weekend passes. Did they find out who did it? What about the insurance that I had on the house?"

"Aunt Hazel spent that, too. She got back on drugs."

"Damn! I don't know what to say." Tears fell heavily down my face. Ray wiped them with his hand and said, "You can live here, baby."

I looked up and said, "Thanks, but I'm going home, even if we all have to sleep in one room. Tell me, who got the restaurant and how did Aunt Hazel let it get away from under her?"

"A nigger named Nick," Sugar said. "Do you remember him?"

"Yeah. I know the low-down motherfucker. I have never been able to deal with him. I don't see how Aunt Hazel fucked with him again after he tricked her and she ended up in the penitentiary."

"Well, baby, those are the breaks."

"Where is she now?"

"She's on Jefferson Street."

"Jefferson Street, for what?

"Heroin sales."

"Now she knows better. You haven't told me about the restaurant."

"Nick's got it."

"I'll be damned."

"She owed him money for the drugs and she didn't want nothing to happen to your family. That's why the money's gone."

"Thirteen thousand dollars in the bank ...at least $10,000 in fire insurance, all gone, huh?"

"Ain't nothing left, baby. But look, baby, just thank the Lord for your family, your health, and your strength."

"I guess the house is fucked up pretty bad, huh?"

"Yep, the back is."

"I ain't got but $4,000 that I saved from when I worked. I can ..." I couldn't finish for the heaviness I felt and the tears that were rolling down my face.

Then Ray said, "Go on and let it out, baby. Get it over with and come out of it strong."

"What's Big H doing?"

"Nothing. He didn't give up a thing."

"That's all right. I'm going to make it."

Ray said, "Here," handing me a hit of cocaine.

"I don't want none ...hand it here." Sniff, sniff, "It's gone now," I said. "Well, how much time did Aunt Hazel get?"

"I think she has two years to serve."

"I guess she was ashamed to tell me, huh? Damn, that'sa lot of money to go through. I wonder who forged my name?"

"You know Nick is tough when it comes down to forgery."

"Fuck it! I'll get some more."

"Now that's my San." Ray played a record for me: Diana Ross's "I'm Coming Out—I Want the World to Know." That really cheered me up. Then I said, "Y'all really kept that a secret. Starting all over again is going to be rough. Hey baby," I said, while blowing my nose, "I've got something to show you." I ran to the car and came back with the box. He held the door open for me while asking, "What's that?"

"Lock the door and come see."

I put the box down on the floor and asked him to open it. He opened the box, pulled the paper out, looked at the reefer, and then looked at me. He stood up with his hand on his hips and said, "Where in the world did you get all this reefer from?"

Between the sniffles I said, "I'll tell you about it."

"San! You know what?"

"What?"

"You are insane."

"No, I ain't."

"Baby, you just got out—goddamn. You got all this?" he said, rubbing his head in amazement. "Hey baby, you are one bad motherfucker! I got to give credit where credit is due." He laughed and said, "Come here and give me a big kiss."

He turned to Sugar and said, "Hey Sugar, my baby got too much nerve. You know she ain't got good sense anyway."

"But—," I interrupted him.

"But—," he put his hand over my mouth and continued, "—nothing. Baby, niggers don't do the shit you be doing. Where did you get all those nerves from?"

"I don't know. Sometimes I feel like I got too many."

We started snorting and drinking cognac. Then I said, "Ray, where is Tonya?"

He took a deep breath and said, "Tonya is dead."

"Oh no! How did that happen?"

"She just started hanging with the wrong people. All three of them got killed."

"Three, who?"

He paused for a minute then I said, "That's all right, baby. I understand. Damn! A lot has happened since I've been gone. Listen, baby, we're going to leave so that I can go see my babies. I'll call you when I get down to mama's house, okay?"

"All right," he said.

Sugar and I left with the box of reefer going down to mama's house. When I got there, Mama, my sisters, my brothers, and especially my kids were waiting on me. My son was in the 10th grade; my daughter was in the 8th. They all were happy to see me. We talked a while and then I gave mama $300. Mama asked, "Where are you going to live?"

I looked at her and answered, "I'm going home, Mama."

Everybody got quiet but mama. She said, "That place is a mess, baby. I know that you don't want to go back over there."

"I'm going back, Mama. I'm going to fix it up, I've got a little money. Trust me. Just let my children stay here for a little while longer."

My baby brother spoke up, "If you're going, we're going, too!"

Then Harry said, "We all can sleep in one room."

Cocoa yelled, "Me too, San!"

I looked at all three of them and said, "Thank you. I love all of you for that. Where's Bay-Bay?" (He's the little mixed baby that I got from the white girl.) Cocoa answered, "He's in nursery school."

My eyes welled and then I said, "I guess my car is gone, too, huh?"

"Yeah. Aunt Hazel let her old man drive it to death. It's all wrecked ...totaled out."

"That's all right. I'll get me another one. Well, what y'all waiting for?" I asked trying to pep things up. I looked at Harry, Tonya, and Cocoa. "Y'all get your things together so that we can go home. Mama, you know what? I'm going to build everything back up again."

"You ain't going to mess with that stuff anymore are you?"

"Not right now, maybe a little later. Right now I've got something new."

Mama started looking funny.

"Hey!" I said as I framed her face with my hands, "I want you to have everything that you deserve. Mama, it's usually the boys that do for their mamas, but my brothers can't give you the things that I can give you. I want you to have everything, Mama. Me, your daughter."

Tears were coming down her face. I stooped down to look into her eyes. Before I knew it, I had tears rolling, too. I kissed her tears and said, "Don't cry, mama. I'm going to make it, okay?"

She nodded her head and said, "Just be careful, San. You know what happened the last time."

"That's the past, Mama. I'm living the '80s. Hey, here comes the children and they are all ready to go." I wiped her face and said, "Pray for me. I'll make it." I smiled and continued, "Hey Mama, come on smile, now. Your clown is back." I did a little dance to get her to smile and she did. Then I said, "Come on, give your baby some sugar."

I was playing with her and she started to laugh then said, "Girl, you better get your butt somewhere. Stop putting that spit all over me, now!"

"See you later, ma! I'll call you tomorrow. Keep Bay-Bay until we get about halfway finished. Okay?" On the way out the door I stopped and said, "Ma, tell him (Bay-Bay) I'm home and that I love him."

"Okay, Dokey."

We all left to go to Eugenia Street. When we got there, I had to climb in the back window to get in. From inside I opened the door. The house had burned badly in the kitchen. The rest of house was damaged from smoke. Everybody was silent for a while as if to see how I was going to react. I broke the silence and said, "Oh well, let's start somewhere else."

"How about the front?" Sugar asked.

"Yeah, let's get us a place to sleep first," I said. "Hey, Sugar?" I said. "No, that's all right. Ronnie?"

"Huh?" he answered.

"Get that box out of the back seat for me."

"Okay."

The next day was Thanksgiving. I let the kids go down mama's house to eat. I didn't want to go. I wanted to get the house in order. Sugar came over. I was sitting in the front formerly known as the living room. She said, "Hey! Snap out of it."

"What?"

"Ah, you know."

"Well I can't help thinking about it."

"Right, but you got to ...hey come on, let's throw all this shit out. Hey, I've got a surprise for you."

"Believe me, sister, I need one right about now."

Sugar went to the door and opened it. I could hear footsteps. I asked, "Who is that, Sugar?"

"It's the working crew! Who the fuck else you think it is?" said a familiar voice.

I got up and turned around to see, and to my surprise there were at least six people dressed to do some serious work. They were all people that bought cocaine from me. Behind them, Ray entered with his work clothes on and had three guys with him. I was so happy. I didn't know what to do. Nip was one of the guys that Sugar brought. I knew all of them, but Nip was the one who appeared to be calling the shots for the crew. Turned out, Nip was the one answered me when they all came in.

Nip asked, "Where do we start?"

"First, let me call my children so that they won't come."

"Damn right," Nip said, "because we are going to work all night long."

I called the children and canceled their trip. Ray said, "Okay, let's get everything in here—out."

Sugar's mother had fixed enough dinner for everybody. They worked that night and the next several days and nights. Ray gave them cocaine to shoot plus pay. They stole paint, panel, and carpet. The ceilings were lowered, closets were built in my bedroom, and Ray helped me install a shower in the bathroom. He and I went to the store to look for some crystal doorknobs. He saw some and said, "Block for me, baby."

"Block what?" I asked while laughing.

"No, no, on steal, c'mon, here."

I laughed again and said, "I'm scared."

While I was laughing, he was busy 'getting' the knobs. He said, "I'm going to get you. Goddamn!"

"What, baby?"

"Here comes the man, girl."

He walked over to me and said, "You got all the nerve when it comes to dope."

"Yeah, but that stealing makes my nerves bad."

He laughed and said, "My big baby ...come on, let's go."
We stared out the door, then, while looking up at him, I said, "Did you get it?"

He stopped, turned around, put his hands on his hips and said, "Damn, girl, you talk loud as hell."

He grabbed my hand and pulled me out the door. We got in the car and laughed then kissed me. He said, "Hey, you know that it's been a long time, baby."

"Nah! You're lying, we just did it week before last when I was on pass."

"But baby, you know what I'm talking about."

"Well can't it wait until—"

"Oh you don't want none, huh?"

"Now did I say that?"

"No, but you're talking shit."

"No, you are ...hey I'll help you. You want me to take them off right here?"

"Yeah. Take them off."

I began to take my sweater off. He snatched it back down and said, "You were going to do that for real, huh?"

"Yeah."

We laughed, then he said, "You're a crazy ass woman."
I looked at him and twitched my nose and said, "Ah, nigger, you love it!"

"Damn sure do. Okay, baby. I can wait."

We stopped and got some cotton candy, cigarettes, wine and beer for everybody. We headed back to the house then Ray said, "Hot damn, baby! We forgot to measure the windows."

"So what? We can't do it all in one week baby. Let's save something for next week. That way we can make love in the empty house. The carpet will be laid by then."

"Oh yeah!"

"I got to get more drapes for the whole house."

We were very busy in the house and I didn't even bother to sell none of the reefer. I called Mary at the halfway house and told her to call me back on the pay phone. She did. "Hello?"

"Hello, San?"

"Yeah."

"What's going on?"

"Well I haven't started working, yet, but I will this week, okay?"

"Sure," she said, "I know it's going to take a little time, so don't worry about it, okay? Just let me know when you are ready to reup."

"Okay, Mary. I'll be talking to you."

Two weeks had gone by. We went to storage to pick up all my furniture. The entire inside of the house was refurbished and furnished. All that was left to do was the back porch, the roof, and a paint job on the outside. I had gotten cold. Ray said, "Let's break until after Christmas."

"You mean New Year's, don't you, baby?"

"Well everybody knows what I mean."

We all had a nice X-mas and I still hadn't made no money. All we did was pay for the fixing of the house. Mary called: "Hello?"

"San! Merry X-mas and Happy New Year."

"Same to you."

"Well, what's going on? It's been a month."

"I know, but I had to get thing together here. I'll be seeing your brother after New Year's. I promise."

"Okay. We'll be talking to you."

The house was beautiful on the inside. I had all my children with me—even little Bay-Bay. My money was very low. I only had about $1,200 left. Now that I had transportation, I decided to get busy. Who of all people came to the house all shamed and scared? Knock. Knock. "Who is it?" I asked.

"Lil' Man," he yelled.

I opened the door, hugged and kissed him. "I ain't made no more," I said, "what's been happening?"

"Ah, nothing but the rent."

"I know that's right."

"Are you going to be doing anything else?"

"Yeah, but I got to get my money together first. Then I'll be back in the pen. I got some reefer."

"Well, let me help you with that."

"Hell nah, motherfucker. You might fuck up again, then I'd have to kill your ass for 'sho."

"Hey, I ain't talking about like that. I know some people who buy big weight."

"Oh yeah?"

"Un-huh. Let me use the phone."

"Go ahead."

He talked to somebody and within his conversation, placed his hand over the mouthpiece and asked, "How much is it?"

"Hell nah! Hang up and call back."

Returning to the phone, he said, "Hey man? Let me call you back." Lil' Man hung up the phone and asked me again, "So how much are you selling it for?"

"Damn, I didn't even ask her. Let me call to find out."

I called Mary's brother, Joseph. He told me $300 per pound. I got off the phone and said, "Okay, Lil' Man, my cost is $300 per pound. You can easily sell it to a nigger for $450 per pound."

"Nah, I'm going to say—"

I looked at him, then he said, "Okay, $450, and if they buy more then I'll go down. Let me call Rock back."

Lil' Man called the man back. Turns out he wanted three pounds. Rock came over to the house, picked up the reefer, and left. I called Big H to see had he heard from Julio and he said that Julio had left the country. The reefer money was too slow for me. I wanted to work with some cocaine. Ray called: "Hello?"

"Hey, baby. I got a nigger who wants five pounds of that smoke. How much is it?"

"Four-fifty per pound."

"How about ...nah, I'll be over there in a little while, okay?"

"All right."

I called Jeff, Duey, and Fat Bob to let them know that I was back in town and would have a sack in a little while.

I only sold reefer during the day hours. Some of the people that I used to sell cocaine also pushed reefer. It was the end of January. I had sold 40 pounds and had ten left. I called Mary and told her that I was ready to pay her.

"Mary? Listen, I appreciate what you're doing for me, okay? I'm sorry it took so long for me to pay you. I owe you $15,000, right?"

"Oh, huh, yeah. You had a 50 pound bale, didn't you?"

"Yep."

"Okay. I'll call Joe to tell him where to meet you."

"Okay. I'll see you later." I hung up the phone and said, "Goddamn reefer ...only $7,000 profit, sh-h-it. I got to get some girl ...this is too much work ...Let me call Ray."

"Hello?"

"Hey, baby. I got to make a run to pick up some more reefer. But you know what, I'm tired of that shit. Can you find some cocaine? I'll have $7,000, nah, $5,000 to invest. I've got to have mama some money for my sisters and brothers."

"When you get through with your smoke business," Ray said, "come over here. Okay?"

"All right. I'll be over there as soon as I pick up."

"Well, drop it off first."

"I ain't because that will be out of the way."

"Baby, you better riding around with all that shit."

"Okay, baby. I'll see you in a minute." I hung up the phone and called Joseph so that we could arrange to meet at the stadium. I told him I needed 25 pounds this time. He agreed to meet, and as soon as I got off the phone, I left out.

I got in my car and went on over to Ray's house. He answered the door: "C'mon in. Let me fix you a drink," he said.

We sat down, drank and snorted. He said, "Listen, baby. I can get a big sack on consignment. Will you help me move it?"

"Hell yeah! Why didn't you just tell me?"

"Because I didn't know where you were coming from."

"What? You've got to be kidding. When can we get started?"

"I'm suppose to meet with him tomorrow."

I heard footsteps coming down the stairs. I looked at Ray and asked, "Who's that?"

"Oh, that's Barbara."

"Talking about that other 'friend' you had when Tonya was living, huh?"

"Hold on, now. Let's not get loud, please."

Barbara had made it down and I looked at her and him ...she was tall, dark and skinny and actually an attractive young lady. She spoke, "Raymond, can I listen to some music?"

He turned around to her and said, "Don't you see that I have company?"

"I'm sorry, I thought they were gone."

"Oh! I'm leaving!" I got up and continued, "Check on 'that' and let me know, okay?"

"Wait a minute," Ray said to me. He turned to Barbara and said, "I got some business to see about," as he grabbed my arm.
I pulled from him and said, "Let me go!"

I rushed to the door and let myself out. I ran to my car and as I was pulling away, I noticed him standing in the door. I didn't look back as I pulled on off. I drove as fast as I could without a tear. I was mad as hell. I said to myself: "Why didn't he tell me? Why?" I looked in the mirror and continued, "I'll show him, just wait."

10

From that night on my love for Raymond remained the same, but I didn't want anything else to do with him. I only wanted his friendship. It was where I had to buy cocaine. I had sold all the reefer that I had and didn't get anymore. I would buy three ounces and get three on credit. Sometimes we even had long talks, but I just didn't want it to be the way it was.

It was May when I met this guy named Melvin. He was six feet tall with long hair; he was chocolate brown and fine. He weighed about 175 pounds and was sho' nuff built. He was larger than Ray. My softball coach introduced us. We were on the ball field when I noticed him sitting in the bleachers. I was on the mound, pitching. I could see my coach trying to tell me something, but I couldn't make it out. It was three up and three down. I went to the sideline. There he was—this fine ass nigger in Kelly Green. Coach Mattie was about 43 years old, dark-complexioned and must have weighed about 185 pounds. We won the ball game. Our uniforms were gold, white, and green. After the game, she introduced me to Melvin: "Melvin," she said, "I want you to meet San, our pitcher. San, this is Melvin."

He looked good. He was a cocaine dealer, also. Melvin said, "Are you riding?"

"Yeah, but if you want, I can ride with you. Let me give Sugar my keys. Hold on for a minute, okay?"

"Sure."

I found Sugar and said, "Sugar, here are the keys. Take the kids home for me. I got a ride."

"Is Ray here?"

"Nope. I've got a new prince ...look," while pointing at Melvin.

She looked around me and asked, "Where?"

"The one in the green!"

"Oooh, that's tough. Girl, you know how Ray is."

"Hey, he's got somebody else, so I can get me somebody else. Anyway, I still love him and I always will. But the way he did really hurt—deeply."

"Honey, Ray ain't going to let you have nobody else and you know it."

"Ha! I've got to go."

"See ya' when you get there."

We walked to his car. He had a 1979 green on green Seville. While driving, he said, "Mattie tells me that you have some good blow."

"Yep, I like it."

"How much for a quarter of an ounce?"

"Four hundred fifty."

"Can you get it now?"

"Yeah, as soon as we get to my place."

As soon as we pulled up I could see the back end of Ray's car turning as he left. I said, "Damn! There's Ray."

"Who's Ray? You want me to catch him?"

"No! He probably didn't want anything."

We got out of the car and another one pulled up full of cracker. I said, "Damn! I wonder who they want?"

When the woman got out, I noticed it was White San, Bay Bay's mother. She said, "Hey, girl, I heard you were home. Did your mama tell you that I've been calling?"

"Yeah, she told me. Come on in. Who's your friend?"

"Oh, that's a friend of mine who sings with a rock group. He wants to buy some cocaine for the guys."

"Well, tell him to come on in. Hey, how much does he want?"

"I think maybe a half ounce, but I'm not sure. Let me get him, okay?"

"Okay."

Melvin and I went into the house. I left the door open for White San. There were two white guys with long hair with her when she came in. She introduced us: "San, this is Joey and Bobby, the singers with a rock group that were at the concert. They want to check out some good cocaine."

"Y'all have a seat. I'll be with you in a minute." I brought back the half ounce anyway—just in case they wanted to snort out of what they were buying. Joey tasted it and Bobby snorted some. They liked it and got the half ounce. Sonya said, "San, we're going to run, okay, but I'll be back tonight."

"All right."

"Hey, you didn't introduce me to your friend."

"Oh, I'm sorry. This is Melvin, Melvin this is Sonya, Bobby, and Joey."

He stood up and shook their hands then said, "Pleased to meet you all."

I let them out then I came back into the living room where Melvin was. He said, "Listen, San, can I see a quarter?"

"Yeah. Hold up a minute."

I went into my bedroom and got it and returned back.

"Here you are."

He checked it and liked it. "You said $450, right?"

"Un-huh."

"Okay, I want it." He counted out four one-hundred-dollar bills and a fifty. We snorted out of his bag, then he asked for a mirror. When I gave it to him, he laid out about a gram for us to snort. I said, "Would you like some Pepsi or orange juice?"

"I have some cognac out in the car. Would you like some?"

"Yes, please."

"Let yourself out while I get the ice and soda." He was a sexy nigger with hair all in his chest. I liked that. It really turned me on.

He locked the door back when he returned with the drinks. He sipped a little cognac then said, "Listen, San, I've got to make a few stops, right? Can I come back if it's not too late?"

"Yeah. Here's my number." I wrote the number down for him.

"I'll call you when I'm on the way, okay?"

"Okay."

I let him out and called Ray.

"Hello?"

"Hey."

"Hey, baby. I've been over your house and the ball field. Sugar said that you had given her the keys and left."

"Yeah, I had some business to take care of."

"What kind of business?"

"None of yours. Hey, I don't question you."

"Are you seeing someone else?"

"Why?"

"Because I have a right to know."

"Well, yeah. I met a guy tonight and I like what I saw."

"What's his name?"

"Melvin."

"What am I suppose to do?"

"Nothing but what you are doing."

"But baby, you knew about that in '77."

"So, I want to be able to have someone else when I can't have you."

"Bitch, you crazy. I'll come over there and kick your god-damn ass. You won't even go to bed with me. You've been fucking that nigger!"

"You wrong, now. I just met the man!"

"Let me catch him over there."

"You ain't my husband ...!"

SLAM! He hung the phone up in my face. I looked at the receiver and said, "Ah, hell!"

I started pacing and thinking. Then I put my hand on my hip and said aloud, "What am I worried about? We ain't never been in a fight." I went to the bathroom to shower. As I was coming out, I heard a knock on the door. I grabbed a big towel, opened the door and yelled, "Hold on, I'm in the shower. I'll be there in a minute!" I just wrapped the towel around me and went to the door.

"I see you finally made it back, huh?"

The children came in telling me how they like the game. Bay-Bay said, "Mama, can I please tell you what the lady did ...she did like this!" He slid on the floor and yelled, "Safe, Mama, safe, and they won!"

I smiled and kissed him. Then I said, "Y'all get ready for bed, okay? Cocoa, how about bathing Bay-Bay?" They went on in the back talking among them. I said, "C'mon Sugar—"

"Girl, let me tell you ...did you know that Ray came out there asking for you: 'Where is she? Who she leave with?'"

"Yeah, I called him."

"What did he say?"

"Let me tell you this, first. I told him that I was seeing someone else. He wants to say that I've been fucking the nigger all the while. He said that's why I don't go to bed with him. But that's why a lie. I've just met the man ...then he hung the phone up in my face."

"He did? He just might come over."

"I don't give a damn."

"C'mon and run me on home."

"Go ahead and drive the car. I ain't got nothing to do tomorrow."

We got up and walked to the door then Sugar said, "I hope that everything go all right."

While opening the door, I said, "I ain't worried about it. Hell, he got other women. I'll see you later."

I locked the door and watched Sugar pull off. Bay-Bay got in bed with me and I turned the lamp off.

The next morning I was awakened by, "Mama, Mama, wake up. I gotta go to school." I looked at him smiling. I got up, woke the other kids up, fixed breakfast and sent all of them out the door. As for me, I got back in bed. The phone rang: "Hello? Hello? Hello?"

I hung up and said, "Stupid ass." A few minutes later, I heard knocking at the door. I went to door and asked, "Who is it?"

I peeped out from the curtain and saw Ray. He said, "Open the door."

I opened it and said, "Lock it back."

I went back to bed. He followed me and asked, "What's going on?"

"Nothing."

He started taking his clothes off and I sat up with my PJ's on and asked, "What are you doing?"

"What in the fuck it looks like?"

He stripped down to his underwear and I said, "I ain't doing nothing."

He snatched the covers off me and got on top of me, kissing me. I said, "Stop now, it's too early."

He looked at down at me and said, "You're going to do something."

"Not me."

He snatched my PJ top off and tossed it. Then he pulled the bottom off and slapped me. He grabbed me all over my face and neck. I was fighting back for a while, then it got good to me. He said, "Pull them off, baby. Don't fight me anymore. Please, I need you. Come on give it to me."

I pulled everything off and we started to make love. The phone rang, he knocked it off the hook and we continued to make love.

"This time, baby, it's going to be like the first time we fell in love."
He sucked my breasts, going from one to the other. He climaxed first and he was mad with himself. He said, "Why do you do me this way? If you hadn't made me wait ..."

He got up, went in and took a shower. I got up and by the time I joined him he was finished. He said, "I don't feel your love like I use to."

"That's because you have more than one to love, now."

"I'll make it up to you, baby. I love you. San, please try to understand."

After he got dressed, he went out the door and slammed it. I put the phone back on the hook after I got off the shower. The phone rang. "Hello?"

"Good morning."

"Who is this?"

"Melvin."

"Well, hello there. What happened to you last night?"

"I got tied up with some people. I called you earlier. Someone picked up but didn't say anything."

"Oh, I probably knocked it off the hook."

"I need to get another quarter. Do you have it?"

"Yeah. Come on over."

Melvin came over, picked up his quarter, and left.

Lil' Man came over. The white girl, San, came over and bought some cocaine. They shot right there in my kitchen. Lil' Man got up from the table went to the bathroom, pulled his clothes off and called me, "San! Come here! Hurry up."

"Go on and do yours, San, let me go see what's up with Lil' Man."

When I got to the hallway door, Lil' Man had on nothing but his jockey shorts and a T-shirt. He was dancing and skipping and singing. I laughed and asked, "What do you want, man?"

"You need to put more cut on the dope. I didn't run but ten lines. You better check on the white girl."

"Sh-hit, crackers can handle way more than niggers."

"Let the bitch shoot if you want to. She's going to be dead, motherfucker."

I went in the kitchen. She was there with the work in her hand. Her head was moving from side to side looking like a bell should be chiming from it.

"Ding, dong," I said, "Hey, are you all right?"

"Sh-h-h, be quiet."

"Well, are you?"

She put her index finger to her lips and said, "Sh-h-h, don't talk."

I went to check on Lil' Man. He was peeping out the front door wearing nothing but his shorts, T-shirt, cap, and shades. Lil' Man had a fat ass. I said,

"Lil' Man?"

"What! Leave me alone."

I laughed as he continued to peep out the door. Just then the white girl came to the door and said, "San, come here. Somebody's at the back door."

"Ah, ain't nobody back there."

"Yes, it is. Go see."

I went to the kitchen and I laughed for a while. She had put two chairs, a softball bat, and a ball behind the door. She came to the kitchen door peeping at me and asked in a whispering voice, "Who is it? Did you check the door?"

"Girl, ain't nobody out there."

Lil' Man came in the kitchen. He looked out of the two windows. The white girl asked, "Lil' Man, do you see anybody?"

"Shut up. I'm trying to see, now."

After they both came down, they wanted to shoot some more. This time Lil' Man got on the floor under the table thinking that some cocaine had fallen. He went in the bathroom and came back with his socks and tennis shoes on. They were some dirty white All-Stars high tops. I asked, "Lil' Man, why do you have your shoes on, cap'n?"

"None of your damn business, that's why."

White San started laughing. Lil' Man asked, "What you laughing for, bitch? You trip harder than I do."

"Nah. Hell no, I don't."

"Fuck it. I don't give a damn. Let me trip."

The white girl asked, "San, go in the front with me."

"For what?"

"I've got to go to the bathroom."

"Ain't nobody in there."

"Shit, you don't know that 'cause you're in here. This is a big house. C'mon, please?"

"Okay, girl. Y'all getting on my last nerve, now." I went in the front and white girl went into the bathroom. Knock. Knock. I heard something say, "Bam, bam. Bing, bing." First I asked, "Who is it?"

Lil' Man and White San came running out. The white girl was pulling her drawers up and Lil' Man had a knife. I fell out laughing.

"Who is that?" Lil' Man asked. "Y'all want me to check, 'cause I got a knife? C'mon, let me check the motherfucker. See, I'll stick them in the head."

I fell out laughing and said, "Honey, sit down. It ain't nobody but Nip."

I opened the door for Nip. He had on some overalls, a plaid shirt, and some tennis shoes. Nip was a brown skinned nigger with nappy hair. He was five feet nine inches tall and skinny with a funny made chest. He had one tooth in the front of his mouth and it had started to decay. "What the fuck is this?" he asked. "What are those stanking motherfuckers doing down here?" Nip laughed and continued, "Ah ha! It got your stanking ass."

"Nip, kiss my ass, motherfucker, and shut the door."

"Here, I ain't got but $20. Gimme a hit."

"Get me ten lines," Lil' Man said to Nip.

"Hoe, you must be crazy," Nip said, "you ain't going to give me none of yours."

"Okay, bastard. You're going to want something from me, you dirty son-of-a bitch."

"Man, I ain't got but $20. Damn! What you thank I'm going to do? Split it? Gimme my shit. I'm gonna take it with me ...away from these begging motherfuckers."

"You can kiss my begging motherfuckin' ass, you one tooth motherfucker," said Lil' Man.

I gave Nip a fifty and he flashed it in front of Lil' Man and said, "See ya', evil Bulldigger."

We all laughed. Lil' Man said, "Your mammy's a bulldiger, motherfucker."

"Let me out, San. This bitch wants me to fuck him. C'mon, give me some pussy and I'll give you ten lines."

"Nigger, kiss my ass. My dick is bigger than yours, anyway."

Lil' Man had a homemade dick. He grabbed it and showed Nip the print of it. Then he said, "Let me fuck you in the ass, bastard."

I opened the door and Nip said, "Bye, baby."

"Just go to hell, fucker," Lil' Man said, "That goddamned Nip is crazy."

"That motherfucker's got good sense," I said, "you see that he didn't give up none."

"That's all right. I'll fix his stanking ass. Gimme me another lil' hit, please, sis?"

"Clean up the house for me. I'll give you one."

"Okay."

Lil' Man started cleaning. The white girl asked, "San, can I talk to you for a minute?"

"Yeah, c'mon in my bedroom."

We went into the bedroom and she said, "Listen. I don't have a place to stay. Can I live here with you?"

"Yeah. You can sleep in the big bedroom or with Cocoa."

"Cocoa is mean. I think I'll sleep in the living room."

"Okay, but don't burn up my shit."

"Oh, I won't," she said, "Do you want me to do anything for you?"

"Nah, I'm paying Lil' Man to clean up for me."

"San, do you have anything that I can wear? I've got to turn some tricks tonight."

"Why don't you work at the club any more?"

"Honey, that cracker fired me."

"Have you tried another spot?"

"I hadn't, but I am tonight. You know, before you went to jail, you made lots of money."

"Uh-huh."

Time went by and folks were running in and out all day. Sugar bought her a car with her income tax return. We went to look for another car for the kids. I saw Ray whenever I saw him, like whenever I had to re-up.

Softball season was over. I dreamed a number and played on it. It fell. The number's man came over to my house that day. "Hey, San! San!"

I ran to the door. "You busted the number, babe!"

I jumped up and down and yelled, "How much will I get?"

"Seventy-two hundred!"

"What?"

"Yeah! I'll be here tomorrow with it, okay?"

"Okay. Bye."

I called Sugar, Ray and my mother with the great news. It was September 1981 when I went to a used car lot and bought a black Fiat; black with a rust interior. It was a four speed. My son could drive a automatic, but I had to teach him how to drive the stick.

He and his sister went to school in December. My baby brother went to City High and Bay-Bay went to the nursery around the corner. Harry learned how to drive the stick with ease, just in one day.

He was in the 11th grade, my brother was in the 12th and Cocoa was in the 9th. Things started going good for us. All the shoplifters knew me and all the burglars, credit card workers, robbers, you name it, they knew me. I bought a van for two grams, then a car for an eighth, another van. I even got a 1936 Chevy for two ounces.

Thanksgiving rolled around and passed. I wanted to get another place for my kids, but decided to wait until after the New Year. I got two of my brothers, Nip, and Lil' Man to work with me because I was getting plenty of business. All five of us had a meeting. It didn't last long, but issues had to be addressed.

"Listen, y'all," I got right to the point, "It's Xmas time and y'all know what that means. Okay, Larry, you hold the front door; James, you sit in my bedroom; Nip, you're in Harry and Tony's room; Lil' Man, you're in the hallway."

"But San, why all the watch out?"

"We've never been robbed and I don't want to be caught off guard. My sister had a dream about what Lil' Man said. She dreamed that five women and one man robbed me. So I was told to turn the dream around so here we are—five men and one woman. Now that's that. Here, Larry," I said as I threw him a .44 handgun. "James, you be the shotgun man; Nip here's your .38; Lil' Man the .25's for you."

"That's right, Lil' Man, you take the little one," Nip said.

"Fuck you in the nose, bastard," Lil' Man responded.

Everybody laughed. I continued, "As for me, I'll have my .45 automatic and lay the sawed-off besides me. Listen! I don't want no female on the door at any time—unless it's me! Now, let's go to work."

It was December and I was selling about $4,000–$6,000 a day. I paid everybody $100/day and if they had a good week, they got $700. I paid for all the hot clothes that came through for them and paid their bills once a month. We even had a grocery man. I bought their groceries, too.

X-mas had passed and I was all out of cocaine. Therefore, there was no work for them. The New Year came and left and I was still out of cocaine. On January 2, 1982, I talked to Ray early that morning. He said that it would be later on before we would have any cocaine. Harry had basketball practice this particular night. Sugar, Ann, Tony, Lil' Man, one of my sisters, my brother, Larry, and Bay-Bay were there. Sugar and I were leaving but before I left I announced, "Hey, I ain't got nothing so don't let nobody in, okay?"

"All right," they answered back.

We got in the van going to Dekalb High School to pick up my son. On the way back home, we stopped by Ray's house and The Elephant Man was on TV. Sugar was looking weird. Ray asked, "What's wrong, Sugar?"

"Nothing."

I wasn't saying too much, either, and since nothing was going on, I said, "Well, baby, since we've got to wait, better get on back to the house."

He didn't have any objection, so Harry, Sugar, and I left.

When we pulled up to the house, I saw Lil' Man opening the door. Harry and Sugar got out and went inside. I could sense that something was wrong because no one was on the porch. I went to the dumpster to put some trash from the van in. I looked at the door again. I took a deep breath and said, "Lord! Whatever it is, I've got to go inside and face it because my children are in there."

I went up the steps, walked in, looked to the right and saw a female dressed like a cowboy with the hat and all. As I reached for her, I noticed a nigger was standing behind the door and he yelled, "Big Man, San thinks we're teasing!"

A big, black-bearded man came from the back with a narrow shotgun wearing a brass-knuckle-plated gun. The woman had a .25 and another one in the middle room had a .45. The one behind the door had a pump shotgun. I threw my hands up and asked, "Where are my kids?"

The big red one behind the door said, "They're all right as long as you cooperate. Where's the money, diamonds, and the cocaine?"

I stared at the big black one very hard until he appeared nervous. Then he said, "Tell her to quit looking at me. Tell her to stop!"

"Come on, San, where is it?" the skinny one asked.

"Where is my family? I want to see them!"

Big Man opened the bathroom door and said, "Don't look at me. Here they are. Man she keeps watching me."

I looked to the ceiling and said to myself: "Lord, have mercy. Please don't let nothing happen." Then I went into Psalms 23: "The Lord is my shepherd, I shall not want. Lord, we're walking through the valley of the shadow of death, for I will fear no evil ..." I then walked out and said to the apparent leader, "You're late. Your informant should have told you about our Xmas robbing, plus I've just got out of prison. Let them go and keep me."

"It don't go like that, San. You know it."

Then the one behind the door said, "Come on up here and answer this door. Maybe the big dope man will come through."

One guy came to the door and said, "Hey San! Gimme a fifty!"

I looked on the side of the door, the robber shook his head "no." On that cue, I answered with the truth, "I ain't got nothing right now."

He left. Then one of the robbers pulled me by my jacket and said, "C'mon, where is it? I know that you have a little money."

"Here, search me!"

I unzipped my jacket and pulled my pants down.

"Pull your clothes up," he said, "take us to the dope man's house."

"Okay, who's riding with me?" I asked.

"Nah, man. It's a trick. We'll call him and let him bring it over." He handed me the phone and Big Man gave another phone to the little skinny one who had a limp. Every number that I dialed, no one answered. I resulted in calling Ray with all intentions of giving him a hint to what was happening, but he didn't answer either.

Just then there was a knock at the door. Big Man waved the gun at me motioning me to answer it. I did.

"Who is it?"

"Charlie boy."

"What do you want?"

"Just a little fifty."

The robber shook his head, "no."

"Ain't nothing happening."

He left. As I watched him leave, I noticed Duey coming up. The robber was checking him and his jewelry he had on. He said, "Let him in."

"That's not real jewelry he has on, he only wants a fifty," I explained.

"San, let me get one of those things 'til tomorrow."

"I ain't got none right now. Check back tomorrow."

He left.

My uncle came to the door next. "Hey baby. How you been doing?"

"Listen, Aunt Hazel is not here right now. Come back later."

"But it's me: your uncle."

The robber grabbed me, snatched him in and put the gun to my head. Then he said, "Bitch! I should kill you for doing that!"

Then he pushed me and beat my uncle. He kicked him all in his ass. The robber pulled Lil' Man out in the hall and said to me, "San! This motherfucker right here needs killing. He's the one who opened the door."

He started wiping Lil' Man's ass. Then Lil' Man said, "Hey man, I'm a woman!" He opened his shirt and show them his titties.

"Ha, ha, ha, a butch." Big Man laughed. "Look a here will you, a bulldigger."

Then another said, "Get the meat out of the freezer, man. Get all of the TVs, the stereos and the new clothes. They got all of those things—even the watches and chains. Get them all off everybody up in here."

They locked me up in the bathroom with everybody else. I could tell that they were gone. I said, "Let me out, y'all, let me out!" I was heading out the door after the motherfuckers.

"Don't open that door, San!" Sugar yelled as I approached the front door.

"I've got to."

I went out the door and they were nowhere to be seen. I went back into the house and announced that I was calling the police as I picked up the phone.

"How can you call the police with all this hot shit up in here?" my sister asked.

"Just like this!" I said as I dialed the operator. I went on to tell her send the police.

"Look, y'all, they even took the van. If anything happens in it, I'm going to jail. I've got to report it stolen." Then I called Ray, again. This time he was there. "Hello?"

"Baby! I've just been robbed."

"I'll be there in a minute."

The police came and I gave a report. Then Ray came and the first thing he asked was, "Where're my children?"

"They're in there."

He walked through the house and said, "C'mon, y'all, pack your things and let's go." Harry, Cocoa, Ronnie, Bay-Bay and I started packing. Ray questioned everybody—especially Lil' Man. Lil' Man gave his account then Ray asked, "Lil' Man, who in the fuck told you to open the goddamn door, anyway?"

"Somebody knocked and didn't nobody go to the door, so I did."

"Well, did San tell y'all that she didn't have any dope?"

"I didn't hear her."

"Where was Larry?"

"He was on the phone."

"You mean she pays all you motherfuckers to lay around to use the goddamn telephone? Goddamn! Where were you, Lil' Man?"

"I was in the living room watching The Elephant Man."

"So the TV and the telephone nearly got y'all asses killed. I thought that San didn't want no woman answering the door. Did you hear her tell you that, Lil' Man?"

"Yeah, but—"

"But my ass! If I find out that you had something to do with this shit, bitch, I'm going to pull every piece of skin off your ass! Let's go! Everybody ready?"

"Uncle Mac will stay," I explained, "Sugar, will you drop my sister and brother off?"

"Yeah. Come on, everybody. Out."

Lil' Man stayed with Uncle Mac. Ray left a gun with him. Ray drove his car with Cocoa and Bay-Bay in it. I drove the big boys: Harry and Tony. We made it to Ray's house. His children were there for the holidays. He had a daughter named Cookies and his son was Jerry. Ray sent all the kids upstairs and we went in the kitchen to talk. With tears in his eyes he said, "Baby, it's time for you to quit."

Tears were rolling down my face and I said, "Come on, let's go upstairs."

We went into his bedroom and closed the door. Then he said, "Baby, can we do something else?"

"What, Ray? Tell me what else can we do right now?"

"Baby, we ain't got to sell no more dope. We have our children to think about. You've got to move from over there. Let's go find an apartment or even a house out here in Decatur. Yeah, we are going to do that tomorrow."

"Okay, no more cocaine."

"No more dope, period. So, what are you going to do with that you've already paid for?"

"I'll see if he will take it back."

"Nah, baby. You know damn well that nigger ain't going to take it back."

"Hey, we can't stop, not right now. I'm going back! That episode ain't going to stop me! Gimme me some and let me ride."

Ray slapped me and tried to shake me to death as he said, "Bitch, you ain't got no sense. What's wrong with you, San? Girl, I love you!" He was crying. "San, you take care of the kids, I'll make the money. Please, if only for a little while. I don't know what I'm going to do with you. You are, no doubt, crazy. What nigger gets robbed and wants to go back and sell some dope? Tell me! Who?"

"Me. Don't worry, baby. The Lord will shield me from whatever. We need some money, okay?"

"Wow! You're going to do it with or without me. So, go look in the drawer and get that .38."

I kissed him and said, "Thank you."

He gave me a little cocaine. It was about half an ounce. I got the gun and dope and left going back to make my money back or at least what the merchandise was worth (they didn't get any cash). That was my worst experience, yet.

11

I was going back and forth to Ray's house, carrying money and prepared food for the kids. I sold dope harder than ever. All the boosters came through and the burglars, too. I bought brand named colored TVs, microwaves, brass, crystal, bedroom suites, den furniture, sheets, spreads ...I mean, I got the works. This time I had more than before. I went and found a house in Decatur. It was a tri-level with four bedrooms, a living room, dining room, kitchen and a den. It was red brick with white trim. It was gorgeous. Every room was fully furnished except for my dining room. Ray fell in love with it. The den had a huge fireplace. Sugar came over and helped decorate. Mama went and bought some drapes. A friend gave me two Rottweiller dogs. I named one Bushrod and the other Chow. One of my friends from jail gave me a spitz. She was white as snow and we named her Snow. White San helped me whenever she was there. She had started back working a club. I left most of the furniture over at the Eugenia Street house because that was my working house. Sonya stayed there with me whenever she was off. I didn't allow the children to come over that way.

It was March and I was getting ready for the check cashiers. They came in and out all day long. Then Melvin came over. He asked, "Can I use your kitchen?"

"For what?"

"I want to cook my cocaine up."

"Okay. You freebase, huh?"

"Something like that."

I went in the kitchen with him and I watched him very closely: He boiled a pot. He put some baking soda in a little bottle that he had on him then topped it up with cocaine. He added a cup or two of water in the bottle. He tightly screwed the bottle top and put the bottle into the pot of boiling water.

After two minutes, he opened the bottle and added teaspoons of the boiling water. He allowed it to come to a boil and after a few moments he added more water. He went to the sink and ran cold water on the bottle. He held the bottle up to the light and started grinning. He then broke a clothes hanger and stuck it in the little bottle to scoop the cocaine out. The powder had transformed into a solid. He blew it to finish up the transformation to the point that it was hard as a rock. He pulled a pipe out of his bag, some golden grain, and some scissors with cotton in it. He cut the cocaine up with a razor blade. He put a piece of the cooked cocaine in the pipe then he passed me the lighter and said, "Light this after I stick the scissors down in the grain bottle."

He put the fire to the top of the pipe and pulled a little bit ...long enough to melt the cocaine. He blew the torch out and took a deep breath; then he soaked the cotton again with the grain.

I lit the lighter for him; he burned the center of the pipe first then he put the fire to the top and pulled. He pulled until all the smoke was gone. He handed me the torch to blow out. He inhaled and held his breath for a minute then exhaled. He started feeling on the chair, the side of the table and the floor. I had to ask, "What are you looking for?" I got no response but I kept on watching him, as he appeared to be looking for something.

White San was at the door; my brother Larry had sent her back to the kitchen. She saw Melvin hitting the pipe and I could tell she wanted some. He gave her a piece. She hit it and started tip-toeing all over the kitchen. I was watching her and him. I hadn't seen nothing like it.

After he finished, he got up and said, "I'll be back. I've got to go."

"Okay," I said, "see you later."

White San yelled, "San! I got some of my bosses coming by tonight. They want to spend some money!"

"Okay, darling. Hey, White San!"

"Huh?"

"I didn't know that you freebase."

"Yeah, I'm tired of shooting cocaine. That pipe puts you in a totally different world." She left and reminded me that she and her bosses would be back.

I was getting kind of depressed, so I snorted about an eighth all by myself in just four hours ...an eighth of pure rock. My nose was hurting very bad. I was in the kitchen cutting up some cocaine and didn't have anybody test it for me. Then Kela came by. She had some comforters for sale. Kela stood about four feet eleven inches and weighed, maybe, 95 pounds. She was a pretty little lady with a brown complexion. She had about nine comforter sets ranging from $150–$300 in all kinds of colors. They were all pretty. I got her to check the cocaine for me. She fixed the cocaine up, put her arm between her legs, and hit it. Kela got up with the needle in her arm, went to the window, then to the door, peeping through and announcing that someone was coming, but in actuality there was no one and no peephole to see out of.

"I see somebody coming," she announced.

"No you don't."

"Be quiet and come here. Listen." She put her ear to the door and motioned to me to do the same.

"Check it out."

"Girl, you better bring your—"

"Listen, you better get it. They are coming in. I ain't going out 'cause somebody's out there. Every time I come over here you give me that goddamn shit!"

Lil' Man walked in and said, "Kela, baby ..."

"Lil' Man, check the back. Somebody's here," Kela said in distress.

"Ah bitch, sit your ass down somewhere and let me peep a while."

"Go to hell, motherfucker."

"Gimme a hit, sis?"

"Okay. Where's your top?" I asked.

Lil' Man looked inside his socks and got his tools. He tied up a hit himself. Kela was shooting some more. Lil' Man pulled his shirt off. Kela unzipped her pants and went to the door again. She and Lil' Man were tripping hard. I was snorting and laughing with the gun under my left arm. I was tripping and didn't even know it. Kela said, "Hurry! Come and listen."

I went to the door and peeped out of the crack to see if I could see anybody. Lil' Man's lips had turned white. He was pointing at the window, the door and the hallway. Then I caught myself.

"Damn! Y'all mother fuckers got me tripping!" I yelled.

"Bitch, you trip anyway," said Lil' Man.

"Motherfucker, be quiet," said Kela.

"Ah hoe, you just glad San let you test some."

"You's a goddamn lie. I got money and anyway, San asked me to test the shit out. San, honey?"

I looked at Kela and she went to ask, "You gonna get some of those comforters?"

"Yeah."

"Well, let me go before I cuss this motherfucker out. What? Do you want all of them? Well just gimme me an eighth and $75."

"Okay, here you go," I said as I handed her the money from my tiddy.

"Thank you, San. And bye, you ugly motherfucker," she said as she rolled her eyes at Lil' Man.

Lil' Man turned around holding the print of his homemade dick and said, "Suck my dick, bitch."

Kela went into the middle of the room and walked on out the door.

"Come on, Lil' Man. Put these comforters in my room."

Lil' Man walked over by me and said, "Let me see who that hoe is riding with."

He looked out of the window of the kitchen door and I said, "Man, let that car go and get this shit out of here before somebody walks with it."

He picked up four comforters at a time, peeped, then walked until he got to my bedroom. When Lil' Man finally moved all the comforters, he went back to peeping. He handed me the cooker and said as he looked all around, "Put a little bit in here, sis."

"Let 'that' wear off, first. Damn!"

It was about closing time. I could hear Nip's voice. He was coming through, heading to the kitchen. When he got in, he said, "San? You got that motherfucker Lil' Man back there, ain't you?"

At this point, Lil' Man was at the back kitchen door and answered, "Man! You better quit fuckin' with me. I ain't your bitch."

"Fat as your ass is, baby, you sho' can get five of my lines."
"Give it to your mammy, you one-tooth-bastard. You need to get your mouth fixed."

"If I get my mouth fixed, I want be able to suck your pussy."

"San, you better tell these motherfuckers to leave me alone 'cause I ain't the one," Lil' Man ordered.

Ignoring her for the moment, Nip threw his cooker on the table for me to put some cocaine in it as he said, "Fix me up, babe." Then he looked over to Lil' Man, "All you need is for somebody to give you a good fuck," he said laughing.

"It won't be you, you ugly ass nigger."

Nip was stirring the cocaine in this cooker as he said, "Ugly? Ugly? Bitch, you called me ugly? You better look in the mirror, hoe."

"Come on, y'all, now," I said, "go on and shoot this shit."

He stared at me first. Then Lil' Man said, "But San ..."

"I know, but I'm gonna have to get through."

"Can I go with you?" Nip asked.

"Hell nah, bastard. Who wants your ugly ass out there?" Lil' Man asked.

Nip had tied his arm up and got a hit and said with eyes bucked wide, "Aah hell, Lil' Man, the room is turning yellow."

"Motherfucker, it's gonna turn black you keep on fucking with me."

"I'm gonna fuck you, baby, don't get mad."

"How you gonna fuck me, nigger: your dick won't even get hard."

Lil' Man grabbed his and continued, "You see this dick right here?" Nip was looking all over the room then Lil' Man commanded, "Look, bastard! This motherfucker stays hard."

"Ah bitch," Nip responded, "you got the herpes."

"All I got to do is throw the motherfucker away and make another one."

"I'm gonna fuck you, yet. Wait and see."

I got up from the amusement and walked around to pay everybody. At the same time I told them what time to come back tomorrow. I left and went home to get in the bed. The next day I woke up to the phone ringing. "Hello?"

"Were you sleep?" Mama asked.

"Yeah, what time is it?"

"Honey, it's 12:30."

"What? Dog Mama, I done overslept ...Listen Mama, I don't mean to rush but did you need something?"

"We need some more meat. I'm about to run out with all these greedy children down here."

"Okay, Ma, I'll make you my first stop. Okay? I'll be there in a minute. See ya' later, Ma."

I got up, combed my hair into a ponytail, and put on a beige and brown warm-up with tennis shoes. I then fed my dogs and gave them water. As I left I said, "Take care, Chow."

I jumped into the brown car and left, going to my mother's house. I was moving fast 'cause I had to get to work. When I got to mama's apartment, I blew the horn. She met me at the door. I kissed her and gave her $200 then I left right back out. As I walked away I said, "When the meat people come through buy you some meat, okay?"

"Thank you, baby. You be careful, Sandra."

"Okay, Ma."

I jumped in the car and took off pretty fast. When I got to the work house, everybody was there. There were ever customers waiting in their cars. The street was full. They all started getting out of the car when they saw me. I parked the car in the driveway. I got out announcing, "Give me a minute!" It was about seven people who wanted 50 grams. "Come on in, Lil' Man," I said while unlocking the door. "Larry! You hold the door. James, you get the back and Nip, you ah...let me see... you walk the block."

"Why don't you let that motherfucker walk?" Nip questioned, referring to Lil' Man.

"Just kiss my ass and walk, bastard," Lil' Man answered.

"Come on, y'all. I've got to fix some up." I cut in. Nip started walking the block, my brother James watched the back for me.

"Lil' Man, get your works out," I said.

I went into my jacket. I went in the kitchen, looked in the cabinet, got the cut, looked in the bottom cabinet, and got the scale. I looked in the drawer and got the sifter and in the dish rack I got a plate. I put it all on the table. Lil' Man gave a card.

He looked in his pocket slowly. I said, "Hurry up, you moving too slow."

I pulled an ounce out of my tiddy and poured half of it into the sifter. It weighed 14 grams of cut up. I mixed them together. Lil' Man was acting like he wasn't really there. It was like I had to tell him every move to make.

"Damn, Lil' Man, pass me the bags."

"San," Larry said, "hurry up. More people are lining up."

"Okay, gimme a minute."

I got the bags, tore them one by one. I used all four corners of five bags so that I could get the people that were already waiting. I was sweating as I worked fast. I bagged five fifties and five grams first. I went into the hallway asking, "Who wants fifties?"

Four of them wanted fifties. One nigger wanted a gram and a half. I gave him a gram and two fifties. Three wanted a gram apiece. Duey wanted a quarter. "Hold on, Duey," I said because I had to go back and fix him up.

"Okay, babe, make it quick."

"I'll be right back." Sweat was falling from my face. I grabbed a towel, wiped my face and went back into the kitchen with the towel around my neck.

Lil' Man was at the back window.

"Honey, sit down," I said.

"Somebody's out there."

"Ain't nobody but James."

I weighed up seven grams for Duey and put it in a bag and gave it to him. I came back into the kitchen, laid the money on the table without counting it. I sifted the other half of cocaine up, weighed up 14 grams of cut and sifted the cocaine and cut. I made up four eighths, one quarter, and the rest in fifties and grams out of that one ounce. I had served up everybody that was waiting and came up with about $4,000. I cleaned up everything but the plate. Lil' Man wanted it.

"Come on, Lil' Man, get done so Nip can get him a hit. I need some help."

Lil' Man was scraping the plate and asked, "Help? For what?"

"I need somebody to stay here at night and be ready for the early morning traffic."

"I'll stay for you."

I looked at him and said, "I'd have to kill your goddamn ass and you know it. You'd be shooting dope all night long. Hell naw! I'll find some one that's gonna get through the night."

Nip had returned from walking the block. "Hey, it's your time to walk, Lil' Man. Come on from back in there." He was heading toward the kitchen. "Just kiss my ass!"

When Nip got to the kitchen, he said "Oh, you just gonna shoot dope all day, huh?"

"If I do, it's my business."

I grabbed Nip's arm and said, "Here, Nip. Come on so I can go up front. I need to get some more guns. If y'all know or hear of anybody got any, let me know."

I gave Nip a good shot and went up front to wait on customers. My brother, Larry, and I were on the porch. White San showed up. I looked at Larry and said, "I got it ...damn! I can let White San stay here and sell the dope for me in the mornings, you know, until I get here."

She walked up the stairs saying, "Hey Rose."

I looked at her and asked, "Who in the hell is Rose?"

"Oh honey, we call all the girls in the club Rose."

"Oh. Hey listen. How would you like to live here and sell dope in the mornings until I get here?"

"Sure, darling, you know that I would do that for you. Hey, listen. You got a gram?"

"Yep. Step inside."

We went inside the door. I handed her the gram and she gave me $80 and said, "Thank you, San. I'll be back tonight before you leave, okay, hon?"

"All right. Don't let me down."

She went on out of the door. I stayed in and got me a good hit of cocaine then I went into the kitchen to see what Lil' Man and Nip were doing. They were cleaning up the kitchen ...together. They didn't see me, so I tiptoed back out into the front and got me another hit. I went back in the kitchen and asked, "Will one of you come down here early tomorrow morning help White San out?"

"Yeah, but I don't want that white bitch giving me no damn orders," Lil' Man said.

"Look, she's going to be the one who holds the sack, so she will call the shots while I'm gone. You're getting paid my way, so what's the gripe?"

"I'll stay all night if you want me to 'cause I want to fuck her anyway," Nip said.

"Nigger, you know damn well that girl don't want no ugly motherfucker like you," Lil' Man said. "Anyway, she sure as hell don't want you with that false ass dick you got," Nip said.

"Don't worry. She ain't do no fucking up in here, anyway. She'll be here to work and live so don't fuck with her."

"Ah, San. We were just kicking the game around," Nip said.

"Okay, game kicker. Well who will be here?"

"It'll be both of us."

"Okay, that's a deal. Listen, I'm going to get something to eat. Y'all want something back?"

"Yeah. Bring me anything and a pack of cigarettes—Benson & Hedges," Nip said.

"Just bring me some Newport News and a Pepsi Cola," Lil' Man said.

"Okay. I'll leave some stuff here with Larry. Y'all go on and get finished. I'll be back in a minute." I went to the front and said to Larry, "I'm going to get all of us something to eat. Here, hold these fifties and grams for me. If anybody comes by with some guns, hold them here 'til I get back."

"Okay."

I got in the car and yelled back, "Tell James that he can stay here until I get back, okay?"

Just as I turned the corner, I saw Ray's car at the light. I pulled over to the side. He looked like he was pissed off about something. He got out of his car leaving the door open and said, "Since you've moved into the house you've been acting shitty. What's going on? Tell me. I want to know."

"Baby, it ain't like that. You know that I had to get everything in order and fixed all up."

"Yeah, but that's no excuse. The only time I see you is when you re-up. I'm jealous."

"What?"

"You heard it right ...jealous."

"Of what, baby? Tell me."

"You usta come to me for this and that ...but now, I don't see you anymore."

"But you know that I still love you and I always will."

"You're going have to take some time off and I mean tonight. I'll be back at 12:30 A.M. and you be ready."

He walked back to his car.

"But Ray ..." I said.

"Twelve-thirty tonight, San ...be ready," he yelled while pointing his finger, "I ain't playing with you either. You don't stay home. You're always over here. That shit is going to stop and I mean it." He drove off.

I went and got the food, stopped by the service station and bought cigarettes for everybody, and came back to the house. White San was waiting with another white girl. Larry came to help me with the food. I was studying the other white girl. I walked on the porch and asked, "Who is this, White San? You know that I don't want to meet nobody. Why you bring her here?"

"This is Cookie. She works at the club with me. She's all right."

"I don't give a fuck. I went to prison the last time for some shit just like that."

"Girl, you know that I wouldn't do nothing like that."

"Yeah, that's what they all say."

"Well, your brother James knows me," Cookie said.

"Oh yeah? Where is James?"

I yelled through the door, "James, come here!"

James came to the door and asked, "Who called for me?"

"Me." I said, "Do you know this girl?"

"Yeah. Why? What's wrong?"

"Oh nothing. I just wanted to be safe because I ain't going back to prison for no bullshit. Those motherfuckers ain't playing now.

"As for you, Cookie, I'm pleased to meet you, but you must understand where I'm coming from. Can't you? I be damned if I want to go back."

"Yes, San, I understand where you are coming from," Cookie said. She was a pretty white girl with blue eyes and blond hair. She weighed about 125 pounds standing five feet six inches. "But I ain't no police," she continued.

"Well, what's up?" I asked, looking at both of them.

"I want to get an eighth," Cookie said.

"Okay. Help me put this food in the kitchen," I said while handing bags to her and White San. We went into the kitchen to eat some chicken. I offered them a seat and they sat down. Then Nip said, "Oh! What's dis? You gonna fire all us niggers and hire all white girls? Or should I say folks."

"Man! What the hell are you talking about? Fuck that shit. Whoever I hire, it's my business. Anyway, white girls bring more money than any of these niggas around here." Nip was still running his mouth. Lil' Man came in and said, "Do you want me to take care of this old punk ass one tooth nigga?"

Nip said to Lil' Man, "Shut the fuck up, Lil' Man, and come on and get yourself some real man."

Lil' Man looked at Nip then at me and bust out laughing. Then we all started to laugh. Cookie got what she came for then she left. Nip said "Damn, San, you got a bunch of crackers coming in and out for real."

"Hey! This is the ghetto and you know it. Man, those girls might draw the heat."

"Ah, shut up, you scary ass motherfucker," Lil' Man said as we went into the house.

And as I was sitting on the porch on Eugenia Street, I saw about three ladies walking toward my way, one which looked a lot like me. Upon reaching the steps, the one that looked like me said, "Hey! You must be San?"

I answered her, "Yes, but who are you and your friends?"

"My name is Sandra, I'm your first cousin, and Tommy is my father."

I looked at her and said, "Oh, what a pleasure. Uncle Tommy should be back in a little while."

"These are two dancers. They work with me downtown Atlanta in the 'HotBar.' I heard that you have the best blow in town, is that true?"

"Hold up honey, now we do look alike, but let me find somebody that knows you because I sure as hell don't."

"That white girl, San, knows me. But I don't know where she is right now."

"I'll call Aunt Hazel, she will know."

"Oh yeah, she knows me, she use to come over when I was little."

I called Aunt Hazel and asked her to come over. While waiting on Hazel, cousin San said, "Hey baby, I'm your kin' folk. You might as well get use to a lookalike; the only difference is you have long hair, and I wear wigs."

"Listen, Rose."

I looked at her and said, "Who in the hell is Rose?"

Cousin San started laughing and so did the other two ladies. Cousin San said, "In this life, we call all the ladies Rose so when and if the cops come they have really got to search for their person."

"Oh yeah! Hey I think that I'll like that."

Cousin San said, "Now with three Sans, you, the white girl, and myself all have the same first name." So you will be Big San, she'll be White San, and I'll be Lil' San." By then Aunt Hazel walked up shaking all hands. Hazel said, "Girl, where in the hell have you been?"

Lil' San said, "Out there trying to make me some money. Oh yeah! Meet Diamond and Star, they dance, too."

Aunt Hazel said, "Yeah, San baby, this is your first cousin, my brother's daughter."

I said, "Now, Rose, (laughing) what can I do for you?"

She said, "We want three separate grams, okay."

I gave her what she wanted, then we exchanged phone numbers and she left us with a smile and a kiss.

Lil' Man came in and wanted something to do to get a hit. It was about 2:30 when the number man showed up. I said "Hey, did I hit the number again?"

The number man said, "Yeah, but only for $300.00." Lil' Man started doing his little dance. I looked at Lil' Man and said, (laughing), "What in the hell are you dancing for? You ain't gon get no more dope."

Lil' Man looked all crazy, but that's usual.

Then the number man said, "San, check this out, I need to talk to you privately."

Lil' Man said, "Bitch, you ain't no private nigga, you are just a little number runner fucker."

"Lil' Man, shut the fuck up," I said. Number man said, "Yeah, little whore, shut up."

"Kiss my ass, nigga, you ain't shit."

I said, "Wait, goddammit. Lil' Man, go on and do what you've got to do."

Lil' Man walked into the house, looking back, rolling his eyes, and cussing. The number man and I went into the living room. He said, "San, my boss has a lot of cocaine in the raw form. Number man he has access to keys, plus he has two keys right now. Now listen at this, San, he didn't know anything about cocaine at all. So he sent me over here to talk to you about selling for him."

"Wait now," I said, "I don't sell for nobody, San sells for San, so I can't help you with that. Anyway, why would a rich motherfucker want to get into this too much time game?"

Number man said, "See San, I told him about you and how smooth you operation is."

"Nigga, you don't know me or how I operate, so how in the fuck you can tell a nigga about me? Hey! I don't like that not a bit. Man you are wrong for that."

"San, I'm sorry, I just thought you might want to get more than what you are getting."

"I do, but damn, man, your boss doesn't even show his face, so how the hell we are going to take care of business? Now what I need to know is, how much per ounce, how much per quarter, how much per pound, and how much per kilo? Now you tell him that. I don't deal with no middle man. It must be him, if he wants my business. So you already told him about my operation, then he knows what time it is with me."

Smiling, Number man said, "San, baby, I am trying to move up in the world. If I get you, girl, I'll be in the house. I won't be ripping and running all around town with that number thing (two paid)."

"Hey, you want be dropping me off nothing. I told you I don't deal with no middle man."

Lil' Man came in as I was mentioning middle man. Lil' Man said, "Hell, naw nigga ain't no middle man."

"Bitch shut up and gimme my business back," I said. "What now, Lil' Man? You got about three people out here that want some dope, and are you gonna serve them, or keep talking to this jive ass number man?"

"Number man! Man, leave me alone, or should I say woman? (Laughing) Kiss my woman ass ugly fucker, I bet your wife like it."

"Hold it now," I said, "here we go again."

Number man said, "Come on, little bitch, you wasn't always a bulldigger. See, San, she used to be a whore."

Lil' Man said, "You're a goddamn lie bitch ass nigga, you ain't never fucked me."

"I done had your sister and your mammy." We were all laughing, but Lil' Man was serious. So I then went out of the living room. Lil' Man was still in there fussing and cussing, tooting his nose. I quickly put Lil' Man out and closed the door. I said, "Listen, take that info to your boss. Get back with me and let me know what is what." I let him out and went into the kitchen where Lil' Man was. I called Hazel from the kitchen phone and asked her to come down 'cause I needed to know about the bossman. Lil' Man and I talked about what the number man had talked about, and then Hazel showed up. "What you want baby?"

I said, "Tell me about the number man's boss, Willie." Her eyes got wide. "Honey, he's a big number man, I mean he'sa rich. He has property all over Atlanta and in the country."

"What has happened?"

I said, "Oh nothing, the number man said that Willie wants to supply me with cocaine."

Hazel said, "What? That nigger doesn't fuck around."

"Well, the Number man talks. He's now into cocaine and wants me to sell for him, but you know me better than that, San sells for San."

Hazel said, "The only thing that I can tell you about him is he's good people. He will help you in any way he can, only if you are trying to help yourself. Give it a shot, hell, Ray only gets so much, and you are trying to get from under him, aren't you? Hey baby he, I mean we, ain't what we use to be. I ain't got time for Ray's bullshit. I'm about the money honey." We were laughing. Lil' Man said, "I'm the tester."

Hazel said, "You can sit your testing ass down, 'cause you peep too damn hard."

Lil' Man said, "So what, it takes you 30 minutes to get a hit, your hand is too big, and you hardly can find a vein. Bitch we are on the same kind of time. You peep 30 minutes, and it takes me about 30 minutes to get a hit. So what the fuck you talking about?"

"Wait ya'll, I ain't got it yet. Hopefully I'll know something later on this evening."

Days had passed by. On Saturday morning Melvin called and said that he was coming over. I had in mind to go and get some practice shooting these guns that I got. I had a 9mm, an ozzie, a 45, and a 25 automatic. I called Sugar and told her I would pick her up. When Melvin got to the house it was about 11 A.M., I kissed him on the jaw and said, "What's up for the next two hours?"

Melvin said, "Nothing baby, just wanted to holla at you, or take you to lunch or something."

Sugar was in the back. "Check this out Melvin, will you take us to the shooting range over in Conyers?"

Melvin said, "Sure, but do you have license for your gun, or should I say guns?" (smiling).

"Hell naw, I ain't got no license and I don't need none until I get caught. Anyway, honey, ex cons are not allowed to carry weapons, I mean no kind."

"Hey, if anything happens, I'll take the weight."

Melvin said, "That's not the problem."

I looked at him. Then ok, I called Hazel and Lil' Man and left Hazel four quarter ounces, and ten fifties that should hold her until I get back. I got the guns and the ammo, and off we went. I thought that it would be like going to a game room, but I found out different and so did Sugar. Melvin knows how to shoot, and that helped us a lot. My favorite gunslinger was and still is Clint Eastwood. He always carried the 45 and that was the one I practiced with last, but guess what, I hurt my shoulder trying to do what I saw Clint do. Anyway we made it back home after stopping by the chicken place.

Hazel had sold all of the quarter ounce, and six of the 50's. She was smiling. Lil' Man was in the bathroom. I knew then that they had been in the bags. I gave Hazel a gram and Lil' Man a 50, and believe me they were ever too happy. Melvin bought a half ounce, then he went home or wherever. My arm was still hurting. Hazel looked at it and put some witch hazel on it and some heat. She rubbed it down and told me what to do to get it well. By then the phone rang. It was Lil' San and the white girl. "Hey cous. What's going on?"

"I went to learn how to kill a nigga."

Lil' San said, "What Girl, who been fucking with you?"

I said, laughing, "Oh no, baby, I'm learning how to shoot. In fact, I believe that I know how to hit my target."

"Cous, Big San, I need a place to live just for a little while until I get myself together. I can help you sell that dope."

"Wait a minute now," I said. "What you are saying?" Lil' San said, "I got into a fight with one of them white girls down at the club, and I beat the shit out of her for fucking with my money, so that punky ass white boy fired me. Hey, I ain't got to go to the big house, just let me stay here. I'll sell dope 24 hours for you."

I said, "Just come on over and bring White San with you." I hung up the phone, my mind was really racing. Yeah! That will work, I can be with my children more often. Well, well, it's time to get this thing rollin from town to town, city to city. I jumped up and said out, "Yes, yes, yes." I went through the house screaming, "Money, money, money, money. Some people got to have it, some people really need it, and I'm both," (laughing). Talking out loud to myself, "Bright lights, big cities, I'm going there. I'll be able to put my mother in a house furnished off, yes sir." A knock at the door. I said, "Ain't no way in the hell Lil' San done here that fast, hell naw." I didn't even look out the window, I said, "Who it is?"

From the other side he said: "The Number Man."

I opened the door very fast with a smile and said, "Hey! What's up? Well, baby girl, you're on." I unlocked the burglar door and kinda snatched him in the house. "Come on, man, tell me what did he say?"

"He's out in the car right now."

I said, "What! Shit, damn, let me get my shoes."

Number Man said, "I'll be on the porch." I ran out to the car while the Number Man stayed on the porch. I opened the door of a 1982 four-door caddy. Wow, it was beautiful triple blue. The top was a darker blue rag like top. He was a mid-height, dark-skinned man with gold on every other tooth, with a thin mustache, little sideburns, and well in his 50th he was a nice looking man. He was Willie. "What and how you want to do this thing? You see, baby, cocaine is very new to me it's a fast lane for me and I'm a bit slow when it comes to that. You will have to teach me a thing or two, ok?"

"First of all, I have ten keys," I said, interupting him. "Hey Willie, I can't buy no ten keys, man."

He laughed and said, "Oh! I know that, I'm just letting you know that we won't run out."

I smiled and said, "Ok, buddy."

Willie said, "Sandra, how much money do you have?"

I said, "How much is a kilo?"

"For you, $42,000," said Willie.

I said, "So two keys is $84,000, right?"

"Wrong," Willie said. "$42,000. The less you buy, the more it cost."

"Oh, I see. Now if I pay you $15,000 cash, can I get the other for $10,000 on time?"

"Sandra, Sandra, you've got a lot of nerve. You're just meeting me and you ask me for a $10,000 loan."

He smiled and said, "I'll tell you what, cut up five keys for me, I'll give you $1,500 per key." Five times 15 is $7,500. I said, "Oh, so I would only owe you twenty-five hundred."

"Yeah," said Willie.

"Ok, you've got a deal. When do you want to start?"

"Now I don't want all ten cut up at one time, only one at a time, maybe two."

"All right," I said.

Willie said, "When do you want yours, Sandra? Listen how about doing a key for me this evening?"

"Ok, but I won't be ready for mine until Thursday."

"Sure, baby, that will work for me. Here," he said handing me his number direct.

I got out of the car smiling. The Number Man walked down the steps going to the car, and said, "Get rich, kid, get rich!" I ran up the steps, but I didn't get real excited until I got in the house and locked the door. I jumped up and down running all around the house after taking a breath; I picked up the phone then called Hazel and Lil' Man. I called my brothers Carey and Rick. Lil' San and White San were on their way. I told all of them that it was time to get down. When Lil' San got there, I told her what time it was. I showed her where she would be sleeping, and her duties. Everybody that came into the house Lil' Man checked them off so that she could remember their faces. Willie called and was ready for me to fix up two keys. I fixed the two keys for him and I bought five ounces for myself. Business was getting bigger and better. I enjoyed every bit of what I was doing. An old friend of mine came by with a guy. His name was Kiley and they called his friend Fancy D. Kiley was a jewel thief. Fancy D. was known for robbing, and taking jewelry also. Fancy D. was handsome, a bit lighter than me, with hazel colored eyes. About six feet, three and a half inches tall and nicely built. Fancy D. said, "So you, San!"

"Hun," I said, "So what's it to you?"

"Oh hey, baby, I've heard a lot of talk about you, and I'm gonna make you mine."

I laughed and so did he. Kiley got a 50 and said to Fancy D., "Come on, man, let's ride."

Fancy D said, "When can I take you out, Ms. San?"

"Nigga, we've just met."

Fancy D. said, "What's that got to do with us going out and getting to know each other?"

Lil' Man walked up and said, "San, do you know this crazy motherfucker."

"Fucker? Oh! Man, shut the fuck up."

"Hey, motherfucker, this is my sister, and I am gonna be your brother in-law."

Lil' Man said, "You a godddamn lie. You ain't gon getting my sister."

Kiley was outside calling Fancy D. Fancy D. said, "I'll be back," and I said, "Ok."

Lil' Man said, "Bitch! You better have some money when you come back."

"Fuck you," Lil' Man said to Fancy D as he was leaving. He then got into the car and winked his eye at me. I asked Lil' Man, "what's up with that jive ass nigga?"

Lil' Man said, "All I can say is the motherfucker gets paid. Yeah, but he snorts drugs, so what. The little dope that nigga snort won't harm a fly. Hell! You snort more than any of the ounce buyer that you have. This is my dope; I do what I want to."

Lil' Man said, "I'm gonna tell Ray."

I said, "Fuck Ray. I told you that I ain't got time for no bullshit. Fuck Ray, I don't need him. Then Melvin, a little scary fucker, I don't need him, either. I'm looking for a new thing, young and tender." We started laughing. "Come on, Lil' Man, get Lil' San and go into the back so that we can break these down." We cut up and bagged the 50. Once finished, I had ten ounces. I was getting paid, the people that work for me got paid, also. Lil' San was very good and dependable. I could really trust her just like Sugar. We sold dope 24/7 nonstop. We got so busy here in this house; we had to separate the dope. Lil' Man sold all the 50's and I had on about $40,000 worth of diamonds. I had to find out the hard way that this nigger can't drink. Oh did he show his ass, that nigga got drunk and loud. I saw that it was gonna be a fight, I pulled off my diamonds, put them in my bra. Fancy was fighting one bouncer and two guys was getting ready to help the bouncer out. I pulled the little 25 automatic out and said nobody move. Fancy D. was still fighting, and I was screaming, "Let's go, baby, let's go." His clothes were all bloody. We backed out like gangstas, and I drove off. Fancy D. said, "San, I'm sorry, please forgive me."

"Man, you are crazy as hell. I don't like shit like that. The next time, let's go downtown Atlanta. I said what in the hell have I gotten myself into." While driving, Fancy tried to kiss me, but I wouldn't let him because his breath was smelling really bad. We were almost to my house when Fancy threw a diamond in my lap. I said, "Fancy, what's up?"

"Hey baby, that will make up for what I put you through."

I said, "Oh no, baby, you don't have to give me that." I then reached between my lap to get the ring out.

I stopped the car and said, "Damn Fancy, is this thing real? Shit, look at this bitch. Oh hell yeah, I want it. Man, this ring must cost about $30,000." Fancy smiled and said, "Almost, I was 37.5."

"Hey, Fancy, you ain't gon clown tomorrow, are you?"

"Hell naw, San. I want you and I need a woman like you. You are just what a nigga like me needs."

"Well, I'll see you tomorrow?"

Fancy looked at me and said, "Yeah, I'll call you, ok?"

We got out of the car. Fancy went to his car, threw me a kiss, got in his car, and drove off. I didn't have a doorbell. I banged on the burglar door until someone came to the door.

Lil' Man opened the door. "Bitch, you should be tired of opening doors. Anyway, I told you about opening my fuckin' door."

"Goddamn, San, what in the hell happened to you? Where in the fuck is that gray-eyed motherfucker?"

"Shut up, that nigger took me to a club on Pryor Street, a fucking hole in the wall and got into a fight."

Lil' San came into the foyer and said, "What in the hell?" We all started to laugh. Lil' San pulled the diamond and said, "Goddamn! Let that nigga fight some more. He gave you that ring, too?"

"Yeah, baby girl, ain't this bitch bad?"

"Girl, but that motherfucker is crazy," Lil' Man said. "I told you, but that nigger will take good care of you."

"I don't know if I can hang, 'cause he's crazy as hell." People started knocking on the door to buy dope. Lil' San was really taking care of my business. Man, when we check out, she gave me $3,500. The next morning Fancy D. called. I could hear Lil' Man talking, "Hey man, the next time you take my sister out you better know where you are going." Click. "San! This ugly bitch hung up in my face. Anyway fuck him." Lil' Man went into the kitchen to fix some breakfast. Lil' Man cooked grits, pork chops smothered in gravy, and homemade biscuits. Breakfast was done. Lil' Man yelled out at everybody to come and eat. We all washed up and were entering the kitchen when someone knocked on the door. Lil' San answered it. It was Sugar. Before we could close the door, there was another knock at the door. It was Fancy D. Sugar looked at Fancy D. and said, "Baby boy, your name is?"

"Fancy Dancer," he replied.

Lil' Man said, "Fancy Dancer my ass, that nigger name is shit 'cause that's all he do is keep up shit."

"Fuck you, lil' bastard," Fancy D. said.

"Fuck you back," said Lil' Man.

"Hey honey, fuck that shit and let's eat. Shit on both of you motherfuckers. Come on Rose, let's eat."

"Who's Rose?" I said.

"Oh, that's what we call all the dancers."

Anyway, we all ate, but not Fancy because he don't eat pork. He ate cereal. Once we finished eating, Lil' Man said, "Hey sis, can I get a hit?"

"Yeah, Lil' San will give you one," Fancy said. "Come here, baby, let me out, I've got to go and take care of some business."

"Let me let the red motherfucker out."

"Man, fuck you," said Fancy D.

"Come on, Fancy, I'll see you to the door."

Lil' Man went into the bathroom to take a hit. We were on the front porch when Fancy kissed me.

"Listen, Fancy, I'm not with all that." Fancy left waving bye to me. Cocaine was selling very fast. Ray called and I did not talk to him. Sugar came over we sat at the table when a phone call came. It was someone from the Plaza that said that Fancy had got stabbed in the side. "Bring him around here. You know what I can take care of him." I hung up the phone. When Fancy got here I looked at the wound, and it didn't look good. I had just bought three ounces, and was about to cut it up when all of this happened to Fancy. I asked Sugar would she take Fancy to the hospital for me. Sugar took Fancy to the medical center. Sugar called me and told me that they had him in the emergency room. They had to call in a specialist. Sugar said that Fancy was acting all crazy because when the specialist came he was dressed in a tuxedo. He had to leave a call. Boy did Fancy clown. Fancy said, "What in the fuck this suppose to doctor gonna do to me? This motherfucker is all dressed up, he can't work on me." The doctor told Sugar that she would have to calm Fancy down before he can operate on him. The knife cut through his appendix. Sugar called me again and gave Fancy the phone. "Hey baby," said Fancy.

"Don't 'hey baby' me. Man, you have got to be cool, and let that doctor operate on you. Fuck what he has on, sick ass nigga. Damn dancer, what in the fuck is wrong with you? Please, baby, let the doctor do his job." Sugar was back on the phone and said, "He'll be all right; they've just given him a shot."

"Sugar, keep in touch and let me know what's going on. When I finished this thing (dope), I'll be down there. God you think that I'm gonna be involved with a crazy fucker like that?"

I hung up the phone and began to tell Lil' Man and Lil San what was going on at the hospital. While I was bagging up the cocaine, people were steady buying and bringing merchandise. Once I finished bagging up the cocaine, I cleaned up everything and I told Lil' San to take care of the business because I had to go to see what was going on with Dancer. I got into my car and headed down to the hospital. While driving I was playing some Whitney Houston, smoking a cigarette, and then I took me a two and two hit of cocaine. When I got to the hospital I began parking my car. Before getting out I looked into the mirror to make sure that my nose was clean. After entering the hospital, I went straight to the emergency room to find Fancy D. I saw Sugar. "Hey! What's up?"

Sugar said, "They've rushed him to surgery. Whatever he was hit with (stabbed) punctured his appendix, plus they're trying to stop the bleeding. Thank God for us being here for him, girl. How did you get involved with a nigga like Fancy D? Honey, that nigga ain't nothing but trouble for you."

"But wait, let me tell you, Sugar."

"No, baby girl, let me finish. See, San, that nigga drinks heavy, do drugs, smoke cigarettes, and all other kinds of shit, you don't need no man like that. I don't care how good he is. Damn girl, what in the hell did he do to you? Hey, he must have a monster head, huh? 'Cause I know that it can't be all about the fuck?" We both start laughing. I then said, "Sugar, for some reason I like that old bum ass nigger. His bed action is very, very good. That head job, me! He's not the man for that. Now, let's see what's going on. There's the doctor." Doctor told both of us that he'd lost a lot of blood, the surgery went well, but he would need to stay there for about three more days, maybe four. "Oh God! Thank you, doctor, thank you so much. Can we see him now?"

The doctor said, "Well, he's in the recovery room now and will be there until the medicine wears off, which will take about 30 minutes to an hour. After that they will give him a room and yes, you may see him then." I looked at Sugar and said, "Do you want a hit?"

Sugar said, "Hell yeah." I went into my bra and gave Sugar the gram bag, and she went into the bathroom. I went out to smoke me a cigarette. We met back up; they told us that he would be on 5B. We got on the elevator going to the floor where Dancer was. Layed all back, "Man, what in the hell were you doing up in that plaza fighting? You need to stop drinking so much, Fancy. Damn!"

Fancy said, "Now, can I get a word in? I don't want to hear all that shit you're talking about. I ain't gonna let no motherfucker disrespect me. Fuck that dumb shit, San."

Sugar said, "Wait, ya'll, stop all that fussing and just be cool!"

Fancy said, "Hell yeah, I'm in pain and you come here with all that shit."

I said, "Man, can't you see we care about your ass? Damn Fancy, I don't know why you came into my life."

"What, you want me out?"

We looked at each other, I then went closer to him. "I'm sorry, Fancy, just a little scared that's all." I got the face pail and began to wash him up. After washing him up, I then kissed him. I ran my hand under the cover; his eyes bucked. "Please, baby, don't tease me like that, you know that I'm sore. Wait 'til I get home."

"Well, Fancy, we see that you are going to leave, so I guess I'll—no, we will—go and get you some PJ's and house shoes."

Fancy said to Sugar, "Thank you for taking out time to bring me here."

She smiled and said, "Hey! That's what friends are for. If San is my friend and you are a friend of hers that means we are all in this together. We love you, Fancy D., or should I say Fancy Dancer?" We laughed, and then Fancy said, "Hey Sugar, how come you call me Fancy Dancer?"

"Well, everytime I see you, naw every time you come back from your lick or hit, you come back dancing. So I went with the Fancy Dancer and I love it. Ok baby, we've got to go and get your stuff."

"Look, San, I want to apologize to you."

"Hey man, I don't want to hear that shit. We will take care of you. You will be coming to my house on Eugenia Street until you get well, so we will see you in a minute. Let's ride, Sugar," I said. We went and bought Fancy the hospital thing, took them back to him, gave him cigarettes, and left. "Now it's back to what I'm about to be very good in and that's cocaine. Sugar, girl, you are the best."

"Look, San, when have you heard from Julio and Big Hawk?"

"Honey, I don't know what's going on, since I've been out, they've been on a low key. Maybe because they think that I'm bad news, meaning no good for them anymore. I just don't know. But anyway, baby girl, it's all about the dollar. Let's go home and make some money." As we were driving down from Walt Street onto Eugenia Street, cars were lined up. Sugar looked at me and I at her. "What in the hell is going on? Park the car, Sugar." I jumped out of the car with my 9mm cocked back as usual. I went to the door and hollowed through it. I saw people all in the foyer, and it looked like they were all over my house. "Lil' Man, it's San."

"Wait a minute."

"San, I'm coming. Bitch, open the fucking door."

Lil' Man said, "Naw, whore, you said for me not to open your fucking door."

I hit the burglar door and said, "I pay the cost to be your motherfuckin' boss. Open the goddamn door, hoe."

"Who in the fuck are you calling a hoe?" San came to the door and opened it. Sugar came up and said, "Hey, to hell with what Lil' ugly motherfucker Lil' Man."

"Damn Rose (Lil' San), what's going on with all the cars?"

"Hey, honey, they want half ounce and ounces. You didn't leave me with all that, so let's get busy." I went into my room and got the package and began to work. Everybody knew the prices of the cocaine. I gave Sugar about four half ounces, and I took care of the ounces. Lil' San took care of all the other. Once we got rid of all the people inside, I said to Lil' San, "Baby, thank you. But don't get caught up like this, these niggers could have taken you out. Man, you had robbers and killers all one time. Hey, and Lil' Man ain't gon bus a grape, (laughing). So the next time think before you act, ok?" Money was coming so fast I called my brother to come help me. I told Sugar, "Girl, this cocaine business is growing."

"You are right, San, but think you've the best cocaine in town, and you are the cheapest. You're pretty, too, and so is Lil' San."

Three days had passed and Fancy was on his way home. We cleaned my bedroom very well for Fancy D. His wound was still fresh. Lil' Man said, "San, how long are you gonna be tied up with that stupid ass nigger, Fancy D? Honey, you got pure D hell on your hands, San. Girl, you better get your act together because you know that it is about time for Ray to show up."

"Damn Ray, he don't give a fuck about me, and you, Lil' bitch, Lil Man, don't you say a goddamn thing about me and Ray. Don't tell him shit about me and the man in my life, and for Melvin, honey, he's a bitch nigga anyway."

"San," (I looked up at Lil' Man) "why are you so down on Ray?"

"That's none of your fucking business. Damn man, you talk too much." A horn blew. Lil' San went to the door, and it was a cab with Fancy D. We went down the steps to help Fancy out. After paying the cab driver, we took him into the house and into my bedroom. Once into the bed, "Oh boy," said Fancy, acting like a king. Plus, we treated him with good old-fashioned love. Now Lil' Man and Fancy was always going at it. Fancy was down for a week. We sold dope, changed bandages, cooked, cut up dope, and whatever was need to keep the business going. Fancy was better. It was late and everybody was tired, the business had slowed down, then Fancy called out to me. "Come here," he touched my hand and said, "hey baby, I want to thank you again for taking care of me. I'll always love you for that." We kissed and I could feel the body heat coming from him and I know that he felt me. Then it happened, I was in the bed with Fancy. I whispered to him, "Baby, just lay there." I began to pull my bra off; our lovemaking was so tender and passionate. There was a feeling like never before. I became very dizzy. Fancy said, "Are you all right?"

"Oh yeah, I have never ever had sex like that." I went into the bathroom, got a pail, and came back into the room to clean Fancy up. I then took a shower myself. I found myself fallin' in love with Fancy, but I had to control my feelings because that man is foolish. I've got to get out of this. Two more weeks and he will be back on his own, thank God for that. Time was moving quite well. Fancy was up and moving around. A week had passed. Finally Fancy decided that he was well enough to get up and go and get some money. "Thank you, baby, for letting me live in, I'll repay you."

"It's not all about the repay. I would have done that for anyone." Fancy D. said, "I thought that I was special to you." I looked at him real crazy and said, "All people are special to me, especially if they need help the way you needed it."

"Oh! I'm just kickin' it with you, San, don't get so uptight."

"So, when are you leaving?"

"Let me call my boy, and then I'll let you know. Would you pass me the phone?" I said, "Yeah," while passing him the phone. He called Kyle. Fancy hung up the phone, jumped up, and said, "Hey baby, I'm leaving, Kyle will pick me up then we'll be going to South Carolina. Will you loan me four or five hundred dollars 'till I get back?"

"Ok, Fancy, just be careful." I went into the other room to get the money for him. I was kinda glad that he was going, but the feeling that I had for him was deeper than I thought. I couldn't let him know. Anyway, life goes on. It didn't take long before Kiley got there. There was horn blowing outside of the house.
Lil' Man said, "Hey, bitch, your ride is here."

Fancy said, "Fuck you, Lil' Man." He then turned and kissed me, and said, "I love you, San, you mean the world to me."

"Ok, Fancy, I'm gonna tell you just like this, you're special, and I do care a lot for you, but all of that drinking, oh man! That got to go. Baby I just can't take that."

He looked without saying a word, just smiled and walked off. Fancy turned around and said, "There's too many Sans in that house, change the names, baby. See you later, baby." They drove off; I went into the house yelling, out, "Let's get busy. Hey, Lil' Man, come here. Where's Hazel? Tell her to come here." She had started to stay home. Her apartment was just in the back of my house. Lil' Man lived further on back with his wife. Hazel came in and said, "Honey, I heard that you had crazy ass Fancy here."

"Yeah, but that over now, he's gone."

"Oh, but that nigger will be back."

"Lil' Man, shut up."

Lil' San was asleep in one of the bedrooms. I asked Hazel, "Why I didn't know anything about San being related to us?"

She said, "They call her Sandy Boo."

"Oh, ok, that's a name change. Anyway, here, take this gram; I hadn't given you anything lately."

"Where's mine?" Lil' Man said.

"Sit your ass down. I'll tell you what, clean up my room and I'll take care of you." Lil' Man did his little dance, spinned around, and almost did a split, but couldn't. We laughed and laughed. Sandy Boo came out said, "Hey," and went into the bathroom to get fresh. Hazel went out of the door; I went into the kitchen to check to see how much cocaine was left. It was time to reup. I made a phone call for five ounces. By that time Sandy Boo came into the kitchen. I said, "Sandy Boo."

She looked at me and said, "Who told you that my name was Sandy Boo?"

We smiled. I said, "Hazel told me. Anyway I've got to go and pick up some cocaine. So I'll leave this package with you. Hey it's about ten grams and 15 50's. That should hold you until I get back. Don't let Lil' Man open that door, please." I made a phone call. I needed more cocaine; I talked to the man with the plan. He told me that he would meet me in the plaza in 20 minutes. Damn nigger must ride dirty all the time. I went on up to the plaza, and went into the grocery store. I bought me $1.00 worth of soude meat, saltine crackers, and a Pepsi. As I left the store eating on the outside, Will pulled up. I walked over and got in the car. We exchanged hellos and goodbyes. He got the money pouch and I got the cocaine. Back to Eugenai Street. People was everywhere when I got there. I parked the car and jumped out with my 9mm in my hand. Sandy Boo was waiting at the door. "Hey, honey, I'm glad that you are back, what up? You have ounce buyers, quarter ounce, and half of ounces."

Damn all those cars. "Come on, Sandy Boo, let's do it." Lil' Man had already set me up in the kitchen. The sifter cup and the bags were laid out. That's how Lil' Man got his extra. I mixed everything up. Fix three ounces to go, four quarters, two half ounces. I decided to fix the rest up and then call for more. We sold so much cocaine I decided that we needed more guns and manpower. I got my god brother to work with me, plus a well-known bodyguard that moved whenever I moved. He was good; he carried a nickel-plated shotgun that was beautiful. Days was going by, I was snorting more and more each day. Money was coming so fast. Police started to ride kinda regularly; I started to see things that I could not explain. Sugar would say, "Baby girl, you need to slow down."

"S-h-h-h-h-h, be quiet, I think that someone is out there."

"Oh shit, San, you're started tripping like the rest of them."

"Oh no, it just that I'm working pretty hard."

"Ok San, give me a hit." We both started to laugh. I passed the little bag to Sugar.

"You're right, Sugar, that shit has me peepin' like Lil' Man and Bippy. Man I don't like that, but that shit makes me feel different. But anyway, let's get busy." So many people was coming and going, I hired a doorman that did nothing but open and close the door. I paid people to walk the block for me. I bought walkie talkies so that they can let me know what was going on in the streets. Fancy came by with much money talking all kind of shit. As usual, he and Lil' Man had it out. Fancy did good in his own way, it's just that I can't take it. He's a good man, but that alcohol gets the best of him. "Hey, baby girl, can I take you out?" Looking at me all sexy with a medium blue suit on. Shoes and cap the same color.

"Naw Fancy, as much as I like you, I just can't do it like that no more, baby. Your drinking is a bit much for me. Plus, you are jealous for nothing." He looked at me and walked off.

Sandy Boo was in the front; he bought a gram from her and went on out of the door. I went in the foyer looking for Fancy. Sandy Boo said, "Oh, he's gone. He got his little shit and left. Girl he had $100 bills going to bed. Fuck that red motherfucker, the bitch wouldn't give me one little hit. I gave him my shit."

Lil' Man said, "Honey, hush up, that's all you talk about." Sugar left, she had to go to work. I found myself snorting more and more. My nose became very sore. It even started to bleed. My face would ache. Money was coming so fast, I was buying cars, vans, jewelry, clothes, furniture, and even food. TV's, vcr's, or they were very cheap. All of the people that worked for me was dressing very well. There was merchandise all over this house, in every closet, even in the hallway. I went looking for Fancy D; I wanted to be with him. This time I couldn't find him. I checked all the places that he would be, but no luck. A week passed and no Fancy; two weeks passed. I was in my bedroom in the bed; my bodyguard let him in. He knew how Fancy and I was. Fancy was all over me. Boy, was I happy. We made love in the bed, and on the floor, all the way to the bathroom, in the tub and shower. Did we make love? Oh yeah, he rubbed his stomach. Lil' Man said as we laughed, "Well, bitch, we eat pork now, ugly red motherfucker! Man, kiss my ass. Hazel, I mean San, you know that."

"Wait, baby, I didn't know that you didn't eat pork, so you ate some pork."

Dancer said, "Please, don't do that to me no more.

"Ok baby, now we know."

A horn was blowing. We went to the door; it was Kiley waiting on Dancer. Dancer said, "I'll call you baby, love ya'!" We threw kisses. Dancer was gone. I would ride and deliver cocaine. I would clear seven to ten thousand in two days, not counting the merchandise that I was buying. Oh man, this business was good. I loved it. My nose was hurting very badly, but I would still snort. My son and daughter was playing basketball, I would go back and forth to see them play. My brother and mother would always babysit so I could sell dope 24/7. I was always buying something no matter what. I even bought cases of shoes strings.

Things were getting kind of shaky. The police would ride by, and then the narc's started to ride also. It was as though I didn't give a damn. I had to sell some cocaine. Cocaine became my life. I enjoyed snorting, I enjoyed looking at people snort dope and the way they tripped made me laugh. my nose would bleed everyday. My face would ache like a tooth ache, but I continued to snort cocaine. I had bags of money; I would take thousands of dollars down to my mother's house to hide it. I would put thousands over to Sugar's mother house and keep some at home. Cocaine was getting low. I called Will, he said that he was coming over, and that he had someone that he wanted me to meet. I thought to myself, "He knows damn well that I don't want to meet no one. What the fuck is going on?" Anyway, Will came on in with a slim-built woman, very pretty. Will said, "Say, San, this will be your connect from now on."

"Hey, wait a fucking minute. I don't work for no one, who in the fuck do you think that you are? You gone bring a bitch to me, telling me that she and I will work together. Hell naw, anyway what kind of work we supposed to be doing?"

Will said to Cookie, "Baby, I told you that San would snap, that's just her way, but she will be all right." I looked at Will and rolled my eyes. "See, you won't be seeing me anymore when you come to reup."

"Wait just a goddamn minute. Re-up on what? Hey buddies, you better know what you are doing. Honey I'm gonna tell you right now, she's a narc (undercover). Your ass is going to jail."
Cookie said, "San, girl, I know that you don't like to work with no one, but I know everybody that you know."

I cut her off, "Let me tell you something sister cup, you don't know a damn thing and anyway, I don't sell dope so what do yall want with me? You aren't no number girl. Just leave me the fuck alone, and get the hell out of my house. Man, you're gonna be sorry for letting this whore work you. Don'tdo it 'cause if you do, your ass is going to jail."

Will said, "Come on, San, you can make big dollars."

"Hey nigger, I got my own number book, and I ain't stupid. I don't want no part of what you are talking about." I looked over at her and said, "And you can get the fuck out Ms. Police, I can smell you sister."

Will said, "San, baby, this will help me out, trust me."

"Man, you've got the police with you and want me to ...hell naw, ya'll get out. I ain't got time for this trouble you are trying to get me in."

"But San ..."

"But my ass." I opened the door mad as hell; Cookie went out first saying, "Maybe I'll come back later when you are feeling well."

"Hey! Just go."

Will looked at me and said, "San, baby."

I cut him off saying, "That bitch is gonna get you busted man, you'll see. You have let your dick go to your heart. Please don't ever do this again, you'll see." They left. I felt deep in my heart that she was undercover. Two weeks passed, a month passed, and I hadn't heard from Fancy D. I was selling dope as though I had license. The money got bigger. I even hired more gunmen; we were 24/7 nonstop. Buying cars was my hobby.

I started to get a bit lonely. I found a game room in Decatur. I would go there to play, I played for hours. After leaving there, I went home. Lil' Man, Sandy Boo, Sugar, and all of the workers were outside. I always rode with my 9mm between my legs. I reach for the gun and jumped out of the car yelling, "What's wrong?" Everybody was trying to talk. (Talking loudly) "Wait a fucking minute. Sandy Boo what's up?"

"San, Will got busted over at his place. They raided it. They got all of the dope and the money that was there. It will be on the 6:00 o'clock news. Tell me this; did ya'll see that police bitch that came with him over here?" Lil' Man said, "Hell yeah, that's the bitch that handcuffed him."

"Oh my God, thank you, Jesus. I told that dumb ass nigger, damn I tried to tell him. Man, I'm so sorry. How much dope did they get? It was about six keys and 300,000 dollars. Damn, I've got to get another connect now. Shit, Lil' Man call Ray."

I looked at Lil' Man and rolled my eyes and said, "Girl, I ain't thinking about Ray. But then again, business is business." One of the guys from the plaza came by and said that Fancy D. had got busted in the windy city (Chicago).

Oh my God, my heart fluttered. Oh no, maybe he will call soon. I asked the guy what name was he in and what his charges were. He didn't know a thing.

Man, was time flying. I started to deal with Ray on a business style. School was out; my mother was always there for me. Harry was ready for college; Cocoa went to stay with Mama alone with the white girl's son. Tony had his own apartment. Oh man, I was ready for anything. At least I thought I was. One night a woman we called Big B was getting high. She went out of the door and said, "Tell San that the police are out here in the trees." We all laughed because Big B always tripped very hard. She yelled out again, "Clean that shit up and get out of there." We didn't pay any attention to her. She left walking toward the plaza. Thirty minutes later we could hear a loud noise; someone was trying to break in. Oh no, it was the cops. I was yelling everybody, "Go, go out of the back door." They got what they could and out of the back door they went. I kept a clean dope house and a hiding place for everything. Of course, Lil' Man remained there. I went to the door, opened it, and they came in and asked for San. I said which San do you want? First narc said, "Oh bitch, don't get smart at the mouth."
"Hey, there's two Sans that live here, which one do you want?"

Second narc said, "Dope dealing San."

I said, "We don't deal dope here, officer."

They pushed me and asked for my name. I told them Sandra Whitt; they said, "You are under arrest."

"For what?"

The 3rd narc said, "You have a sale case honey; you sold dope to an undercover agent on 11–30–83."

"What? That's a lie. I ain't sold no fucking dope."

First narc said, "You have the right to remain silent, anything you say can and will be used against you."

I went to jail. They wouldn't give me a bond. I called my mother and told her to go over with my brothers and put everything that they can in storage that was of value. I knew that I was gonna do some time. I went to court, they wanted me to take five years, but my lawyer got it down to three years to serve. I took those three years and was sent to the State Penn in Georgia (Hardwick). I'll never forget when we boarded the bus going to Hardwick. We started to sing, "I'm going to Hardwick, Georgia, Hardwick, Georgia, here I come! They got some crazy little women there, and I'm gonna get me one." We all laughed. I fell asleep.

When we reached Hardwick, I was awakened by the guard. "Get up lady and get out, you are home for a while."

While getting off of the bus with my jail bag, I just looked around at the glass house. Inmates were all staring at us; some would holla out my name, San San. They acted as though they were glad to see me, but I wasn't too happy to see them. I went on into control where we were checked in, sprayed down for crabs and lice, then they would give us our own uniforms, etc. Now to the fingerprints and pictures. Once finished, they sent us to the dining hall, walking in line with no talking. If caught talking, you will get restriction. Population could talk, but we were not allowed to do so. Six weeks of diagnostic. I was in G college, which was an educational college.

While I was there I had not received any visitors, but that was cut because I would only be there about one year. We had yard call three times a day. Work detail, I worked out in the garment factory. Some would fight and go to the hole, some would cry and some would just take life one day at a time. As for me, as usual I became the jailhouse preacher, after being here for ten months. They called me to the mail room for legal mail. Oh my God, I got my mail and read it and ran back to my quad jumping up and down saying, "Hey, I'm going home next month."

It was the end of March 1984. My release date was April 12, 1984. I continued to pray with the ladies, all the way to April 11. One girl said, "That night, you Atlanta girl always coming and going, ya'll need to sit down somewhere and get a life."

"Ah, shut the fuck up, I'm going home in the morning."

"You ain't nothing but an old dope selling bitch anyway."

I said to her, "Baby girl, you are right but guess what? I'm going home to sell more dope, and I'll see you when I get back."

"Fuck you, San." I laughed and walked off.

When the morning came, I was ready. The preacher and my son picked me up. We talked all the way to Atlanta. My mind was on getting a package. He let us out and said, "San, get your life right with God."

I got into my car, turned on the cassette, the song, "Street Life" was playing. On my way to do my thing. Dope was the thang and selling it was my game (laughing).

This is only the beginning.

ABOUT THE AUTHOR

Sandra Lee Whitt Horsley is the oldest of thirteen children raised in a one-room apartment of Ma Louise's whorehouse. Not even knowing who her father was, she latched onto the male tricks that frequented her grandma's brothel. Part of a family-run business where her aunts were prostituting, four-year-old Sandra Lee started working as the timekeeper earning a nickel per john. For her mother's sake, Sandra ventured into the "straight life" of nine-to-five work, trying to make a living. When the brothel proves unfulfilling of her hustle mentality of Sandra, she begins embezzling thousands of dollars. Feeling cooped up and confined, Sandra began to seek more creative ways to make money on the street. Now Sandra Lee Whitt Horsley lives with her two sons, Samuel and Deontray Johnson, her Uncle George (Bubba) Whitt, and her dog (Buck) in Decatur, Georgia. She is now an ordained pastor.

This is the first of several more books to come.